D1577659

The Anatomy of Scottish Capital

SCOTTISH COMPANIES AND SCOTTISH
CAPITAL, 1900-1979

JOHN SCOTT and MICHAEL HUGHES
with research assistance from John Mackenzie

CROOM HELM LONDON

McGILL-QUEEN'S UNIVERSITY PRESS
MONTREAL

© 1980 John Scott and Michael Hughes
Croom Helm Ltd, 2-10 St John's Road, London SW11

British Library Cataloguing in Publication Data

Scott, John
   The anatomy of Scottish capital.
   1. Corporations − Scotland − Finance −
   History − 20th century
   2. Capital − Scotland − History − 20th century
   I. Title   II. Hughes, Michael
   338.5   HG4142
   ISBN 0-7099-0043-0

McGill-Queen's University Press
1020 Pine Avenue West, Montreal H3A 1A2

ISBN 0-7735-0528-8

Legal deposit 2nd quarter 1980
Bibliothèque Nationale du Québec

Printed in Great Britain by
Biddles Ltd, Guildford, Surrey

CONTENTS

TABLES

FIGURES

ACKNOWLEDGEMENTS

Our first acknowledgement must be to Allan Maclaren whose innocuous request for a contribution to a book which he was editing led us into a project that has lasted for longer than we ever imagined. Happily the research soon became more concrete than the somewhat grandiose contribution to the Maclaren volume. Our second acknowledgement is to John Mackenzie who was our Research Assistant for the year 1976-7. During that time he worked diligently and enthusiastically on the frequently boring jobs which we asked him to do. We are particularly sorry that we made him spend much of the summer of 1976 working in dingy basements.

We obviously cannot thank all those companies which provided us with copies of Annual Reports, but we are nevertheless grateful to them. We would like to thank most warmly those companies which responded to our requests for further information: Associated British Foods (Mr T.H.M. Shaw), Bank of England, Bank of Scotland (Mr W.T. Liddle), Burmah Oil (Mr B. Jones), Clydesdale Bank (Mr R.M. Sim), Cooper Industries (Mr M. Grey-Smart), James Finlay and Co., Garton Engineering (Mr J.C. Hayward), Ivory and Sime (Mr R.J. Randall), Royal Bank of Scotland (Mr R.J. Boyd), Weir Group (Mr J.D. Sinclair), and Messrs. Wood Mackenzie (Mr H. Buchan). Mr J. Iain Murray kindly provided us with information on his family history, and Garry Runciman provided information on Anchor Line as well as advice and criticism on various aspects of the research.

Various individuals and institutions have provided help and encouragement throughout the project. The Social Science Research Council financed the project for the period 1976-9 under grant number HR4132. Glasgow University Business Archives and the Glasgow Stock Exchange provided facilities for data collection during 1976. Malcolm Thwaite kindly provided some of the data used in Chapter 4. J. Clyde Mitchell provided an early version of his blockmodel computer program. The computing staff at Leicester University, and particularly Sylvia West, have given us constant and cheerful help and advice. Figures 1.5, 2.8, 3.5 and 4.4 have been expertly produced from our own inadequate scribbles by Angela Chorley of the Leicester University Audio-Visual Unit. Colleagues in the ECPR Research Group on Intercorporate Structure have provided many discussions and critical comments on our research. Professor P.L. Payne of Aberdeen University suggested some alterations to Chapters 2 and 3 and kindly sent us a copy of his paper on the early Scottish joint stock companies. An earlier version of Figure 4.4 appeared in *Sociology*, 13, 1, 1980.

We must finally make more than merely the token acknowledgements to the secretaries at the University of Lancaster and the University of Leicester who have typed various drafts of the chapters of this book. The many tables and lists have been typed with considerable patience and they have all shown great initiative in deciphering the many names which have been mentioned in the text.

John Scott, University of Leicester
Michael Hughes, University of Lancaster

INTRODUCTION: CAPITAL, CONTROL AND COMMUNICATION

This book is a study of Scottish companies and Scottish capital in the twentieth century. The study begins with the major companies of 1904-5 and examines their history and subsequent development. The top companies in a number of periods are also examined and the study concludes with an investigation of the major companies of 1973-4 and their response to the recent oil developments. It is perhaps necessary to begin with a discussion of the nature and significance of the joint stock company.

The joint stock company is a form of business enterprise in which the capital is subscribed jointly by a group of shareholders. It was introduced as a way of raising funds for projects which were too large for the resources of an individual family. As compared with the older legal form of the business partnership it permitted 'investors' to remain detached from day-to-day management and, most importantly, gave the business a legal existence independent of its owners. Whilst Scottish law was more conducive to this form of undertaking than was English law, both Scottish and English law were consolidated in a series of Companies Acts from the 1840s to the present. The spread of the joint stock principle was uneven, being first concentrated in railways, utilities, shipping and large scale undertakings, and becoming the predominant form of business enterprise by the end of the nineteenth century. Equally, the principle of stock exchange quotation, and the status of 'public' as opposed to 'private' company, spread slowly and unevenly. Although much of the big business sector consisted of public companies from a fairly early date, a number of important companies remain private today.

The joint stock company is the central institution of modern capitalism. It is the means through which the wealth of many individuals can be mobilised as capital and put to work under a unified direction. It is precisely this centrality of the company to modern capitalism which makes it the focus of our study. The joint stock form points to the relationship between ownership and control. It is frequently held that the company form of enterprise permits the 'divorce' of control from ownership. While this is certainly a possibility, a more realistic view is that the joint stock company leads to a transformation in the

13

relationship of control to ownership. Control remains linked to ownership though not in a direct or immediate way. There is considerable evidence from a number of countries that individual families may retain control of a company even when they no longer have full ownership of it. The continuity of families in the context of a system of joint stock companies shows that the company is the public and impersonal means through which private and personal control can be maintained. At the same time, the company can also be the means through which control itself becomes impersonalised. The joint stock company, and the interweaving of share ownership and credit relations which it permits, indicates the gradual transformation of property from a specifically personal relation to a more social relation. Private property is gradually and imperceptibly 'socialised': from being the property of particular individuals, capital becomes the property of a class. Or to put it differently, the class ownership of capital is transformed from a personal form of ownership to a collective form of ownership.

Marwick has shown in a number of his books (see Bibliography) that the rise of the business partnership and, particularly, of the joint stock company led to a complex system of 'interlocking directorships' in the Scottish economy. The interweaving of share ownership between companies was complemented by the interlinking of company boards. Marwick argued that during the late Victorian period there emerged a class of 'professional' company directors, men whose sole occupation was that of sitting on two or more company boards. Our study aims to investigate this phenomenon in a systematic way. It is necessary to show the actual structure of interlocking and the characteristics of the participants in this structure. Underlying our investigation is the claim that the pattern of interlocking directorships is a significant phenomenon in its own right, as well as being an indicator of the other relations between companies. We argue that capital and control relations are associated with particular patterns of interlocking which constitute a distinct level of business organisation. Interlocking directorships constitute relations of communication between companies which may have no legal connection with one another. An interlocking directorship is a channel of communication through which business information can be transmitted; a network of interlocking directorships is a complex web of communiction which no one has designed or intended, but which is an important constraint upon business decision-making. It is in this way that company strategy may be influenced. Thus, it is the interplay of capital, control and communication which is the focus of our attention in this book.

This book in not intended as an economic history of Scotland, though we hope that it may contribute to the further understanding of the Scottish economy. Our approach has been to sketch in some of the well-known features of the Scottish economy over the course of the last 100 years or so as a backdrop to our own empirical investigations. We try to get behind the broad trends to the particular companies and people who made those trends. The book is intended to fill the gap between detailed company histories, which are of variable quality, and broad historical interpretations. The concern of this book is with the major companies and figures which make up the system of Scottish capital. Throughout the book we see Scottish capital as a distinct system with its own characteristics and which follows a distinct pattern of development. This pattern is investigated through the changing structure of the business system.

The data relate to the top Scottish companies at five points in time: 1904-5, 1920-1, 1937-8, 1955-6 and 1973-4. Chapter 1 looks at the development of Scottish companies during the nineteenth century and relates this to the structure of the business system as it was during the first decade of the present century. Chapter 2 discusses the inter-war period, from the post-war boom to the end of the 1930s, and compares the nature of Scottish business at the beginning and at the end of this period. Chapter 3 looks at the immediate post-war period and Chapter 4 brings the picture up to date with an analysis of capital, control and communication in the 1970s. Each of these chapters adopts the same structure so as to permit the maximum amount of comparison to be made by the reader. Finally, Chapter 5 gives a brief account of some of the most important features of Scottish participation in the development of North Sea oil. This chapter does not pretend to give a comprehensive account of oil activities, it is merely intended to discuss some of the features most relevant to the 1973-4 data discussed in Chapter 4.

So far as possible we have avoided technicalities of theory and technique in our text, though a necessary minimum of technicalities have been introduced at the relevant points. More detailed definitions and points of explication are covered in the Appendix, which may be disregarded by the general reader. The book is very much a data book. We have tried to provide as much of the basic data as possible so that future investigators and interested persons may return to these data themselves in answering different questions to those we have tackled here. In order to help the reader to follow the details of the narrative we have provided a large number of diagrams which we hope will function as 'visual aids' to the text.

1 THE DEVELOPMENT OF SCOTTISH CAPITAL UP TO THE FIRST WORLD WAR

The Scottish industrial revolution was centred on west central Scotland and was based upon textiles and heavy industry. Cotton had been the first growth industry and had led to developments in dyeing, calico printing and thread manufacture. As Lancashire competition caused problems for the Scottish cotton industry, firms moved into wool and flax production. The development of the textile industry stimulated the production of spinning and weaving machinery, though the engineering industry did not really take off until coal and iron deposits began to be worked commercially. The production of goods for export led to an early development of marine engineering and shipbuilding, and this industry in turn, in association with the growth of the railways, stimulated the development of the basic coal and iron industries. Scottish capital emerged in these industries, and firms began to grow in size mainly through the internal accumulation of capital rather than through bank credit.

The period from 1870 to 1914 saw the consolidation of the basic structure of the Scottish economy. The main interests of Scottish capital were in heavy industry, textiles, railways and the booming investment company sector. These industries, together with drinks, tea trading and chemicals, were dominated by joint stock companies, and the joint stock principle was making inroads into industries where private partnerships remained the main form of business enterprise. As Scottish industrialisation had occurred in alliance with English imperial power, so the relative decline in British industrial supremacy, which followed the rapid industrialisation of America and Germany, had its repercussions in Scotland. Scottish capital came to exemplify the problems of the British economy as a whole: the economy was centred around export oriented heavy industry which faced increasingly aggressive foreign competition, and had a massive outflow of invest-ment funds into foreign agriculture, railways and mines, much of which exacerbated the domestic problems.

Our aim in this chapter is to discuss the most important Scottish companies in the period up to the First World War. We shall give a detailed discussion of the largest companies of the year 1904-5 and we shall trace the development of these companies and the connections

between them. We shall show how the main areas of Scottish capital
were linked together through common ownership, interlocking directorships and bonds of kinship. This analysis will make clear the basic
structure of the Scottish economy which has been briefly sketched
above.

Scotland's Top Companies, 1904-5

The top Scottish companies for 1904-5 are listed in Table 1.A, at the
end of this chapter. A total of 64 non-financial companies had issued
share capital in excess of £300,000. Together with the eight Scottish
banks, 14 large insurance companies, and 22 investment and property
companies with capital over £300,000, the list of 'top companies'
comprises 108 companies. Table 1.1 shows the size distribution of the
non-financial companies.

Table 1.1: Size Distribution of Non-Financial Companies (1904-5)

Companies by Rank	Total Share Capital (£)	Cumulative Total (£)
1-10	132,137,155	132,137,155
11-21	14,340,297	146,477,452
22-30	7,869,755	154,347,207
31-40	6,472,894	160,820,101
41-50	5,364,453	166,184,554
51-64	5,600,182	171,784,736
TOTAL	171,784,736	

Over three-quarters of the share capital of the 64 companies was
accounted for by the ten largest, and the two largest companies –
the North British Railway and the Caledonian Railway – accounted
for 53 per cent of the total capital. The massive capital requirements
of the railways are clear from the fact that the 11 railway companies
together accounted for 71 per cent of the capital of the non-financial
companies. The North British and the Caledonian were amongst the ten
largest railways in Britain, and the Glasgow and South Western was the
15th largest. Of the top ten Scottish companies no fewer than six were
railways, the remaining four comprising two textiles companies, a tea
merchant, and an oil company. Table 1.2 shows the industrial activities
of the top companies.

Outside railways, the largest sectors were textiles (accounting for

Table 1.2: Industrial Distribution of Non-Financial Companies (1904-5)

Industrial Sector	Number of Companies			Total Capital (£)
	Top 30	Top 50	All 64	
Plantations and Merchants	4	4	4	4,808,400
Coal Mining	2	3	4	3,498,822
Non-coal mining	0	2	3	1,796,278
Iron and Steel	2	4	7	4,744,703
Engineering	1	4	6	4,035,000
Oil	1	1	3	2,637,808
Chemicals	2	3	3	2,620,000
Textiles	3	3	5	13,624,590
Paper	1	1	1	900,000
Food and Drink	3	6	9	6,619,350
Electricity Supply	0	3	3	1,800,000
Railways	10	11	11	121,267,110
Shipping	0	4	4	2,401,390
Theatres	1	1	1	1,031,285
TOTALS	30	50	64	171,784,736

27 per cent of non-railway capital), food and drink (13 per cent of non-railway capital), tea plantations (ten per cent of non-railway capital), and iron and steel (nine per cent of non-railway capital). The importance of heavy industry, however, is understated by these figures since it is difficult to separate companies engaged in iron and steel production from those engaged in coal mining and engineering. Many of these companies were vertically integrated concerns with operations throughout the heavy industry sector. The proportion of non-railway capital accounted for by these three sectors together was 24 per cent. Thus, the main areas of involvement for Scottish joint stock capital were railways, textiles and basic heavy industries.

The eight banks included in the list of top companies had total deposits of £96m and a total note issue of £7,075,434. The two Scottish banks not included in the list – the Town and Country Bank and the Caledonian Bank were both very small. The largest bank in terms of both deposits and note issue was the Bank of Scotland, though size differences between the banks were not great. The only exception was the North of Scotland Bank which had most of its customers in Aberdeen and the north east. The life and general insurance funds of the 14 insurance companies were in the region of £100m, about a half of this resting with the four largest — Scottish Widows, North British and Mercantile, Scottish Provident and Standard Life. The 22 investment and property companies had a total share capital of £15,335,000 and this comprised an important sector of Scottish capital. The companies were divided between the older land and property companies and the newer general investment trusts.

Table 1.3: Size of Board (1904-5)

Sector	Mean Size of Board
Non-financial (by rank)	
1-10	12.3
11-21	7.5
22-30	6.7
31-40	6.1
41-50	5.8
51-64	5.2
All Non-financial	7.2
Banking	10.9
Insurance	11.9
Investment and Property	5.5
All Companies	7.1

Turning from the companies to the people who ran them, Table 1.3 shows that insurance companies and banks had the largest boards of directors, followed by non-financial companies, with the investment sector having the smallest boards. The boards of the ten largest non-financials were comparable in size to the banks and insurance companies. Size of company and size of board were directly associated with one another. Of the 108 companies, 92 (85 per cent) were connected through interlocking directorships. A total of 612 men held 833 directorships divided evenly between financial and non-financial companies. Men sitting on more than one board held just under a half of all directorships, but these were not distributed evenly amongst the sectors. Multiple directors held two-thirds of all bank directorships, a half of investment directorships, just under a half of all insurance directorships, and a third of non-financial directorships. Table 1.4 shows that virtually all of the financial companies were interlocked, and that financial companies had the highest number of multiple directors on their boards. The average number of multiple directors on a company board was 3.3, although the banks averaged 6.9 each.

Table 1.4: Interlocked Companies (1904-5)

Sector	No. of Companies	Number interlocked	Mean no. of Multiple Directors per Company	
			All Companies	Interlocked Companies
Non-financial	64	49	2.6	3.4
Banking	8	8	6.9	6.9
Insurance	14	14	5.0	5.0
Investment	22	21	3.0	3.1
TOTALS	108	92	3.3	3.9

From Table 1.5 it can be seen that the distribution of multiple directors according to size of company is more or less as expected. The ten largest companies had an average of 5.3 multiple directors, though if the two major railways are excluded the proportion of multiple directors shows little significant variation across the top 30. The 34 smallest companies not only had a lower rate of interlocking, they also had fewer multiple directors sitting on each interlocked company. Interlocking was most extensive and most intensive amongst financial companies and the largest non-financials. The five companies with the most multiple directors on their boards were Caledonian Railway (13), Scottish Widows (12), Union Bank (10), Royal Bank (9), and Standard Life (9). These were followed by the North British Railway and the rest of the top five banks, with eight multiple directors each.

The capital of the top Scottish companies in 1904-5 was to be found mainly in railways, textiles, basic industries and investment. A very high proportion of these top companies had director links with one another, interlocking being particularly characteristic of financial and large non-financial companies. These companies, moreover, each had a considerable number of multiple directors sitting on their boards and so formed a well-connected network. In the following sections we shall examine this network in more detail.

Table 1.5: Directorships in Non-Financial Companies (1904-5)

Companies by Rank	No. of Directorships	No. Held by Multiple Directors	Mean no. of Multiple Directors on each Interlocked Company
1-10	123	53	5.3
11-21	83	30	3.0
22-30	61	32	4.6
31-40	61	17	2.1
41-50	58	9	2.3
51-64	73	24	2.4
TOTALS	459	165	3.4

The Financial Sector

The financial companies will be examined by first taking the bank and insurance sector, and then the investment and property sector

(i)   The Banking and Insurance Sector

Before the nineteeneth century, Scottish banking was dominated by the two big chartered banks, the Bank of Scotland and the Royal Bank. The so-called 'Dundas system' of politics through which British rule was imposed on Scotland, was closely linked with these financial interests, both the 1st and the 2nd Lords Melville (one of the Dundas family peerages) having been Governors of the Bank of Scotland. By the end of the nineteenth century these two banks had been joined by the British Linen Company Bank, though Edinburgh private bankers such as Ramsays, Bonar and Co., remained important in Scottish Banking. The first challenge to this system came in 1810 with the foundation of the Commercial Bank, the first joint stock bank in Britain. The nominal head of this bank was the Liberal economist Lord Lauderdale, though its main promoters were James and Henry Dunlop the iron-masters, Archibald Russell the coalmaster, Peter Denny the shipbuilder, and Sir Nathaniel Dunlop the shipowner. In 1825, similar interests founded the National Bank. The founding of the Union Bank in Glasgow in 1830 was associated with the Edinburgh paper and publishing interests of Charles Cowan and Adam Black, together with the mercantile Ewing family. In 1838, the Union Bank merged with Sir William Forbes and Co., a major Edinburgh private bank, and in the same year the Clydesdale Bank was founded, also in Glasgow. The

main promoters of the Clydesdale were James Lumsden, one of
Glasgow's political bosses, and John King, both of whom were later
associated with the Glasgow and South Western Railway. By the 1840s
the tradition of aristocratic governors was firmly established: the
Lauderdales at the Commercial Bank, the Dukes of Buccleuch at the
Royal Bank, and the Melvilles at the Bank of Scotland.

The major insurance companies developed in close association
with the banks. The Scottish Widows was founded in Edinburgh in
1811 by David Wardlaw, a lawyer, and Patrick Cockburn, an
accountant. Many of its honorary directors were clergymen, but two of
the vice presidents were managers of the Royal Bank and the British
Linen Co., and the president was Lord Primrose, soon to become
the 4th Earl of Rosebury and governor of the British Linen Co. The
Scottish Union Insurance was founded in 1824 by Alexander
Henderson, the Lord Provost of Edinburgh and a major mover in the
National Bank. Its governor was the author Sir Walter Scott, the deputy
governor was John Hope, Solicitor General for Scotland, and one of
the main directors was Adam Black. In 1841 the Scottish National
Insurance was established with Holmes Ivory as manager and John
Inglis, later Lord Justice General of Scotland, as a director. In 1877
the Scottish Union and the Scottish National amalgamated to form
the Scottish Union and National. The Scottish Amicable was founded
in Glasgow in 1827 by William Spens, a Glasgow lawyer, and Edinburgh
Life was founded by Edinburgh lawyers five years later.

Thus, banking and insurance developed in close association with
one another. Finance for the insurance companies came from the
banks, and managerial expertise was provided by partners in the larger
legal and accountancy firms. By 1852, total Scottish bank deposits
were £36m, and Scottish life insurance obligations were £34m, these
two sectors being closely connected through interlocking directorships.
In 1904-5 these links remained strong, particularly in Edinburgh (see
Figure 1.1). These links were most obvious at the level of their
governors and presidents: the Marquess of Linlithgow linked the Bank
of Scotland and Standard Life; the Duke of Buccleuch linked the Royal
Bank, Standard Life and Scottish Equitable; the Earl of Mansfield
linked the National Bank and the Scottish Equitable; and the Marquess
of Tweedale linked the Commercial Bank, Edinburgh Life and Scottish
Widows. Insurance companies such as Scottish Widows, Standard Life,
Scottish Equitable and Edinburgh Life each seemed to have strong
connections to two banks and so to 'bridge' the space between the
banks, the banks themselves not being interlocked with one another.

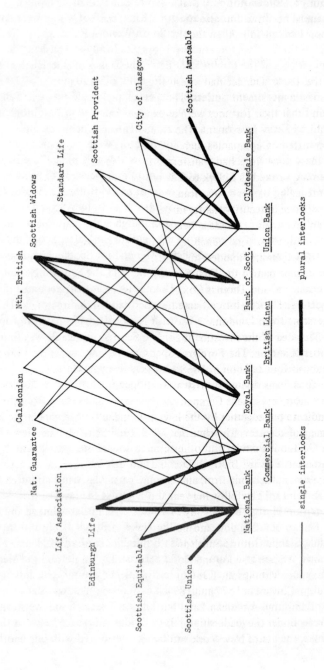

Figure 1.1: Bank and Insurance Interlocks (1904-5)

Scottish Amicable

City of Glasgow

Scottish Provident

Standard Life

Clydesdale Bank

Scottish Widows

Union Bank

Nth. British

Bank of Scot.

Caledonian

British Linen

Nat. Guarantee

Royal Bank

Life Association

Commercial Bank

Edinburgh Life

National Bank

Scottish Equitable

Scottish Union

single interlocks   plural interlocks

Figure 1.1 shows not only that Edinburgh was the centre of this financial network, but also that the largest insurance companies had closer banking links than the smaller companies.

(ii)   Investment and Property Companies

In the 1870s, Dundee had massive surplus funds available with declining domestic investment outlets. The 'juteocracy' of wealthy textile families found that their fortunes were expanding but that their firms no longer required heavy investment. The Dundee linen industry had been dominated by companies such as Cox, Baxter, and Gilroy, and most of these same firms had transferred their interests to jute. Robert Fleming worked as a clerk to Edward Baxter and Sons and was involved in managing Baxter's American stocks and shares. It was from his experience in security management that Fleming developed the idea of an investment trust as a means of channelling Dundee's surplus funds to American pastoral, ranching, mining and above all, railway concerns. In 1873 Fleming founded the Scottish American Investment Trust (later to be named the First Scottish American Trust) with John Guild as chairman, and Thomas Cox, Thomas Sharp and Thomas Smith as directors. Fleming himself acted as secretary to the trust, latterly operating from London.

The idea of the investment trust was not purely an invention of Robert Fleming. The Foreign and Colonial Government Trust had been established in London in 1868, and the Scottish American Investment Company was floated shortly after the Fleming trust. The Scottish American Investment Company had been organised by an Edinburgh syndicate put together by the lawyer William J. Menzies, who acted as managing director. The chairman of the company was the banker Sir George Warrender and other directors were Thomas Nelson the publisher, Edward Blyth, J. Dick Peddie, John Cowan of the Cowan paper manufacturing firm, and two lawyers, Alexander Hamilton and A.R. Duncan. The following year another syndicate founded the Scottish American Mortgage Company. This trust was jointly managed by an American, H.I. Sheldon, and an Edinburgh lawyer, J.D. Smith. The chairman was John Guthrie Smith and the board included two Dundee merchants, William Lowson and Robert Mackenzie, an Edinburgh merchant, Alexander Thompson, T.J. Gordon WS, and Charles Cowan MP, brother of John Cowan. In 1877 and 1878 the American Mortgage Company and the Edinburgh American Land Mortgage Company were founded, the former under the leadership of James Tait, and the latter being financed by a syndicate of New York bankers headed by John Paton. The board of Edinburgh American included Alexander Cowan, father of John and Charles, John McLaren, James S. Darling WS, and William Wood CA.

All of these trusts show the strong alliance between Edinburgh and Dundee interests, the importance of lawyers and accountants in trust management, and the role of family connections in linking the separate companies. These features recur in all the Scottish trusts formed before the First World War. The overlapping membership of the financial syndicates, reflected in interlocking directorships, became a prominent feature of the growing investment sector in Scotland. A syndicate headed by Holmes Ivory had set up the United States Mortgage Company in 1884 and the Scottish Investment Trust in 1887, the latter company invested heavily in other investment trusts and two years later was involved in the flotation of the Second Scottish Investment Trust. 1888 saw the consolidation of various Dundee land investment companies into the Alliance Trust, in which William Mackenzie soon became the dominant figure. The first chairman of the Alliance was John Guild, and other directors included James Prain, a jute manufacturer, and John Leng of Dundee, Perth, and London Shipping. William Reid, who had been associated with some of the predecessors of the Alliance, had joined with James Tait to form the Oregon Mortgage Company in 1883. Similarly, John Guild and Robert Fleming organised a syndicate to back the British Investment Trust in 1889, its board comprising John Cowan, R.D. Balfour (a London stockbroker), George Dunlop WS, J.P. Wright WS, and Sir M. Mitchell-Thomson. John Guild was also associated with the founding in 1892 of Investors' Mortgage Security, a company backed by the Alliance syndicate.

The period of expansion of the investment trust sector, which ended with the crisis of Baring's bank and the US depression of 1893, was characterised by prominent promoters such as Robert Fleming, John Guild, Holmes Ivory, William Menzies and William Mackenzie, and major financial backers such as the Cox and Cowan families. During the period 1873 to 1900, a total of 19 trusts and a number of mortgage companies were established in Scotland, and these companies had begun to attract much English capital.

The outcome of this growth in Scottish investment and property companies was that by 1904-5 the pattern of overlapping syndicates could still be seen. The trusts tended to be run independently, with lawyers and accountants acting as managers or secretaries. Even when trusts were run from the offices of a firm of lawyers or accountants, it appears either that one of the partners was manager or secretary, or that the firm provided secretarial and administrative services only.

Figure 1.2: Investment Company Management (1904-5)

Manager or Secretary	Trust(s)
Wm Mackenzie Dundee (Sec.)	Alliance
Douglas Murrie 36 Castle St, Edinb. (Sec.)	American Mortgage
A.J. McConachie 64 Queen St, Edinb. (Sec.)	Australasian Mortgage
Moncrieffe and Horsburgh 46 Castle St, Edinb. (Sec.)	British Investment Trust
W.A. Wood, CA 4 Melville St, Edinb. (Sec.)	Edinburgh American
Wallace and Guthrie WS 1 Nth Charlotte St, Edinb. (Sec.)	Edinburgh Investment
Guild and Shepherd 63 Castle St, Edinb. (Sec.)	Investors' Mortgage
W.S. Davidson 69A George St, Edinb. (Man.)	New Zealand and Australian Land
Jas. Muirhead 205 St Vincent St, Glasgow (Sec.)	North British Canadian
W. Smith 201 Union St, Aberdeen (Sec.)	North of Scotland Canadian
Adam Hunter 13 Albert Sq., Dundee (Sec.)	Northern American Second Scottish American Third Scottish American
Auld and MacDonald WS 21 Thistle St, Edinb. (Sec.)	Oregon Mortgage
E.A. Davidson 4A St Andrew Sq., Edinb. (Man.)	Realisation and Debenture
Scott-Moncrieff, Thomson and Shiels 141 George St, Edinb. (Man., Sec.)	Reversionary Association
Chas. D. Menzies 123 George St, Edinb. (Man., Sec.)	Scottish American Investment
Thos F. Binnie 8 Castle St, Edinb. (Man.)	Scottish American Mortgage
Holmes Ivory WS 6 Albyn Place, Edinb. (Sec.)	Scottish Investment United States Mortgage
J. A. Robertson Durham CA 33 Charlotte Sq., Edinb. (Man.)	Scottish Reversionary
J. M. Murray 188 St Vincent St, Glasgow (Sec.)	Transvaal Proprietary

The management of each major trust remained independent, though subject to constraints imposed by the system of interlocking directorships. Figure 1.2 shows the distribution of the 22 largest investment companies according to their management. It is clear that, whilst smaller trusts may have been allied with these same management groups, there was little sign of grouping amongst the larger trusts. A partner in one firm was just as likely to be the director of a trust administered by another firm as he was to be on the board of a trust administered by his own firm.

Of the 22 investment and property companies, 17 were interlocked with one another, four had only non-investment interlocks, and one had no interlocks with other top companies. The three Dundee Fleming trusts formed a separate clique, whilst the remaining 13 companies formed a continuous network. It is clear from Figure 1.3 that the large component was centred around Scottish American Investment, Scottish American Mortgage and Investors' Mortgage, all three being connected to the Alliance. The three Fleming trusts were closely linked to one another through plural directorships, as were Scottish Investment and US Mortgage. In both cases these plural connections were associated with common management. Although there was little obvious pattern in the connections between the investment sector and the banking and insurance world, certain links can be discerned. There was a definite connection between the grouping formed by Investors' Mortgage, British Investment and Scottish Investment, on the one hand, and Bank of Scotland, Scottish Widows and Scottish Provident, on the other. Standard Life was most closely linked to the grouping formed by Scottish American Investment and Realisation and Debenture.

Many of the investment trust interlocks involved the original trust promoters and their descendants: the manager and secretary of Scottish American Investment was Charles Menzies, and the company board included James Ivory and A.R. Duncan; David Cowan was chairman of Realisation and Debenture, John Cowan was chairman of British Investment, and R.D. Balfour and Sir M. Mitchell-Thomson were both directors of British Investment; R.M. Guild and William Mackenzie were directors of Investors' Mortgage; Charles Menzies sat on Scottish Investment along with J.M.D. Peddie, and this trust had Holmes Ivory as secretary. Managers and secretaries were often involved in interlocks, even if they did not sit on the board of the trust which they administered: Wallace and Guthrie, secretaries to Edinburgh Investment, had Alexander Wallace on the boards of Realisation and Debenture (along with P. Guthrie) and Scottish American Mortgage, and

Figure 1.3: Investment Company Interlocks (1904-5)

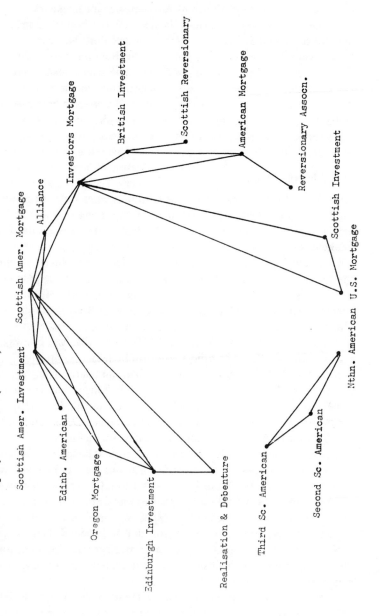

Sir James Guthrie was chairman of Alliance; William Mackenzie
continued as secretary of Alliance; James MacDonald, of Auld and
MacDonald, sat on Scottish Investment and US Mortgage; and
E.A. Davidson sat on Investors' Mortgage and Scottish Investment.
Finally, many of the trusts had interlocks with smaller trusts, this often
being associated with common management. Thus, Investors' Mortgage
was interlocked with the American Trust Company, both having Guild
and Shepherd as secretaries, and Holmes Ivory's Scottish Investment
was interlocked with British Assets Trust, for which Ivory and Sime
were secretaries.

The Industrial Sector

As we have already shown, the single most important sector of Scottish
capital was the railway sector. The nineteenth-century railway boom
had been an important stimulant for the English capital market and for
joint stock company legislation. Much of the capital for the Scottish
railways therefore came from England. Initially lines proliferated, but
the 1860s saw a number of amalgamations. By the 1870s the railway
system was dominated by the big five: Caledonian, North British,
Highland, Glasgow and South Western (closely associated with the
Midland), and Great North of Scotland. Together these companies
owned or controlled most Scottish lines. The West Highland Railway,
for example, was backed by the North British and was eventually
absorbed in 1908. The North British had been associated with the
construction firm of Sir William Arrol in the building of the Tay and
Forth bridges in the 1880s and 1890s, and the Forth Bridge Railway
was one-third owned by the North British, the remaining shares being
held by three English lines — Midland, Great Northern and North Eastern.

Railway development generated other important links with industries
such as coal, iron, steel and engineering. Many of these links are obvious
from the 1904-5 data. Figure 1.4 shows the interlocks between railways
and heavy industry. Of the 23 companies in railways, coal, iron, steel,
heavy engineering and allied industries, 20 were interlocked with one
another. The exceptions were Glengarnock Iron and Steel, Lanarkshire
Steel and Summerlee Iron. The network formed by these companies was
divided into two components centred around the two large railway
companies.

The North British Railway was connected not only to its dependent
mainline railways but also had a double interlock with Glasgow District
Subway, a company which was linked to two private companies —
G. and J. Weir and William Baird. Bairds had been founded in 1833 to

Figure 1.4: Railway and Heavy Industry Interlocks (1904-5)

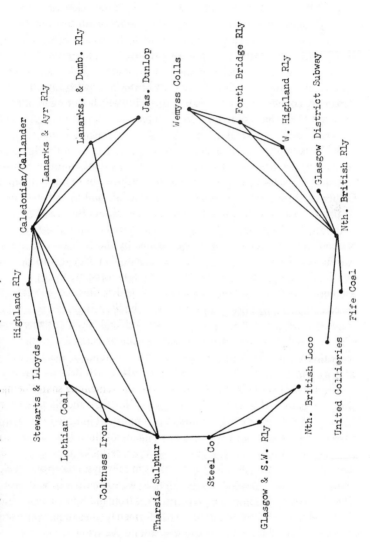

operate blast furnaces in Lanarkshire and Ayrshire. The Baird family
did not continue with the business and it passed into the control, in
turn, of William Weir, Sir William Laird and Andrew McCosh. The
subway company and the North British were linked through McCosh
and Alexander Simpson, the chairman of Glasgow District Subway.
Henry Grierson, chairman of the West Highland Railway linked the
North British to other railways and to Wemyss Collieries, a company
set up to operate the Fife coal interests of the Wemyss family. The
remaining connections of the North British in this sector were to Fife
Coal and to United Collieries. Fife Coal had been formed in 1872, with
Charles Carlow as general manager and then chairman, in order to mine
on Wemyss land and in other collieries. This firm had been the dominant
element in the Prices Association formed to regulate supply in the coal
industry. Outside the largest companies it was connected to Edinburgh
Collieries, through the chairman, Henry Mungall, and to Melville Coal,
Arniston Coal, and Robert Addie and Sons Colliers. The board of
Edinburgh Collieries brought together many coal interests such as the
Nimmo and the Dixon families. Carlow linked Fife to Shotts Iron, the
two firms having been associated for many years. United Collieries, also
chaired by Mungall, included Sir David Richmond on its board.
Richmond had founded the steel company North British Tubes (later
Scottish Tubes), had been Lord Provost of Glasgow from 1896-9, and
connected United Collieries with Clyde Valley Electrical and Broxburn
Oil. Fife Coal, United Collieries and Edinburgh Colleries were the
co-ordinating points of many Eastern collieries and were their main link
with the North British Railway, of which Carlow was deputy chairman.

The Caledonian Railway had links to three main parts of the heavy
industry sector: to Lanarkshire rail and coal interests, to the Highland
Railway, and to the Tennant 'empire' and its associates. The Caledonian
operated the lines of both of the Lanarkshire railways, as well as operating
the Callander and Oban. The Lanarkshire and Dumbartonshire was
chaired by W.A. Donaldson, and the Donaldson family ran the coal and
iron firm of James Dunlop which had been founded by the Dunlop
family of Glasgow colonial merchants. The Highland Railway was
connected closely to Stewarts and Lloyds, which was run by Andrew
Stewart and Sir William Arrol and which had grown out of the 1902
amalgamation of A. and J. Stewart and Menzies with the Birmingham
firm of Lloyds. The main product was steel tubes and its major rival
in this field was Scottish Tubes. Stewarts and Lloyds' main interlock
was with the engineering and bridge-building firm of Sir William Arrol,
which fell just outside the list of top companies. The functional nature

of these interlocks between railways and companies engaged in engineering and in the production of coal, iron and steel is obvious.

Functional links of vertical integration are an even more prominent feature of the links between the Caledonian Railway and the Tennant empire. The Tennants had set up the St Rollox alkali works of Charles Tennant and Co., which in 1885 had become a part of the Liverpool-based United Alkali Company on its formation as the world's largest chemicals concern. Sir Charles Tennant had put together a syndicate of alkali producers to form the Tharsis Sulphur and Copper Company in the 1860s which was organised to operate Spanish pyrites mines and, following its take-over of the original French company, had French minority shareholders and directors. Tharsis had considerable surplus funds, much of it invested in the shares of the Caledonian Railway, which had originally been established by William Baird and the chemical producer John Orr-Ewing. Just as Tharsis provided the pyrites required for Tennant's chemical production, so the Tennant syndicate set up the Steel Company of Scotland and Cassel Gold Extracting to use by-products of chemical production. Although the original aim of using a copper derivative in steel production failed, the Tennant interests remained closely integrated. The remaining companies in the Tennant empire were Young's Paraffin Oil and Nobel's Explosives. Young's had been formed in 1866 and was run by John Orr-Ewing, although James Young retained a 25 per cent stake. Nobel's was set up by the Swede Alfred Nobel together with the syndicate behind Tharsis, and by 1900 Sir Charles Tennant was both the chairman and a major shareholder in Nobel's.

The constituent companies of the Tennant empire were heavily interlocked with one another, and Figure 1.4 shows that both Tharsis and the Steel Company were linked to the Caledonian and that each of these companies had further heavy industry interlocks. The Steel Company was connected to the Glasgow and South Western Railway and to North British Locomotive. The Glasgow and South Western had been founded by men associated with the Clydesdale Bank and with the chemical industry — James Lumsden, John King of Orr-Ewing's Campsie Alum Company, and Sir Andrew Orr. North British Loco was formed in 1903 as the unification of Neilson's Hyde Park Locomotive works at Springburn, the North British works at Cowlairs, and the Caledonian works at St Rollox. The link between these companies was carried by William Lorimer, who chaired the Steel Company and North British Loco. The rationale for his connecting a railway company, the major Scottish locomotive builder, and a large steel concern is clear. Tharsis was involved with the Caledonian in numerous mutual interlocks with Lothian Coal and Coltness Iron. Lothian Coal was chaired by Sir James King, son of John King and a director of many Tennant companies, and through its managing director, J.A. Wood, was linked to Scottish Central Electric Power and to Lothians Electric Power. Like the North British, the colliery connections of the Caledonian were linked with the new electricity generating concerns. Coltness had been formed by the Lancashire textile manufacturer Henry Houldsworth to produce textile machinery and soon became an important iron works and colliery. In 1904-5 it was still very much a Houldsworth family concern and was linked to the Caledonian through both Sir William Houldsworth and the ubiquitous Sir James King.

The Tennant empire was the core of the many interlocks between the Caledonian Railway and heavy industry. The vertical integration of related processes was an important feature of these interlocks. But the Tennant concerns themselves had a low level of vertical integration. The Steel Company was unable to use the by-product which United Alkali produced from Tharsis pyrites, and the Cassel process for refining gold, into which Tennant put much money, remained unintegrated. The products of the St Rollox chemical works were under competitive pressure from Brunner-Mond and Lever. The empire was built around the wealth and personal power of Sir Charles Tennant: this had been its strength in the past, but it was to prove a fundamental weakness after Tennant's death in 1906.

Outside the railway spheres of influence there were a number of other interlocked industrial groupings. The largest of these was a group of five companies associated with James Finlay and Company. The first James Finlay and his partners were involved in Indian colonial trade from Glasgow and Liverpool. The firm became prominent, however, under his son Kirkman Finlay who entered into partnerships with James Ewing, Archibald Buchanan and Alexander Kay. Under the leadership of Kirkman Finlay the company's main activity became the importation and processing of cotton. In the 1860s the last of the Finlays ceased to be associated with the company, control passing to John Muir, the son-in-law of Alexander Kay. Muir soon became sole proprietary partner in the firm and extended the company's interests into tea, jute and shipping, as well as taking on various insurance agencies. Although James Finlay remained a partnership until 1909, the four main tea companies set up in the 1890s were all to be found amongst Scotland's largest companies in 1904-5. Sir John Muir, as he had become, died in 1903, but his son, Sir Alexander Kay Muir, was chairman of Consolidated Tea and Lands, Amalgamated Tea Estates, Anglo-American Direct Tea Trading, and Kanan Devan Hills Produce. The boards of each of these companies were identical and included James Finlay Muir (Sir Kay Muir's brother), Sir R.D. Moncrieffe (whose brother was married to one of Sir Kay's sisters), A.M. Brown (senior partner in James Finlay), Robert H. Sinclair (originally personal assistant to Sir John), and J.T. Tullis (vice chairman of United Collieries). Brown sat on the board of Clan Line, the Cayzer shipping firm in which Finlays had a substantial holding, and a number of the Finlay directors sat on the board of Champdany Jute, a small company wholly-owned by Finlays. Apart from United Collieries, links between the Finlay group and other companies were limited to the insurance sector, both Scottish Imperial and General Accident being linked to the companies.

An important group of vertically integrated concerns centred around Burmah Oil. Burmah was engaged in the exploration and development of Burmese oil fields and was interlocked with a shipping company, the Irrawaddy Flotilla, and the private family shipbuilding company of William Denny. Burmah had been promoted by a Glasgow East India merchant, David Cargill, and developed under his son John T. Cargill. In 1904, the Burmah board was chaired by John Cargill and included Leonard Gow, a shipowner and son-in-law of the New York publisher John Harper, Robert King, brother of Sir James King and son of John King, and M.T. Fleming. Burmah was linked to Irrawaddy through John Innes, managing director of Irrawaddy, and the latter's board included Colonel J.M. Denny and Sir James King. Burmah was soon to rise to prominence as the main financial backer, together with Robert Fleming's London banking house, of the Anglo-Persian Oil Company (later British Petroleum) in which Burmah became the major shareholder.

Connected into the Tennant empire and Clydesdale Bank sphere of influence through Sir James King was the large textile firm of J. and P. Coats. This company had been the leader of the sales cartel for cotton threads, and the Coats family engineered an amalgamation between Coats and its four main competitors in 1895-6, making the company the dominant force in the British thread industry. Archibald Coats and his family became involved in speculative mining and investment ventures and dealt in the shares of Tennant companies, though the main family interest remained the thread company. The Linen Thread Company emerged out of a series of amalgamations in 1898. Predominant on its board were members of the Barbour and Knox family, though the company was linked to Coats through

Sir Thomas Glen-Coats. Many textile firms, particularly in the jute
industry, remained private companies in this period, but Alexander
Gilroy's Victoria Jute appeared amongst the largest public companies.
Gilroy's family concern of Gilroy and Sons was one of Dundee's most
important jute spinners, and Victoria Jute had been set up to process
jute in Bengal — a strategy followed by Thomas Duff in founding
Samnuggur and Titaghur Jute, all these companies eventually competing
sucessfully *against* the Dundee-based spinners. By the First World War,
the Dundee jute industry was dominated by the firms of Cox, Low and
Bonar (based on Baxters), and Caird. We have already discussed the
close links between these firms and the early investment trusts. In
1904-5, Victoria Jute was also connected to the Highland Railway
through Sir W.O. Dalgleish and A. Gilroy, both of whom sat on the
small but important Dundee, Perth and London Shipping.

In the drinks industry the two main sectors, brewing and distilling,
were distinct. Brewing was dominated by three competing but connected
firms: William McEwan, William Younger and George Younger. There
were no interlocking directorships between these companies, but
family and kinship links were important. The board of George Younger
in 1904-5 included the elder James Younger. One of his sons, George,
chaired the company, and another son, William, was managing director
of McEwan. Somewhat confusingly, William had no kinship links with
the family which ran the firm of William Younger. The latter company
was chaired by H.J. Younger, and its board included his three sons:
H.G. Younger, W.J. Younger and J.A.C. Younger. (See Figures 4.6 and
4.7.) Outside the brewing industry, McEwan was interlocked with the
Caledonian Railway and Standard Life, William Younger was interlocked
with North British Railway and the Scottish Union, and George Younger
was interlocked with the National Bank and the North British Mercantile.
The Distillers Company was the product of an amalgamation in 1877 of
six large distilleries. The new holding company replaced earlier trade
agreements between firms such as Haig, Bald and Menzies. Distillers
dominated British whisky production under the general managership of
William Ross. Distillers' main interlocks were with smaller distilleries,
and its only link with a large company was with Arizona Copper, which
was itself linked to a number of smaller land investment companies.
Arizona Copper had been set up in 1882 by directors of Scottish
American Mortgage but soon ran into financial difficulties. The company
was restructured under the chairmanship of G.A. Jamieson, who brought
together the resources of the two main Edinburgh investment
syndicates. It eventually proved necessary to dissolve the company in

1884 and to transfer the assets to a new company with the same name. The links between Distillers and Arizona probably related to investments made by the separate distilleries in mining and land in the USA, the interlocks involving A. McNab and Bald Harvey.

A final set of industrial interlocks involved companies with mainly financial connections. Glengarnock Iron and Steel, which was based on the old firm of Merry and Cuninghame, was associated with the equally old firm of William Beardmore, the headquarters of which had moved to London. Apart from links to small collieries and railway lines, Glengarnock's only interlock was with Standard Life. Lanarkshire Steel, under the chairmanship of John Strain, was linked only to the Commercial Bank and the Reversionary Association, though the latter was interlocked directly with Fife Coal. Scottish Waggon was also connected to Fife Coal, but had no other industrial interlocks. Its most important interlock was with the British Investment Trust through the latter's chairman John Cowan. Although Scottish Waggon was listed in the 'Industrial and Commercial' section of the *Stock Exchange Official Intelligence* and has been treated here as a coachbuilding firm, it is in fact likely that it was a hire purchase finance company set up as a way of enabling collieries to purchase the railway wagons required to transport their coal. Scottish Waggon may be a financial company and not an industrial at all. Similar considerations may apply to Scottish Gympie Gold Mines. This company was the head of a group of companies mining in Australia, and its only interlock was with Transvaal Proprietary, a company involved in the financing of South African mines. Transvaal's only other Scottish interlock was with the smaller Scottish General Investment Corporation, a company engaged in the management of urban property. All these companies were managed from the same office at 112 Bath Street in Glasgow, and may best be seen as components of a Glasgow-based investment group.

The Structure of the Business Network

The company connections which have been documented above have generally involved strong financial linkages between the firms involved, whether this be a shareholding, a credit relation, a common financial dependence upon integrated industrial processes, or a common marketing strategy. These direct interlocks between companies are of great importance in explaining the movement of capital through the system of Scottish companies and, thereby, in explaining the development of the main groupings. When companies interlock with one another they also become elements in a broader network of interlocking directorships. The creation of a direct interlock between two companies induces a set of indirect interlocks between these companies and those to which each of them is separately connected. Repeated throughout the company sector this generates a network of communication between companies. Those who sit on company boards have access to financial information about these companies and are able to 'transmit' this information from one company to another. Control over the flow of information makes companies influential in relation to others: whilst company strategy may be determined by the movement of capital, it is also influenced by the flow of information. Furthermore, companies may be strongly influenced by other companies with which they have no direct interlocks. The cumulation of indirect interlocks may be such as to generate a structure of influence which differs from the structure of direct interlocks. In this section we shall examine the overall structure of the network of interlocking directorships.

Of the 108 top companies, 92 were interlocked with one another. Of the 16 uninterlocked companies, nine were linked to smaller Scottish companies and seven had no links to Scottish quoted companies. There were 135 multiple directors who generated a total of 277 lines between companies. Of these lines, 233 were single connections between companies and 44 were lines in which companies shared more than one director. The plurality, or 'value', of the line between two companies is an important measure of how close the companies are to one another, and Table 1.6 shows the pattern of plurality in company linkages.

The density of the network was 4.8 per cent. That is, of the total number of 11,556 possible connections between companies (each of the 108 companies can be connected to each of the other 107), 554 were actually made. Whilst this appears to be a fairly low density, it is noteworthy that the companies were in fact connected closely to one another: the 'connectivity' of the network (the probability that any two randomly selected companies will be connected to one another, directly or indirectly) was high at 66.3 per cent. The 92 interlocked companies were formed into three separate components of 88, two and two companies each. The two small components comprised the Scottish Gympie-Transvaal Proprietary pair, and the Aberdeen-based North of Scotland Bank and Great North of Scotland Railway. The uninterlocked companies tended to be smaller than those which were interlocked, and they included Alex Pirie the papermakers, Summerlee Iron (the Neilson family ironworks), John Dewar the whisky distillers, and Sir William Pearce's Fairfield Shipbuilding, which was built around John Elder's original company. Also uninterlocked were

Table 1.6: Plural and Single Company Linkages (1904-5)

Value of Line	Number of Lines
1	233
2	27
3	7
4	3
5	1
6	0
7	0
8	6
TOTAL	277

Note: A 'line' exists when two companies are connected through common directors. The 'value' of the line refers to the number of directors in common. See Appendix.

Table 1.7: Distribution of Company Connections (1904-5)

No. of Companies Connected to	No. of Companies	No. of Connections
0	16	0
1	11	11
2	14	28
3	5	15
4	6	24
5	13	65
6	8	48
7	10	70
8	5	40
9	3	27
10	4	40
11+	13	186
TOTALS	108	554

Henderson shipbuilding and Anchor Line, though both were run by the Henderson family.

It is clear from Table 1.7 that the distribution of company

connections is very even. Eleven companies were each directly connected to only one other company, ten companies each had direct connections with seven other companies, and 13 companies were each directly connected to 11 or more companies. The number of firms to which a company is directly connected is a measure of the 'local centrality' of the company: a firm is a central meeting point for many company linkages. Table 1.8 lists the 20 companies which may be considered as the nerve centres of the business system.

Table 1.8: The Twenty Most Central Companies (1904-5)

Company	No. of Companies Connected to	Connections with Other Central Companies
Caledonian Railway	25	13
Standard Life	18	11
Clydesdale Bank	17	11
North British Railway	14	3
Young's Paraffin	14	10
Scottish Widows	14	6
Tharsis Sulphur	13	10
Commercial Bank	13	4
Union Bank	12	5
Irrawaddy Flotilla	12	7
National Bank	12	1
Coats	11	8
Callander & Oban Railway	11	7
Highland Railway	10	3
Nobel's Explosives	10	8
Lothian Coal	10	7
Bank of Scotland	10	4
Royal Bank	9	3
National Guarantee	9	3
Edinburgh Investment	9	4

Note: This list includes all companies from Table 1.7 with nine or more
         connections.

It can be seen that the most central companies were equally divided between the industrial and financial sectors. Two other features stand out from the list. First, seven of the ten central financial companies were banks, and these companies clearly played a key role in the network of influence. Second, many of the industrial companies owe their high centrality scores to the fact that they were part of the system based around the Caledonian Railway, the Clydesdale Bank and the Tennant empire. The relative autonomy of the central companies from one another is measured by the final column in Table 1.8, which shows the number of direct connections which each company had with the rest of the 20 central companies. If a large proportion of a company's centrality score is explained by its connections to other central companies, then it cannot count as a separate centre. Conversely, a central company with few connections to other central companies stands out as an autonomous centre. Taking this into consideration, it may be concluded that the company network of 1904-5 was centred around the major banks and railway companies. These companies were the hubs of spheres of influence, and insurance companies acted as bridges between these spheres. The high centrality scores of both Standard Life and Scottish Widows reflect their extensive connections with the various hubs.

The network of 20 central companies alone was far more dense than the total network, its density being 33.9 per cent. It is clear that the hubs of the various spheres had many links with one another, and that the insurance companies were important means of maintaining this density. The connectivity of the network of 20 central companies was 100 per cent, the network forming one fully connected component. If these conclusions about the core of central companies are put together with the results discussed earlier, it is possible to produce a representation of the main component of 88 companies. Figure 1.5 attempts such a representation.

Figure 1.5 shows the main spheres of influence centred around their company hubs. The network exhibits a clear distinction between the 'Glasgow' and 'Edinburgh' segments. The five Edinburgh-based banks and the North British Railway were the hubs of relatively distinct company clusters, a pattern which becomes more marked if interlocks with small and medium-sized companies are analysed. The major industrial connections of the Edinburgh spheres were with the Royal Bank, the North British Railway, and the Linen Bank, the other banks having mainly financial connections. The two overlapping clusters of investment companies were the main meeting point of the 'Edinburgh' interests. In the same way, Scottish Widows was a bridge between five of the Edinburgh hubs. Whilst the Edinburgh spheres overlapped with one another and were bridged by insurance companies, the 'Glasgow' segment was far more dense. The Clydesdale Bank, Caledonian Railway,

Figure 1.5: The Structure of the Business Network (1904-5)

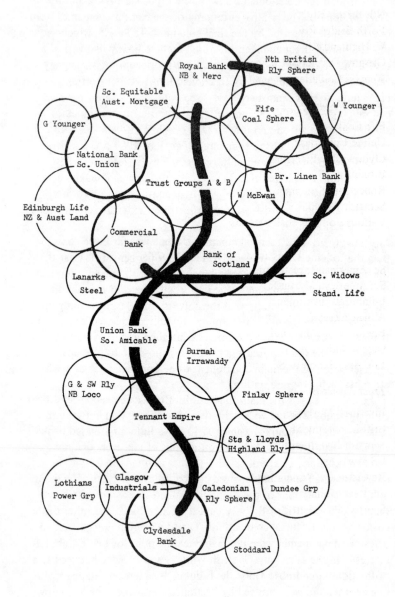

Key to Figure 1.5

North British Railway Sphere

Nth British Rly
Forth Bridge Rly
W. Highland Rly
Glasgow District Subway
Wemyss Collieries

Fife Coal Sphere

Fife Coal
United Collieries
Clyde Valley Electrical
Broxburn Oil
Robertson, Sanderson
Scottish Waggon
Various iron and coal interests

Trust Group A

Sc. American Investment
Sc. American Mortgage
Edinburgh Investment
Alliance Trust
Edinb. American Land
Oregon Mortgage
Life Association of Sc.

Trust Group B

Investors' Mortgage
British Investment
Scottish Investment
US Mortgage
Reversionary Association
Sc. Reversionary
Scottish Provident Trust

Caledonian Railway Sphere

Caledonian Rly
Callander & Oban Rly
Lanarks. & Dumbs. Rly
Lanarks. & Ayr. Rly
James Dunlop

Tennant Empire

Young's Paraffin
Tharsis Sulphur
Nobel's Explosives
Steel Co. of Scotland

Glasgow Industrials

J. & P. Coats
Linen Thread
Coltness Iron
Allan Line

Finlay Sphere

Consolidated Tea
Anglo-American Tea
Amalgamated Tea
Kanan Devan Hills
Clan Line
General Accident
Sc. Imperial Ins.

Dundee Group

Victoria Jute
Northern American Trust
Sec. & Third Sc. American Trusts

Lothians Power Group

Lothian Coal
Lothians Electric
Sc. Central Electric

and Tennant empire cannot be considered as fully autonomous spheres: they overlapped considerably with one another and with other groupings. These spheres were the foci of the predominantly industrial Glasgow grouping, though the Union Bank was an important hub also. Of course, the Edinburgh-Glasgow divide was not rigid: the Glasgow-based Broxburn Oil and Clyde Valley Electrical were in the Fife Coal sphere, and various Dundee and Lothians companies clustered around the Glasgow hubs. Nevertheless, the regional pattern was important and was reinforced by the fact that the two large Aberdeen companies were connected to one another but not to Glasgow or Edinburgh companies.

Many of the basic features of this structure can be confirmed by an analysis of plural connections between companies. Table 1.6 shows that 44 of the lines between companies involved two or more shared directors, and Table 1.9 shows how many companies were involved in the network of plural linkages.

Table 1.9: Distribution of Plural Linkages (1904-5)

No. of Plural Lines per Company	No. of Companies
0	44
1	25
2	12
3	8
4	1
5	1
6	0
7	1
TOTAL	92

The 44 plural lines connected 48 of the interlocked companies, the majority having only one plural link. These 48 companies were divided equally between the industrial and financial sectors. The network of plural lines formed 11 separate components: one component of 19 companies, one of six companies, one of four companies, three of three companies, and five of two companies. The Caledonian, Clydesdale and Tennant spheres had mutual plural linkages, as did the main Edinburgh banking and insurance companies (see Figure 1.6). These two sectors were tied together and were linked to the Union Bank through plural

Figure 1.6: Network of Plural Lines: Two Largest Components (1904-5)

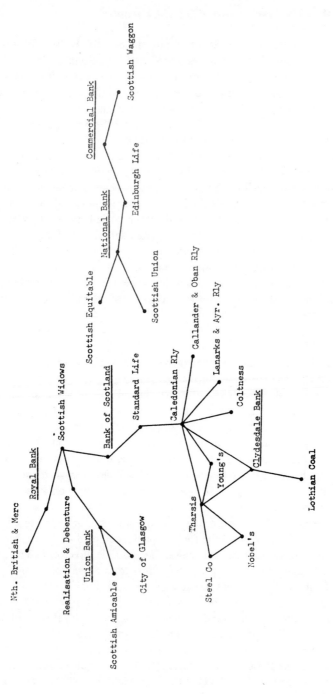

connections involving Standard Life and Scottish Widows. This large component of 19 companies reproduced the skeletal structure of the whole network. The component of six companies involved the National and Commercial Banks and their linkages, whilst the component of four companies comprised the Finlay tea companies.

The network of Scottish companies in 1904-5 comprised a system of regional and functional clusters of industrial companies embedded in a diffuse but well-connected financial system. The industrial groupings often involved the vertical or horizontal integration of technical processes, though the Tennant empire was based largely on the personal wealth and power of Sir Charles Tennant. The regional and functional clustering was even more marked amongst small- and medium-sized companies, resulting in extensive pyramidal spheres of influence centred on the main banks and railway companies. The financial system involved closely linked banks and insurance companies which were tied into the operations of investment, property, and mining companies through the activities of the lawyers and accountants who ran them.

The Men of Business

So far we have discussed the interconnections between companies in terms of the power and influence exercised through control over capital and through the network of interlocking directorships. Inter-company relations are only maintained, however, so long as people continue to interact in specific ways. The 'supports' of the business system are the men of business who run the companies. In this section we shall examine the characteristics of the multiple directors and the connections between them. In particular, we shall describe when and where the men of business meet together, and the kinship connections between them.

Table 1.10 shows that the 135 multiple directors represented 22 per cent of all directors in the top companies and held 43 per cent of all the directorships in these companies. The multiple directors had many of the characteristics of a privileged status group: many of the men were Members of Parliament, Deputy Lieutenants, Justices of the Peace, etc., and were drawn from the landed aristocracy and the established professions. Although data on qualifications is incomplete, at least 14 of the multiple directors were Writers to the Signet and a further six were chartered accountants, most of these men sitting on the boards of investment and property companies. The 11 members of the peerage were to be found on the boards of the banking, insurance, and railway

Table 1.10: Distribution of Directorships (1904-5)

No. of Directorships per Person	No. of People	No. of Directorships
1	477	477
2	86	172
3	27	81
4	13	52
5	7	35
6	–	–
7	1	7
8	–	–
9	1	9
TOTALS	612	833

companies. Table 1.11 shows that 25 of the 32 titled men of business held hereditary titles, 14 being baronets, a title which Queen Victoria had thought appropriate for the middle classes. The baronets were concentrated amongst the men with three or more directorships, whilst members of the peerage tended to have two directorships each and to hold office as chairman, president, or governor. Many of the peers may have been figureheads for the companies over which they presided, but in terms of the network of influence they were of considerable importance.

A total of nine men held five or more directorships, including three baronets and a marquess. The two men with the largest number of directorships were Sir James King, Lord Provost of Glasgow from 1886 to 1889, and Hugh Brown. Both men were involved in directing the core Glasgow companies, sitting on Clydesdale Bank, Caledonian Railway, Tharsis and Young's. In fact, four of the nine directors with five or more directorships sat on the Caledonian Railway, another four having most of their directorships in the Finlay tea group. It is important to know not only which men have the largest number of directorships but also how many other multiple directors they meet at board meetings. The network of interlocking directorships is a network of communication, and it is when men of business meet one another that information can be communicated. These men may well have met on numerous formal and informal occasions, but company board meetings are particularly important forums of discussion. Table 1.12

Table 1.11: Multiple Directors and their Titles (1904-5)

No. of Director-ships per Person	Knights	Baronets	Barons	No. of People Earls	Marquesses	Dukes	TOTALS
2	4	5	2	3	2	1	17
3	3	3		1		1	8
4		3					3
5		2			1		3
9		1					1
TOTALS	7	14	2	4	3	2	32

Table 1.12: Central Directors in the Network (1904-5)

Director	No. of Directors Met
Sir James King	35
Sir M. Mitchell-Thompson	29
Marquess of Breadalbane	27
Hugh Brown	24
Sir T.D.G. Carmichael	21
Duke of Buccleuch	20
A.R.C. Pitman	20
Earl of Dalkeith	19
William Younger	19
Charles Carlow	18
J.S. Tait	18
Sir R. Anstruther	17

Note: The centrality of a director is here measured in terms of the number of other directors he meets on company boards. See Appendix.

shows the central figures in the meeting network of multiple directors.

A number of the central directors were active in the overlapping clusters of Glasgow companies and met one another two or three times on the boards of the Clydesdale Bank, the Caledonian Railway and the Tennant companies. Hugh Brown, Sir James King, William Younger and the Marquess of Breadalbane were points in a system of frequent

meetings with Glasgow businessmen such as J.H. Houldsworth and
Sir Charles Tennant. The heavy industry segment of the network
involved not only tightly interlocked companies, but also a small group
of men well known to one another. The remaining central directors
were people who sat on the banks and railway companies which were
the hubs of the major spheres of influence.

The pattern of interlocking directorships was reinforced through a
complex system of kinship relations which testify to the importance
of family inheritance and to family continuity in positions of power
and influence. Kinship links are not always immediately apparent from
a list of names. The Duke of Buccleuch and Queensberry, and the Earl
of Dalkeith, both of whom appear in the list of central directors, were
father and son, the earldom being a courtesy title for the Duke's
elder son. Together, these two men sat on the boards of the Royal
Bank, North British Railway, Forth Bridge Railway, Scottish Widows,
Standard Life, and Scottish Equitable. Family continuity without
similarity of name is also evident amongst smaller companies: Sir C.
Bine Renshaw, chairman of A.F. Stoddard, was son-in-law of the
A.F. Stoddard who founded the firm.

An important set of kinship ties centred around the Dundas family
who seem to have constituted an Edinburgh business establishment.
The board of North British and Mercantile included Ralph Dundas of
Dundas and Robert Dundas of Arniston. Ralph Dundas, who also sat on
the Royal Bank, came from the main branch of the Dundas family, and
one of his relatives was married to William Younger (of William
McEwan), whose brother George was also on the North British and
Mercantile board. Another relative had married into the family of Lord
Balfour of Burleigh, Governor of the Bank of Scotland. Robert Dundas
was the son of Sir Robert Dundas, who had been a director of Scottish
Widows and the Bank of Scotland and whose family firm, Arniston
Coal, was tied into the Fife Coal group. Another branch of the Dundas
family was represented by the Marquess of Zetland, who was vice
president of North British and Mercantile. Clearly the 'Dundas system'
of patronage in Scottish life, which is supposed to have run from 1775
to 1805, was still a force to be reckoned with in the Edinburgh financial world.

Glasgow also had its family dynasties linking the major industrial
and commercial interests of the region. Figure 1.7 shows kinship
connections between those who were directors of J. and P. Coats, the
Linen Thread Company and the Finlay group of tea companies.
Through Sir James King's directorship of Coats these companies were

**Figure 1.7: Intermarriage in Glasgow Industry and Commerce —
Section A: The Coats, Arthur and Finlay Families**

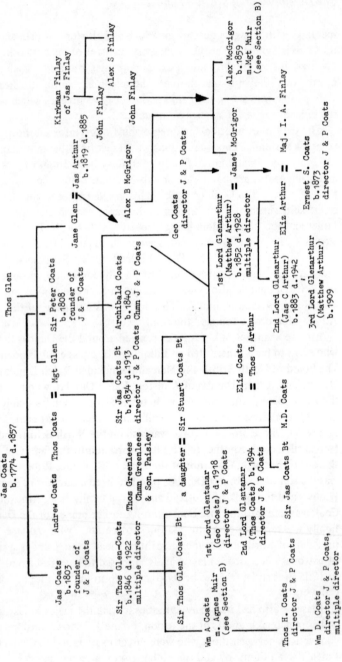

Figure 1.7: Intermarriage in Glasgow Industry and Commerce — Section B: The Muir and Denny Families

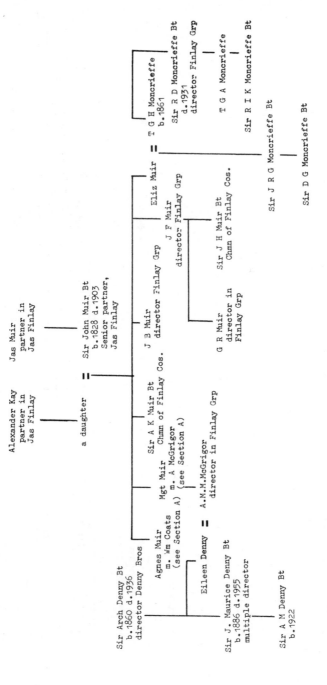

Figure 1.8: Textile and Investment Interests in Dundee

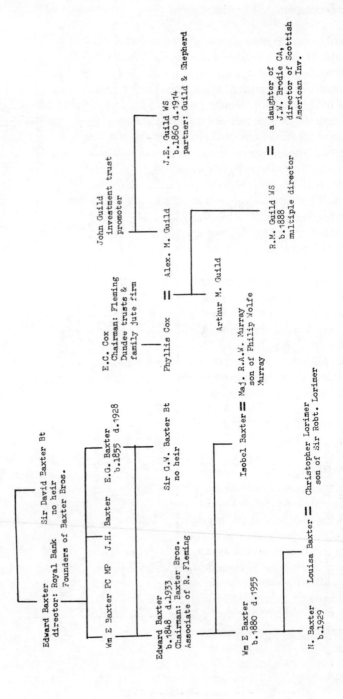

linked to the Tennant empire, and it is interesting that one of Sir
Charles Tennant's daughters was married to a younger son of the Earl
of Wemyss and March, a branch of whose family ran Wemyss Collieries.
Tennant's other daughter, Margot, was later to achieve notoriety as the
wife of H.H. Asquith. Similar patterns of intermarriage can be found
amongst the Dundee jute and investment families. Figure 1.8 shows
some of the family linkages between the Cox, Guild and Baxter family
interests. The linkages were more extensive than can be shown in the
diagram, for Sir David Baxter was succeeded as chairman of Baxters
by Sir W.O. Dalgleish who sat, with Edward Cox and Alexander Gilroy,
on the Fleming Dundee trusts and was an associate of Gilroy on
Dundee, Perth, and London Shipping.

Aberdeen was not without the entanglements of kinship which
linked together the main business interests. The board of the North of
Scotland Bank included two members of the Ogston family who were
prominent shareholders in the bank and who had numerous links to
shipping and investment companies operating in Aberdeen. The bank
was interlocked with the Great North of Scotland Railway through
Thomas Adam and Theodore Crombie. The latter was chairman of
Leslie Steamship and was a director of Culter Mills Paper and Aberdeen
Jute. Adam was managing director of Adam Steamship and other
Aberdeen shipping companies. Ogston family directorships included
both Adam Steamship and Aberdeen Jute. Whilst the Aberdeen men of
business remained separate from those based in the other cities, the
major business interests were perhaps more clearly interlinked than
elsewhere.

Conclusion

The discussion of Scottish companies and Scottish capital in 1904-5
has exemplified in detail the broad features of the Scottish economy
which we outlined at the beginning of this chapter. In this conclusion
we shall draw out some of the implications of our discussion.

The Scottish business system still bore the signs of its origins in small
family enterprises. Although the period from the 1890s to the First
World War involved numerous company amalgamations, the new
combines differed only a little from their predecessors. In the USA and
Germany, bankers promoted company amalgamations and used their
command over capital to bring about a rationalisation and restructuring
of industry. Particularly in the USA, centralised corporate management developed as a means of controlling large integrated concerns.
In Scotland, as in Britain generally, the pattern was different.

Amalgamation involved the fusion of independent family concerns into a holding company structure in which there was little reorganisation at the technical or financial level. The device of the holding company was mainly a way of regulating sales or output, or of enabling a number of small firms to raise capital through the stock exchange flotation of a more marketable holding company. Many dominant firms were either family firms which had adopted the joint stock form, concerns which had grown up on the basis of old family firms, or groups of family firms held together through a holding company. Only in the case of the railways and some newer firms in oil and electricity was the family principle not to be found. The large, non-family concerns tended to be closely tied to the major banking and insurance interests, these financial companies themselves having grown beyond the limits of family capital. Nevertheless, the data suggest that former controlling families and members of established family dynasties continued to be represented on their boards.

When interlocking directorships or the formation of a holding company resulted in horizontal or vertical integration, there was generally little impact upon the industrial structure of the companies. A certain amount of co-ordination between interdependent firms was possible, and considerable power over the market could be exercised, but economies of scale and greater efficiency were rarely achieved. Combination tended to be a conservative defence of existing market shares or a way of maintaining family power. The most notable exception was J. and P. Coats, which had completely taken over its smaller competitors and had become one of the three largest companies in Britain at this time.

The process of fusion between the economies of Scotland and England was already well advanced. Although Scottish capital had been very much the junior partner of English imperial power, Scotland in the nineteenth century still constituted a distinct national economy. The Scottish economy probably had a greater economic autonomy at that time than have many industrialising nations today. Some companies had transferred their headquarters to London or had amalgamated with English concerns, but others, notably Coats and Distillers, were dominant in the British and world markets for their products. Nevertheless, the changing international balance of economic power and the encroachment of English capital were beginning to make themselves felt on the Scottish economy. Whilst the period up to 1914 can be characterised as a story of the 'success' of Scottish capital, this success was laying the seeds of the problems which were later to mark the development of the Scottish economy. The over-dependence on heavy industry and the massive flow of capital abroad meant that Scottish capital failed to move into the newer growth industries which were to become so important after the First World War.

Table 1A: Scotland's Top Companies (1904-5)*

Section A: Non-Financial Companies

Rank	Company	Industry	Capital (£000)	Multiple Directors
1	North British Railway	Railways	47,236	Earl of Dalkeith (C), C. Carlow (VC), A.B. Gilroy, H. Grierson, A.K. McCosh, H.S. Macpherson, A. Simpson, H.G. Younger
2	Caledonian Railway	Railways	42,899	Sir J. Thompson (C), Sir J. King (DC), Sir M. Mitchell-Thomson, D. Tod, Marquess of Breadalbane, H. Brown, Sir C.B. Renshaw, E. Cox, J.H. Houldsworth, Lord Newlands, H. Allan, G.R. Vernon, W. Younger
3	Glasgow and South Western Railway	Railways	14,204	Sir J. Bell (DC), Sir M. Arthur, Earl of Glasgow, W. Lorimer, Sir H.E. Maxwell
4	J. and P. Coats	Cotton thread man.	10,000	Sir T. Glen-Coats, Sir J. King, Sir W. Arrol, S. Clark
5	Great North of Scotland Railway	Railways	4,979	T. Adam, T. Crombie
6	Highland Railway	Railways	4,653	R.M. Wilson (DC), Marquess of Breadalbane, W.S. Fothringham, J.G. Stewart, Duke of Sutherland, Sir W.O. Dalgleish
7	Forth Bridge Railway	Railways	2,325	Lord Balfour of Burleigh, Earl of Dalkeith, H. Grierson
8	Consolidated Tea and Lands	Tea planters	2,000	Sir A.K. Muir (C), Sir R.D. Moncrieffe, J.F. Muir, J.T. Tullis, A.M. Brown, R. Scott, R.H. Sinclair, D.M. Hannay
9	Linen Thread	Linen and thread man.	1,991	Sir J. Knox (VC), Sir T. Glen-Coats

Table 1A: Section A —cont.

Rank	Company	Industry	Capital (£000)	Multiple Directors
10	Burmah Oil	Oil	1,850	L. Gow, J. Innes
11	United Collieries	Coal mining	1,801	H. Mungall (C), J.T. Tullis (VC), Sir D. Richmond
12	North British Locomotive	Engineering	1,750	W. Lorimer (C)
13	Distillers	Whisky distillers	1,419	A. McNab, J.B. Harvey
14	Stewarts and Lloyds	Iron and steel man.	1,400	J.G. Stewart (C), Sir W. Arrol, R.M. Wilson
15	Lanarkshire and Dumbartonshire Railway	Railways	1,389	W.A. Donaldson (C), J.M. Denny, H. Brown
16	Glasgow District Subway	Railways	1,300	A. Simpson (C), J.P. Smith, A.K. McCosh
17	Tharsis Sulphur & Copper	Copper mining	1,250	Sir C. Tennant (C), H. Brown, T. Alexander, J. Couper, Sir J. King
18	'Moss' Empires	Theatre manage.	1,031	–
19=	Kanan Devan Hills Produce	Tea planters	1,000	Sir A.K. Muir (C), Sir R.D. Moncrieffe, J.F. Muir, D.M. Hannay, A.M. Brown, R. Scott, R.M. Sinclair, J.T. Tullis
19=	William McEwan	Brewers	1,000	W. Younger (MD)
19=	William Younger	Brewers	1,000	H.G. Younger
22	Barry, Ostlere & Shepherd	Linoleum man.	934	–
23	West Highland Railway	Railways	929	H. Grierson (C)
24	Anglo-American Direct Tea Trading	Tea merchants	910	Sir A.K. Muir (C), Sir R.D. Moncrieffe, A.M. Brown, R. Scott, R.M. Sinclair, J.F. Muir, D.M. Hannay, J.T. Tullis
25	Alex Pirie & Sons	Paper makers	900	–

Table 1A: Section A—cont.

Rank	Company	Industry	Capital (£000)	Multiple Directors
26	Amalgamated Tea Estates	Tea planters	898	Sir A.K. Muir (C), Sir R.D. Moncrieffe, J.F. Muir, D.M. Hannay, A.M. Brown, R. Scott, R.M. Sinclair, J.T. Tullis
27	Coltness Iron	Iron and steel man.	850	J.H. Houldsworth, Sir J. King
28	Fife Coal	Coal mining	831	T. Aitken (C), J. Jordan, H. Mungall, C. Carlow
29	Callander & Oban Railway	Railways	817	Sir J. Thompson (C), Marquess of Breadalbane, Lord Newlands, H. Brown, D. Tod
30	Nobel's Explosives	Explosives man.	800	Sir C. Tennant (C), Sir R.W. Anstruther, H. Brown, T. Alexander
31	George Younger & Son	Brewers	750	G. Younger (C)
32	Arizona Copper	Copper mining	737	J.B. Harvey, A. McNab
33	Irrawaddy Flotilla	Shipping	720	Sir J. King (VC), T. Aitken, J.M. Denny, J. Innes (MD)
34	Scottish Gympie Gold Mines	Gold mining	660	J.B. Hilliard
35	Allan Line Steamships	Shipping	606	H. Allan
36=	Clyde Valley Electrical Power	Electricity prod.	600	Sir D. Richmond
36=	John Dewar & Sons	Whisky distillers	600	–
36=	Lothians Electric Power	Electricity prod.	600	D. Russell, J.A. Hood, H. Rüffer
36=	Scottish Central Electric Power	Electricity prod.	600	W.S.B. McLaren (C), D. Russell, J.A. Hood, H. Rüffer
36=	Summerlee Iron	Coal mining and iron prod.	600	–
41	Anchor Line (Henderson Bros.)	Shipping	575	–

Table 1A: Section A—cont.

Rank	Company	Industry	Capital (£000)	Multiple Directors
42	British Dyewood & Chemical	Tanners	570	—
43	Acadia Sugar Refining	Sugar refiners	560	—
44	Rivet Bolt & Nut	Engineering	550	—
45	James Dunlop	Iron, coal and steel	549	W.A. Donaldson (C), Sir J. Thompson, W.S.B. McLaren
46	Lanarkshire and Ayrshire Railway	Railways	535	G.R. Vernon (C), H.E. Gordon (DC), Sir J. Knox, D. Tod
47	David & William Henderson	Engineers and shipbuilders	525	—
48=	Clan Line Steamers	Shipping	500	A.M. Brown
48=	Fairfield Shipbuilding and Engineering	Shipbuilders	500	—
48=	Wemyss Collieries Trust	Coal mining	500	H. Grierson
51	Steel Company of Scotland	Iron & steel man.	496	Sir C. Tennant (P), W. Lorimer (C), J. Couper, T. Alexander
52	Dailuane-Talisker Distilleries	Whisky distillers	490	—
53	Young's Paraffin Light & Mineral Oil	Paraffin man.	453	Sir M. Arthur, H. Brown, Sir J. King, H.S. Macpherson, T. Mason
54=	Bulloch Lade	Distillers & merchants	450	—
54=	Lanarkshire Steel	Iron & steel man.	450	J. Strain (C), A. Watt

Table 1A: Section A —cont.

Rank	Company	Industry	Capital (£000)	Multiple Directors
56 =	Glengarnock Iron and Steel	Iron & steel man.	400	J.H. Davidson
56 =	Fresno Copper	Copper mining	400	–
58	Lothian Coal	Coal mining	367	Sir J. King (C), R.K. Stewart, J.A. Hood (MD)
59	Scottish Waggon	Coachbuilders	360	J.H. Buchanan, J. Jordan, John Cowan
60 =	'Argyll Motors'	Engineering	350	–
60 =	Robertson, Sanderson	Wines & spirit merchants	350	A. Sanderson, J. Jordan, W. Blair
60 =	A.F. Stoddard	Carpet man.	350	Sir C.B. Renshaw
60 =	Victoria Jute	Jute spinners & weavers	350	A. Gilroy
64	Broxburn Oil	Shale oil extraction	335	Sir D. Richmond (C)

Table 1A—cont.

Section B: Banking Companies

Rank	Company	Deposits (£000)	Multiple Directors
1	Bank of Scotland	15,198	Lord Balfour of Burleigh (G), Marquess of Linlithgow (DG), W.J. Mure, Sir M. Mitchell-Thomson, J.M. Trotter, Sir R. Anstruther, J.A. Jamieson, G. Dunlop
2	National Bank of Scotland	14,134	Earl of Mansfield (G), J. Mylne, John Cowan, P. Blair, G. Younger, C. Ker, W.S. Davidson, A.D.M. Black
3	Commercial Bank of Scotland	14,025	Marquess of Tweedale (G), Marquess of Breadalbane (DG), Sir C.G. Macrae, J.H. Buchanan, J. Strain, J. Jordan, J. Rankine, J.L. Mounsey
4	Royal Bank of Scotland	13,606	Duke of Buccleuch and Queensberry (G), Earl of Elgin and Kincardine (DG), Ralph Dundas, C. Carlow, J.P. Wright, Sir T.D.G. Carmichael, J. Haldane, Sir H. Cook, C.C. Maconochie
5	Union Bank of Scotland	12,270	Sir C. Tennant (C), H.E. Gordon, Sir L.J. Grant, A.R.C. Pitman, D. Ritchie, J.P. Smith, J.S. Tait, S. Thomson, R. Blyth, R.E. Findlay
6	British Linen Co., Bank	11,917	C.B. Balfour, Robert Dundas, J.J. Cowan, A. Sanderson
7	Clydesdale Bank	10,923	Sir J. King (C), H. Brown (DC), H. Allan, Sir J. Bell, W. Sanderson, R.K. Stewart
8	North of Scotland Bank	4,013	T. Crombie, T. Adam

Table 1A—cont.

Section C: Insurance Companies

Rank	Company	Life & General Funds	Multiple Directors
1	Scottish Widows Fund Life Assurance	17,208	Marquess of Tweedale (P), Earl of Dalkeith (VP), Sir H.E. Maxwell (VP), W.J. Mure, Sir H. Cook, Sir T.D.G. Carmichael, D. Cowan, J.A. Jamieson, C.B. Balfour, Sir M. Mitchell-Thomson, S. Clark, E.A. Davidson
2	North British and Mercantile Insurance	16,351	Duke of Sutherland (P), Ralph Dundas, C.C. Maconochie, Robert Dundas, G. Younger, Earl of Elgin
3	Scottish Provident Institution	13,138	J. MacDonald, P. Murray, J.J. Cowan, Sir L.J. Grant, J.M. Trotter
4	Standard Life Assurance	10,925	Duke of Buccleuch & Queensberry (G), Marquess of Linlithgow (DG), J.H. Davidson, Sir R.W. Anstruther, Sir J. King, A.R.C. Pitman, W. Younger, C.F. Whigham, J. Ivory
5	Life Association of Scotland	5,399	W.C. Johnston, W.H. Murray, J.L. Mounsey
6	Scottish Equitable Life Assurance	5,073	Duke of Buccleuch & Queensberry (P), Earl of Mansfield (VP), J.C. Pitman, P. Blair, J.M.D. Peddie
7	General Accident, Fire & Life Assurance**	Not known	W.S. Fothringham, Sir R.D. Moncrieffe
8	Scottish Amicable Life Assurance	4,670	Earl of Glasgow (VP), S. Thomson, R. Blyth, R.E. Findlay
9	Scottish Union & National Insurance	4,623	W.S. Davidson (C), A.D.M. Black, T. Mason, H.G. Younger

Table 1A: Section C—cont.

Rank	Company	Life & General Funds	Multiple
10	Edinburgh Life Assurance	3,865	Marquess of Breadalbane (P), G. Barclay, J. Rankine, Sir J. Guthrie, J. Mylne
11	City of Glasgow Life Assurance	2,832	Sir J. Bell (C), J.P. Smith, C. Ker, D. Ritchie
12	Caledonian Assurance	2,694	R. Stewart, W. Sanderson, W. Blair, Sir C.G. Macrae
13	National Guarantee & Suretyship Association**	Not known	J. Mylne, W.C. Smith, R. Stewart, W. Sanderson, J.S. Tait
14	Scottish Imperial Insurance	648	L. Gow, D.M. Hannay

Table 1A—cont.

Section D: Investment and Property Companies

Rank	Company	Capital (£000)	Multiple Directors
1	New Zealand and Australian Land	1,550	R. Stewart (C), G. Barclay, W.S. Davidson, J. Haldane
2=	British Investment Trust	1,500	John Cowan (C), Sir M. Mitchell-Thomson, J.P. Wright, G. Dunlop
2=	Scottish American Investment	1,500	P.W. Cambell (C), J. Ivory, T. Maitland, W.H. Murray, A.R. Duncan
2=	Scottish American Mortgage	1,500	A. Wallace (P), A. Whitton, P.W. Campbell
5	Alliance Trust	1,200	Sir J. Guthrie, A. Whitton, T. Maitland
6=	North of Scotland Canadian Mortgage	750	W.C. Smith
6=	Northern American Trust	750	E. Cox, Sir W.O. Dalgleish, A. Gilroy, R.B. Don
8	Australasian Mortgage & Agency	553	C.F. Whigham
9	Edinburgh Investment Trust	504	P.W. Campbell (C), W. Sanderson, W.S. Fraser, J.S. Tait
10=	Investors' Mortgage Security	500	G. Dunlop (C), E.A. Davidson, W. Mackenzie, A. Whitton
10=	North British Canadian Investment	500	—
10=	Oregon Mortgage	500	P.W. Campbell
10=	Scottish Investment Trust	500	E.A. Davidson (C), J. MacDonald, C.D. Menzies, J.M.D. Peddie, R.J. Torrie
10=	Scottish Reversionary	500	Sir M. Mitchell-Thomson, W.C. Johnston
15	American Mortgage Co. of Scotland	428	J. Campbell (C), G. Dunlop, P. Murray

Table 1A: Section D—cont.

Rank	Company	Capital (£000)	Multiple Directors
16	Realisation & Debenture Corp. of Scotland	403	D. Cowan (C), Sir T.D.G. Carmichael, A. Wallace, A.R.C. Pitman, J.S. Tait
17=	Second Scottish American Trust	400	E. Cox (C), Sir W.O. Dalgleish, A. Gilroy, R.B. Don
17=	Third Scottish American Trust	400	E. Cox (C), Sir W.O. Dalgleish, A. Gilroy, R.B. Don
19	United States Mortgage Company of Scotland	375	J. MacDonald (C), R.J. Torrie, W. Mackenzie, J.C. Pitman
20	Edinburgh American Land Mortgage	362	A.R. Duncan
21	Transvaal Proprietary	335	J.B. Hilliard
22	Reversionary Association	325	T. Aitken (C), J. Campbell, A. Watt

* See Appendix for notes on this table.
** Rank estimated since figures for funds are not available.

2 CONTINUITY AND CHANGE IN THE INTER-WAR YEARS

The war-time extensions in company activities and the post-war boom of 1919-20 led to a great increase in the number of joint stock companies and in the significance of joint stock capital. The conversion of family concerns into private or public companies progressed in all industries and continued throughout the twenties. The depression of 1921-31 hit the older export-oriented industries particularly badly and led to a reduction in the number of publicly quoted companies. Concentration and monopolisation proceeded apace and consolidated the position of the large firms and, at the same time, wealthy families began to diversify their shareholdings rather than tying up their interests in one concern. These years saw the beginning of the transition from small-scale family enterprises to large-scale business. Economic recovery in Britain began in 1932 and was concentrated in steel and in the newer industries such as electrical engineering, chemicals, auto-mobiles and aircraft. These newer industries tended to be located in the south and midlands of England, and areas such as Scotland lacked not only growth industries but also their multiplier effects on traditional heavy industry. Thus economic recovery in Scotland was even less marked than that in Britain as a whole, though rearmament generated just enough demand to keep Scottish industry at work. Such new industry that was established in Scotland tended to be owned by English or, increasingly, American interests.

In each sector of Scottish industry this period was a phase of con-centration and monopolisation. The shipbuilding industry had been subject to government regulation during the war and these controls continued into the post-war period because of the over-capacity of the world shipbuilding industry. Through the 1920s and 1930s the industry in Scotland was rationalised and shipbuilding firms became closely linked to the major steel companies. The 'anglicisation' of Scottish industry became a marked feature of this period as Stewarts and Lloyds transferred much of their production to their new plant at Corby and the Scottish railway companies were forcibly merged into the government-regulated LMS and LNER. The falling demand for coal after the war led to various official investigations of the coal industry in an attempt to prevent its total collapse. Although an Act of 1930 was intended to encourage combinations and co-operative marketing, conflicts amongst coal owners precluded effective combination and there was little rationalisation of the industry. The growing electricity industry was closely allied to coal mining. Much of the generating capacity was controlled by municipal concerns, although some large joint stock companies were rivalling the local undertakings. In 1926, the government began to introduce the national grid system and so exerted control over the power companies. A particularly important development in Scotland was the production of hydroelectric power by the Scottish Power Company. In the chemical industry, the biggest single event of the period was undoubtedly the creation of Imperial Chemical Industries in 1926. ICI brought together Nobel's, United Alkali, Brunner Mond, and a number of other companies, and it was the first British company amalgamation to adopt the centralised divisional administrative structure rather than the holding company structure. Through this merger, the last important segment of the Scottish chemical industry passed out of Scottish control.

Three trends stand out: economic concentration, 'anglicisation' of control, and the growth of government regulation. In this chapter we shall discuss the structure of the business system in 1920-1 and in 1937-8 in order to illustrate these general trends in the development of the Scottish economy.

Scotland's Top Companies, 1920-38

The list of top Scottish companies for 1920-1 is given in Table 2.A at the end of this chapter. A total of 76 non-financial companies had share capital in excess of £500,000. Together with the eight Scottish banks, 13 major insurance companies and 17 investment and property companies, the list of top companies comprises 114 enterprises. Table 2.1 shows the size distribution of the non-financial companies.

Railway capital was of slightly less importance than in 1904-5, the nine railway companies accounting for just over a half of the total capital. Of the ten largest companies, accounting for just over two-thirds of all capital, five were railways, two were in oil, two in textiles, and one in steel. As Table 2.2 shows, textiles remained an important sector with eight companies accounting for over a quarter of non-railway capital. Similarly, the 22 companies in engineering, iron, coal and steel accounted for almost a quarter of non-railway capital. Railways, textiles and heavy industry remained the characteristic sectors of Scottish joint stock capital. In 1919, the 50 largest British manufacturing companies accounted for 43 per cent of the market

Table 2.1: Size Distribution of Non-Financial Companies (1920-38)

Companies by Rank	1920-1 Total Share Capital (£)	1920-1 Cumulative Total (£)	1937-8 Total Share Capital (£)	1937-8 Cumulative Total (£)
Top 10	159,881,734	159,881,734	87,941,323	87,941,323
11-20	23,073,800	182,955,534	22,758,377	110,699,700
21-30	13,859,786	196,815,320	16,218,900	126,918,600
31-40	10,191,771	207,007,091	11,996,140	138,914,740
41-50	8,093,112	215,100,203	9,379,384	148,294,124
51-60	6,271,868	221,372,071	−	−
Remainder	8,381,185	229,753,256	6,771,417	155,065,541
TOTALS	229,753,256	(N = 76)	155,065,541	(N = 59)

Table 2.2: Industrial Distribution of Non-Financial Companies (1920-38)

Industrial Sector	Number of Companies 1920-1 Top 30	1920-1 Top 50	1920-1 All	1937-8 Top 30	1937-8 Top 50	1937-8 All
Railways	7	8	9	0	0	0
Tea and rubber	4	6	6	3	6	6
Coal, iron and steel	5	8	14	5	9	12
Food and drink	1	5	8	4	6	7
Non-coal mining	1	2	3	0	1	1
Oil	2	2	2	2	2	2
Chemicals	1	1	1	2	2	2
Engineering and metalwork	1	3	9	3	4	4
Paper	0	1	2	1	2	2
Dyeing	1	1	1	1	1	1
Textiles	2	5	8	2	5	8
Electricity	1	1	2	2	2	3
Shipping	2	3	6	2	5	5
Distribution	2	3	4	2	2	3
Theatres	0	1	1	0	1	1
Road transport	0	0	0	1	1	1
Newspapers	0	0	0	0	1	1
TOTALS			76			59

value of British companies and 17 per cent of British output. Amongst
these 50 were five large Scottish companies (Coats, Nobel's, Stewarts
& Lloyds, Linen Thread and Distillers), and the list also included
Buchanan-Dewar, the London holding company for Dewar. It is clear
that these six Scottish companies, together with the major railway and
oil companies, were important not only in the Scottish economy but
also in the wider British economy.

The eight Scottish banks had total deposits of £286m, and the 13
insurance companies had total funds of about £128m. Whilst there was
little difference in size between the banks, the four largest insurance
companies accounted for over a half of the total funds of the 13 companies. By 1929, these four large companies (Scottish Widows, North
British & Mercantile, Scottish Provident, and Standard Life) were all
amongst the 20 largest British life companies, and the North British
was joined by General Accident, Scottish Union, and the Caledonian
amongst the 20 largest British non-life companies for that year. The
total share capital of the 17 investment and property companies, most
of which had converted to general investments trusts, came to £31m,
about the same in size as the textile sector.

In 1937-8 (see Table 2.B) there were 59 non-financial companies
with capital of £700,000 or more. Together with the eight banks, 14
insurance companies and 30 investment and property companies, 111
top companies were included in our analysis. The total capital of the
non-financial companies actually fell during the period after 1920,
largely due to the reconstruction of the British railway network in
1923. As Table 2.2 shows, the ten largest companies accounted for
just over a half of all the capital. Apart from railways, the main industrial changes were in engineering and metal working, where the number
of companies fell from nine to four over the period. The basic structure
of the Scottish economy, involving a predominance of textiles and
heavy industry, remained but Scottish companies seemed to be losing
their position in the British economy. In 1930, the 50 largest British
manufacturing companies accounted for 64 per cent of the market
value of British companies and 26 per cent of British output. These 50
included only three large Scottish companies (J. & P. Coats, Distillers,
Stewarts & Lloyds) and so it would seem that the large Scottish
companies failed to keep their relative positions in an increasingly
concentrated British economy.

The eight banks had total deposits in 1937-8 of £329m and
insurance funds amounted to £234m. The four largest insurance companies continued to account for over a half of these insurance funds,

and all retained their positions in the top 20 British insurance companies. The investment and property companies, most of which had converted to general investment trusts, had a total share capital of £46m. This figure was considerably larger than the capital of the textile firms (£29m) and was equivalent to almost one-third of the capital of the non-financial companies.

As a result of the post-war boom there was an expansion in the absolute and relative size of the non-financial sector of the Scottish economy. Over the years which followed, many of these companies were brought under foreign control, were amalgamated with English companies, or were absorbed into larger Scottish concerns. As a consequence, considerable funds must have been available to the former shareholders of these companies. This wealth, however, was not put back into industry but was put into the formation and extension of investment trusts. The relative importance of the investment sector in 1937-8 was greater than it had been before the First World War. Scottish capital was not used to broaden the Scottish industrial base but to enlarge the already substantial investment sector.

There are many interesting trends in the characteristics of company boards over the period. Average board size increased from 7.1 in 1904-5 to 7.8 in 1920-1, but it fell back to 7.4 in 1937-8. Although these variations are small, there was a noticeable increase in the size of bank boards between 1904 and 1921, and a noticeable decrease in the size of investment company boards. Thus, bank boards in 1920-1 averaged 11.5 members and investment companies averaged 4.9. These averages remained at this level in 1937-8. The major causes of the overall decrease in board size after 1921 seem to be a fall in the size of insurance company boards, from 11.5 to 10.1, and the loss of the railway companies with their huge boards. Thus, the ten largest industrials in 1920-1 had a board size of 12.0, whilst the average in 1937-8 was 9.9. In 1920-1, 688 men held 893 directorships, 118 of these men sitting on two or more boards. These multiple directors held just over a third of all directorships. Whilst 37 per cent of all directorships were in financial companies, 52 per cent of the directorships held by multiple directors were in the financial sector. In 1937-8, 586 men held 824 directorships, 370 being held by 132 multiple directors. Whilst 46 per cent of all directorships were in the financial sector, 57 per cent of the directorships held by multiple directors were financial. The increasing significance of the financial sector is apparent from this data: whilst the proportion of financial directorships held by multiple directors remained constant at just over a half, these financial directorships became a much more significant element in the Scottish business system. Most noticeable of all was the fact that the proportion of investment company directorships held by multiple directors increased from 62 per cent in 1920-1 to 77 per cent in 1937-8. Not only was Scottish capital moving into the investment trust sector in a big way, but control over this sector came more and more to rest with the multiple directors.

Table 2.3: Multiple Directors on the Board (1920-38)

	Number of Companies			
No. of Multiple	1920-1		1937-8	
Directors on Board	Non-financial	Financial	Non-financial	Financial
0	19	1	23	1
1	23	1	5	4
2	14	9	6	7
3	7	7	6	9
4	2	4	5	10
5	2	5	4	11
6	4	3	1	4
7		3	6	4
8	5	1		1
9		2		
10		1		
11		1	1	1
12			1	
13			1	
TOTALS	76	38	59	52

Table 2.3 shows that, for interlocked companies, the average number of multiple directors sitting on each company board rose from 3.4 to 4.3, the average having been 3.3 in 1904-5. It would appear that multiple directors were occupying a larger proportion of the available board seats, not only at the aggregate level but also in each individual company. Whilst the number of companies with a large contingent of multiple directors fell between 1920 and 1938, the number of companies with just one multiple director fell by a greater amount. The rise in the average number of multiple directors on each board was a

necessary consequence of these two trends. The decline in the number of companies with many multiple directors is clear: in 1920-1 there were ten companies with eight or more multiple directors, by 1937-8 there were only five. The companies with the most multiple directors in 1920-1 were Bank of Scotland (11), Union Bank (10), National Bank (9), Scottish Widows (9), Edinburgh Assurance (8), Caledonian Railway (8), and the four Finlay tea companies (8 each). In 1937-8 the list comprised Scottish Brewers (13), William Younger (12), William McEwan (11), Bank of Scotland (11) and Scottish Provident (8). Excluding the brewing group and the tea group, which appear in the list because they interlock frequently within their own group, the number of widely connected companies which had many multiple directors fell from six in 1920-1 to two in 1937-8. In 1904-5, there had been nine such companies.

The general trends of the inter-war years indicate the growing importance of the financial sector, and particularly of the investment companies. The level of interlocking amongst financial companies increased up to 1920 and then remained constant, whilst the proportion of industrial companies which were interlocked fell between 1920 and 1938. However, those companies which were interlocked in 1937-8 seemed to be more dominated by the multiple directors than had been the case previously. The network seemed to be 'tightening up' around a financial core.

The Financial Sector

(i)   The Banking and Insurance Sector

During the course of their development the major Scottish banks had taken over their smaller competitors and, with the acquisition of Caledonian Banking in 1907 by the Bank of Scotland and the acquisition of the Town and Country Bank in 1908 by the North of Scotland Bank, the eight large banks held exclusive sway. However, the move towards concentration in English banking had its repercussions north of the border. Between 1918 and 1924, four of the Scottish banks were acquired by English banks. In 1918, Lloyds Bank acquired the National Bank through a share exchange scheme as a result of which Charles Ker, chairman of the National, obtained a seat on the Lloyds board and a Welsh landowner, Wilfred de Winton, represented the parent company on the National board. James Tuke, the general manager of the British Linen Bank from 1912, engineered a merger between his own bank and Barclays in 1919. As a result, Tuke obtained a seat on the Barclays board, and R.L. Barclay represented his bank on the British Linen board. The Midland Bank took over the Clydesdale in 1921 and the North of Scotland in 1924. Both of these takeovers were financed through a share exchange deal and so the controllers of the Scottish banks acquired an interest in the Midland. The Ogston family held six per cent of the capital of the North of Scotland Bank, and the Clydesdale directorate held ten per cent of their company's capital. Through the share exchange scheme these men held one per cent of the Midland's capital, and three of the Clydesdale's directors (H. Allan, J. Henderson and Sir James Bell) joined the Midland board. As a result of this restructuring, the two Scottish subsidiaries became interlocked through Reginald McKenna, the chairman of the Midland.

These changes in control were associated with alterations in the relative size of the banks. In terms of deposits, the Bank of Scotland fell from top position in 1904-5 to a 1937-8 position in the middle ranks, and the National Bank fell from second to fourth position. Conversely, the Royal Bank rose from fourth position in 1904-5 to top the list in 1937-8. The Clydesdale Bank rose from seventh in 1904-5 to fourth in 1920-1, though it subsequently fell back to sixth place. The North of Scotland remained the smallest Scottish bank, and the British Linen Bank and the Union Bank were consistently in the lower ranks.

The insurance sector also was marked by a considerable restructuring during the inter-war period. Intensification of competition in the late nineteenth and early twentieth century involved an extension of the branch network and the number of agencies, and so led to increasing costs. The attempt to minimise costs created a tendency towards amalgamation amongst British insurance companies. It was in the period leading up to the First World War that many of the large composite (life and non-life) companies emerged, and this had its repercussions in Scotland. Whilst the Scottish Union took over the smaller City of Glasgow in 1913, two other acquisitions involved English companies: the Norwich Union took over Scottish Imperial in 1913, and the Commercial Union took over Edinburgh Life in 1918. Of these companies, only Edinburgh Life retained its separate legal identity (as a composite group renamed Edinburgh Assurance), and there was no exchange of directors between the company and its parent. The North British and Mercantile had been formed through the merger in 1860 of the North British Insurance Company with the London-based Mercantile Insurance, but had operated as a holding company with separate Scottish and English boards. In 1926 the decision was taken to combine the two boards and to transfer control to London, though the company retained its Scottish registration. As a result, the company was less interlocked with the Scottish banks than previously and became more directly linked to the Arbuthnot, Schröder and Kleinwort banking interests which had dominated the London board. An important change in this period was the conversion in 1925 of Standard Life from a proprietary company to a mutual company, though there was no change in its control: a half of the 1920-1 board were also directors in 1937-8.

The close interlocking between banks and insurance companies remained a feature of the inter-war years. The overall pattern of inter-locking was similar to that discovered for 1904-5: there was a con-siderable overlapping of company linkages and a tendency for 'Edinburgh' and 'Glasgow' interests to remain distinct. The major changes were that the Clydesdale Bank had no Scottish insurance connections in either 1920-1 or 1937-8, and that plural lines between companies became a less marked feature of the network. The 'strength' of an interlock can be defined by its duration, by the number of common directors, and by whether the interlocks involve corporate office-holders. Certain important continuities over the period 1904 to 1938 were apparent for the strongest interlocks. The National Bank had strong links with North British and Mercantile, the Commercial Bank had strong links with Life Association, and both banks had strong links to Scottish Union. The Bank of Scotland had strong links to Standard Life, Scottish Widows, and Scottish Provident, and two of these insurance companies had strong links to other banks: Scottish Widows to the Royal Bank, and Scottish Provident to the British Linen Bank. The other strong links were those between the Union Bank and Scottish Amicable, and between the North of Scotland Bank and Northern Assurance. Throughout the first 40 years of the century, three of the largest insurance companies played an important bridging role between banks: Scottish Union, Scottish Widows and Scottish Provident were of key importance in connecting major banking centres. Despite a turnover in personnel as directors retired, died, or resigned, this structure remained intact.

(ii)   The Investment and Property Sector

Robert Fleming had transferred many of his investment interests to London to form the Investment Trust Corporation in 1888 and Robert Fleming & Co. in 1909, the latter becoming a general financial business. He remained, however, the London correspondent of many of the

Scottish investment companies and was able to use his London and Scottish interests as a way of placing the new company share issues which his firm handled. Fleming continued to be an important figure on the Scottish investment scene throughout its period of expansion between 1924 and 1929, and he remained an active company director until his death in 1933. Along with Fleming, many of the earlier investment trust promoters and their descendants remained prominent figures throughout the inter-war period.

Figure 2.1: Investment Company Interlocks (1920-1)

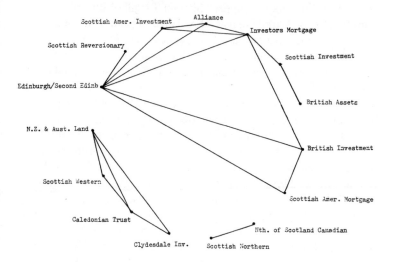

Figure 2.1 shows that the pattern of interlocking amongst investment trusts in 1920-1 was similar to the pre-war structure. All but one of the 17 investment companies were tied into a system of three components, the components being centred around Edinburgh, Glasgow and Aberdeen interests. The isolated trust was the Dundee-based Northern American Trust, which continued to be interlocked with the smaller Dundee trusts. The Dundee-based Alliance Trust continued to form a part of a predominantly Edinburgh group comprising Scottish American Investment, Investors' Mortgage, and the two Edinburgh Investment Trusts. Scottish American Mortgage had become a less central part of this component, and Edinburgh Investment became the focus of many more connections. The 'Glasgow' group centred around the Brown, Fleming and Murray trusts, but also

included the Edinburgh-based New Zealand and Australian Land.
William Mackenzie of the Alliance Trust, and Andrew Bonar Law, MP,
joined with Robert Fleming to form the Scottish Western in 1907 and
the Caledonian three years later. Fleming managed the investments
from his London office and Bonar Law chaired the companies. In
1912, Bonar Law's political commitments forced him to resign, but the
syndicate continued to operate the trusts and also set up Clydesdale
Investment in 1913. These trusts were closely allied with the development of Burmah Oil and Anglo-Persian Oil, and much of their funds
seem to have come from shipping and shipbuilding interests. In the
1920s, their directorate comprised Sir John Cargill of Burmah,
members of two Murray families, H.A. Jamieson, and R.F. Barclay.
As in 1904-5, most trusts had an independent management and secre-
tariat, though the group form of organisation was becoming an
important feature. Group organisation was perhaps least marked in
Edinburgh.

As Figure 2.2 shows, the group form of organisation had become
more typical by 1937-8. The huge growth in the number of trusts,
manifested in the greater number included in our analysis, involved
either the creation of new trusts within existing groups or the emer-
gence of new groups. In addition, formerly independent trusts had
been incorporated into groups. The most important of the new groups
was Baillie, Gifford, which was the largest Edinburgh group. The largest
trust in the group, Scottish Mortgage, was formed in 1909 as the Straits
Mortgage and Trust. In the three years preceding the First World War,
this company changed its name, and the Scottish Canadian Mortgage
Company and Edinburgh, Dundee and Aberdeen Investment were
formed. The group went through a massive growth and restructuring
between 1924 and 1929. In 1924, Edinburgh and Dundee dropped
'Aberdeen' from its title and Scottish Central Investment was formed,
followed a year later by Scottish Capital Investment. In 1927, Scottish
Canadian became Second Scottish Mortgage and the Second Edinburgh
and Dundee was established. Baillie, Gifford expanded into London in
1929 by setting up the Abbots, Friars and Monks trusts and the Winter-
bottom Trust. The central figure in the group, and a key figure in the
British investment trust movement, was T.J. Carlyle Gifford who sat on
three of the four main trust boards as well as being a director of many
trusts outside the group. The group's closest links were with the Guild
and Shepherd families and with the directors of the Alliance Trust.

The Alliance and the Second Alliance were chaired by James Prain,
the head of a Dundee jute firm. Although the trusts remained closely

Figure 2.2: Investment Company Groups (1920-38)

	Manager or Secretary	Trust(s)
1920-1	Brown, Fleming and Murray 175 W. George St, Glasgow Secretaries	Caledonian Trust Clydesdale Investment Scottish Western
	Alex. Clapperton, CA 1 North Charlotte St, Edinburgh Secretary	Edinburgh Investment Second Edinburgh Investment
1937-8	W.D. Macdougall Dundee Manager	Alliance Trust Second Alliance Trust
	Ivory and Sime 9 Charlotte Sq., Edinburgh Secretaries	British Assets Second British Assets
	R.M. Robertson 46 Castle Street, Edinburgh Manager	British Investment Realisation and Debenture
	Brown, Fleming and Murray 175 W. George St, Glasgow Secretaries	Caledonian Trust Clydesdale Investment Scottish Western Second Scottish Western
	Alex Clapperton, CA 3 Charlotte Sq., Edinburgh Manager and Secretary	Edinburgh Investment Second Edinburgh Investment
	Shepherd and Wedderburn 16 Charlotte Sq., Edinburgh Secretaries	Investors' Mortgage Second Investors' Mortgage American Trust
	R.J. Edgar, CA 6 Albyn Place, Edinburgh Secretary	Scottish Investment Second Scottish Investment
	Baillie, Gifford and Co. 3 Glenfinlas St, Edinburgh Manager and Secretaries	Scottish Mortgage and Trust Edinburgh and Dundee Scottish Capital Scottish Central

allied with Edinburgh interests, their ownership was firmly rooted in Dundee. Table 2.4 shows that both trusts had about 80 per cent of their shares held in Scotland and that, within this total, Dundee was most important, particularly in the case of the Second Alliance. It is likely that many of the Dundee holdings were the investments of the local textile magnates who had originally financed the trusts. Share concentration was fairly high: 375 individuals held shares in both companies and accounted for 15 per cent of the Alliance capital and 54 per cent of the Second Alliance.

Table 2.4: Shareholders in the Alliance Trust Group (1934)

| | Alliance | | Second Alliance | |
	No. of Holders	% of Shares	No. of Holders	% of Shares
Dundee and District	888	45.1	436	69.0
Rest of Scotland	952	33.8	143	12.2
London and District	264	10.6	57	12.1
Elsewhere	386	10.9	57	6.7
TOTALS	2,490	100.0[a]	693	100.0

[a] rounding error in original source
Source: J.C. Gilbert, *A History of Investment Trusts in Dundee*, P.S. King, London, 1939, p. 11.

The Fleming Dundee trusts also were dominated by jute interests. The chairman of the Northern American and the other trusts was J. Ernest Cox, whose firm had transferred its registration to London and became Jute Industries. The influence of the 'juteocracy' had been most marked in the 1920s, when three of the four board members had been Cox, George Bonar and William Low. Closely associated with the Fleming trusts in Dundee was the Camperdown Trust which had been set up as a private Cox family trust in 1913 and had grown during 1921 and 1928. In the 1930s, Camperdown still had only 34 shareholders.

The largest group outside Edinburgh in the 1930s was the Brown Fleming and Murray group. During the 1920s, the three original trusts had been joined by five 'Second' and 'Third' trusts, and the Second Great Northern, though not the Great Northern, became part of the group. Sir John Cargill chaired all the trusts in the group and managerial responsibility was shared by R. Alistair Murray and J.I. Murray, the sons of Robert Alexander Murray. Other important group directors included R.F. Barclay, T.P. Spens (brother of H.B. Spens) and M.V. Fleming. Ivory and Sime had been built up by the Ivory family and was based around British Assets Trust. This trust had purchased the whole capital of Edinburgh American Land Mortgage in 1919, and in 1925 the latter's name was changed to Second British Assets. Similarly, British Investment Trust acquired control of Realisation and Debenture, transforming it from a general finance company into an investment trust proper.

Interlocking between groups in 1937-8 was such that the general pattern of Figure 2.1 remained. However, there was much more overlapping of groups, 28 of the 30 investment companies forming a single component. Only Great Northern and North of Scotland Canadian were isolated. The skeleton structure is presented in Figure 2.3, which shows all interlocks generated by trust chairmen. Even at this level, the Glasgow and Dundee groups were connected with the Edinburgh core. It is noticeable that the trusts in the Baillie, Gifford group have distinct patterns of connection, whilst the trusts in the Brown, Fleming and Murray group interlock in similar ways. This distinction between the 'umbrella' form of trust management and the 'collective' form of management became an important feature of later trust reorganisations. In the 1930s, most of the trust groups adopted an umbrella form of organisation and did not impose a common investment policy on the separate trusts. It is for this reason that the three main centres in the network — Edinburgh Investment, Scottish American Investment and Investors' Mortgage — tended not to form exclusive patterns of connection with particular trust groups, and why the whole network of investment interlocks was so densely connected.

In 1920-1, the major link between the Edinburgh investment companies and the banking and insurance sector ran through the Bank of Scotland and its associated insurance companies. Virtually all the main Edinburgh trusts were connected to the Bank of Scotland, though there was some separation between Standard Life and Scottish Widows' 'spheres'. Standard Life was connected to British Investment, Edinburgh Investment and Scottish American Mortgage, and these companies also connected to the National Bank and Scottish Provident. Scottish Widows was connected to Scottish Investment, British Assets, Investors' Mortgage and Scottish American Investment, and these companies also linked with the Royal Bank, Scottish Union and Edinburgh Assurance. Overall, however, there was little sharp separation between these clusters. The Aberdeen trusts were connected not only to one another but also to both the North of Scotland bank and Northern Assurance.

Figure 2.3: Investment Interlocks Involving Chairmen (1937-8)

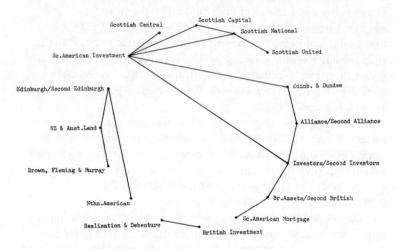

Similarly, the Northern American Trust of Dundee was connected to the Perth-based General Accident. The Glasgow investment companies of the Brown, Fleming and Murray group had close links to the Clydesdale Bank and Scottish Amicable, though their connection with New Zealand and Australian Land linked them to the National Bank. By 1937-8 the dominance of the Bank of Scotland was far less marked, and both the Royal Bank and the Commercial Bank had increased in importance. Scottish American Investment, Scottish Investment and the trusts which now formed the Baillie, Gifford group retained their close links to Scottish Widows. Similarly, Standard Life retained its links to Scottish American Mortgage, Edinburgh Investment and British Investment, and these companies were joined by the Ivory and Sime trusts. The separation of the Aberdeen companies persisted, though the Dundee trust acquired a link to the National Bank. The Brown, Fleming and Murray trusts were linked through New Zealand and Australian Land to the National Bank and to Caledonian Insurance, and they were linked indirectly to Scottish Amicable and the Union Bank through H.B. Spens's directorship in Burmah Oil.

The level of interlocking within the financial sector increased during the inter-war years, probably as a reflection of changes within the insurance sector. Life insurance companies, of which Scotland had many, had experienced a massive growth in their funds and had begun to invest more money in company shares rather than in government stock or company loan stock. This inevitably brought about closer links with the investment trusts, which were suitable vehicles for insurance company investment. This period saw the beginning of a transformation in investment company ownership from wealthy individuals to large insurance companies. At the same time, investment trust directors were experienced investors in ordinary shares and were, therefore, even more welcome as members of insurance company boards. As a consequence, insurance companies and investment trusts were drawn more closely together. Thus, the number of investment connections of Scottish Widows increased from three to ten, and those of Standard Life from four to seven.

The Industrial Sector

Of the 64 large non-financial companies of 1904-5, 46 were still amongst the 76 top companies of 1920-1. A total of 18 companies were lost from the list during this period: six were too small to appear in the top 76, six had been liquidated, four had merged with other large Scottish companies, and we could obtain no information on two of them. Broxburn Oil and Young's Paraffin, were merged with a number of smaller companies in 1919 to form Scottish Oils, a subsidiary of Anglo-Iranian Oil. In the railway sector two companies merged with the companies which already operated their lines: in 1908 the West Highland was absorbed by the North British, and in 1909 the Lanarkshire and Dumbartonshire was absorbed by the Caledonian. Amongst those companies going into liquidation, the assets of Glengarnock Iron and Steel were acquired in 1917 by David Colville & Sons. The 30 companies which were new to the 1920-1 list of top companies included five which had been too small to appear in the 1904-5 list (Edinburgh Collieries, Sir William Arrol, Carron Grove Paper, Lochgelly Iron and Redpath, Brown). The remaining 25 newcomers had previously been partnerships or private companies, or were completely new flotations: thus, James Finlay was converted to a public company, and both Scottish Oils and Scottish Iron and Steel were new amalgamations of smaller companies.

A total of 38 of the 1920-1 top 76 were also in the top 59 of 1937-8. The high disappearance rate of companies is probably due, in part, to the drop in the absolute number of non-financial companies included in the analysis for 1937-8. A comparison of the top 64 of 1904-5 with the top 59 of 1937-8 shows a continuity of 26 companies over the 30-year period. Of the 30 companies new to the list in 1920-1,

12 survived into 1937-8. The 38 companies lost over the period comprised 12 which were too small for inclusion, nine which had been
liquidated, one which had been municipalised (Glasgow Subway), eight
railways which had merged into the English companies, six which had
become unquoted subsidiaries of other companies, and two on which
there was no information. The London, Midland, and Scottish Railway
absorbed the Caledonian, the Callander and Oban, the Lanarkshire and
Ayrshire, the Glasgow and South Western, and the Highland. The
London and North Eastern Railway absorbed the North British, the
Forth Bridge, and the Great North of Scotland. Following the acquisition of its iron and steel interests by Colvilles in 1930, James Dunlop
became an unquoted subsidiary of Nimmo and Dunlop, itself a creation
of Colvilles and the Lithgows. Lowrie became a subsidiary of Distillers,
Fairfields became a subsidiary of Lithgows, the Steel Company of Scotland became a subsidiary of Colvilles, Scottish Tubes was acquired by
Stewarts and Lloyds, and G. and J. Burns became a subsidiary of Burns
and Laird Lines (later to be part of P and O). Amongst those companies
going into liquidation, Carron Grove Paper was reconstructed as part of
Inveresk, Anchor Line was reconstructed by a consortium put together
by merchant bankers Dawnay Day, D. and W. Henderson became part
of the Belfast firm of Harland and Wolff, and two companies operating
abroad were incorporated into foreign concerns (Acadia Sugar, Arizona
Copper). The 21 companies which were new to the list in 1937-8
included five companies which had been small in 1920-1 (Scottish
Power, Scottish Motor Traction, George Outram, Lothian Coal and
Wilsons and Clyde). Only four of the newcomers were holding companies for related concerns — Scottish Brewers, Bairds and Dalmellington,
Nimmo and Dunlop and Federated Foundries — the remainder were
either completely new companies (such as Singer and Scottish Agricultural Industries) or were conversions of former partnerships and
private companies.

The connections amongst firms engaged in heavy industry in 1920-1
were generally very similar to the pattern for 1904-5. The major change
was the break-up of the former Tennant 'empire', which resulted in
the Caledonian Railway becoming an even more important focus than
before. Examination of those links which do not directly involve
railway companies shows the extent to which the Tennant empire had
broken down. Nobel's, like the Steel Company of Scotland, had no
board connections with other top industrial companies, and Tharsis
was connected only to Colville. The break-up of the Tennant empire
had begun in 1885 with the amalgamation of the St Rollox chemical

works into United Alkali, and this was followed by the absorption of
Young's Paraffin Oil into Scottish Oils in 1919. Sir Charles Tennant
himself had died in 1906 and was succeeded in many of his directorships by Sir James King. After King's death in 1911 there was no
individual capable of holding the remaining interests together. W.P.
Rutherford, general manager of Tharsis, became chairman of the
company in 1921 and remained in that post until his death in 1963.
Cassel's Gold and Nobel's both joined with United Alkali to form ICI
in 1926. ICI was largely the invention of Harry McGowan (later
Lord McGowan) of Nobel's, and McGowan virtually ran ICI single-
handed until his retirement in 1950.

Figure 2.4: Interlocks in Basic Industries (1920-1)

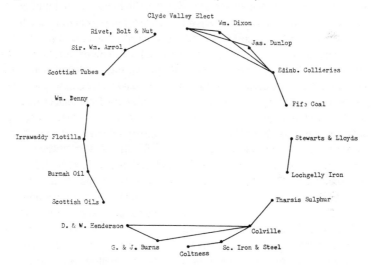

It is clear from Figure 2.4 that the steel firm of David Colville and
Sons had become a new centre for the integration of steel, shipbuilding
and shipping interests in the west of Scotland. The other interlocks in
this sector illustrate the continued importance of vertical and horizontal
integration: the two oil companies were linked to a shipbuilder and a
shipping company; Arrol's bridge building firm was linked to a steel
tube producer and a rivet manufacturer; Stewarts and Lloyds was
connected to Lochgelly Iron and Coal; and numerous heavy industrials
were linked to one another through the North British Railway.

The rise of Colville in steel was closely associated with the rise of

Lithgow in shipbuilding, and together these firms were to become the pivot of Scottish heavy industry. At the turn of the century the four largest Scottish shipbuilders were Alexander Stephen, Barclay Curle, Wm Denny, and Elder. Other important builders were Russell, Beardmore (who had taken over Napier's interests in 1900), D. and W. Henderson, Scott, and Harland and Wolff of Belfast. The rest of the Scottish shipbuilding industry comprised smaller firms such as J. & G. Thomson (acquired by John Brown in 1899), J.H. Lamont, and A.R. Stenhouse. Those firms which were not controlled from outside Scotland tended to be private family concerns and to have close links with other local interests. Alexander Stephen, for example, was firmly controlled by the Stephen family, had built many of the ships of the Allan Line and Clan Line, and had a long-standing connection with the shipowning firm of Maclay and McIntyre. Family control in shipping was still important, but it was beginning to disappear: Anchor Line had been taken over by Cunard in 1911, and Allan Line became part of Canadian Pacific in 1915. Shipping firms such as Donaldson Line remained family concerns, as did smaller private companies such as Bank Line (run by Andrew Weir and Co., of Glasgow), Christian Salvesen of Leith, and Lyle Shipping (owned by the Lyle, Macfarlane and Shearer families).

During the First World War, the shipbuilding industry had been administered by Sir James Lithgow, whose family had acquired a controlling interest in the Russell shipyard, and by Sir Joseph Maclay the shipowner (later Lord Maclay). This government regulation had a considerable impact on the inter-war shipbuilding industry as various attempts at rationalisation were made. In 1930 Sir James Lithgow chaired National Shipbuilders Security, the aim of which was to organise tenders for foreign orders on a collective basis. This was the prelude to Lithgow's undisputed dominance. The widow of Sir William Pearce had died in 1920 and her controlling block of shares in the Fairfield yard (formerly Elder and Co.) eventually passed to Sir James Lithgow in the 1930s. At about the same time Lithgow acquired Beardmore's shipbuilding and steel interest and a large stake in Colville. By the late 1930s, the bulk of Scottish shipbuilding capacity was in the yards of Lithgow, Fairfield (owned by Lithgow), Stephen, Harland and Wolff (which had acquired the Henderson firm in 1935), Yarrow (set up by a Londoner, Alfred Yarrow, in 1907) and the smaller family concerns of Denny and Scott. Denny had for long been associated with the Irrawaddy Flotilla and British and Burmese Steam Navigation, both of which had been set up by the shipowner P. Henderson together with

T.D. Findlay. This group of companies was tied in closely to Burmah
Oil and Scottish Oils, which were headed by Sir John Cargill and which
were closely allied to the Brown, Fleming and Murray trusts with which
Maclay was associated. In shipping, the near-bankrupt Anchor Line had
been bought from Cunard by a consortium headed by the Bank of
Scotland and including Lord Runciman. The company eventually
passed into the full control of the Runciman group.

During the 1920s, Lithgow and other shipbuilders had bought up
many of the Scottish steel plants so as to ensure their supplies. A
consortium of the smaller shipping and shipbuilding companies headed
by Stephen, Yarrow and Clan Line, purchased the Steel Company of
Scotland, F.J. Stephen becoming chairman. The company made per-
sistent losses and was eventually sold to Sir James Lithgow who
subsequently sold it to Colvilles in 1936. The two Colville brothers who
had run the family steel firm died during the war and Viscount Pirrie
bought a majority holding in Colville on behalf of Harland and Wolff.
As a result of the share exchange with Harland and Wolff, Viscount
Pirrie and his family obtained control, although the Colvilles remained
important shareholders and were still represented on the board.
Virtually unaffected by Viscount Pirrie's death in 1924 or by the arrival
of his successor Lord Kylsant, John Craig the general manager had
virtual control and continued to run the company in the interests of
the Pirrie/Kylsant interests, the Colville family and the National Bank,
which had granted the firm a large overdraft. In the late 1920s various
attempts had been made to mobilise the agreement and finance for a
merger of the Scottish steel companies. Eventually in 1930 Colvilles
acquired the Lithgow firm of James Dunlop and was separated from
Harland and Wolff. By the late 1930s, encouraged by the Bank of
England and the commercial banks, Colvilles, under the general
financial control of John Craig, had purchased Beardmore's Mossend
works, the Steel Company, and Lanarkshire Steel (having acquired the
latter from the Clydesdale Bank who held the loan capital). At this time
the company accounted for nearly 90 per cent of Scottish steel
capacity and only Scottish Iron and Steel remained independent,
though this merged with William Baird in 1939.

The movement of concentration in shipbuilding and steel was not
unique. A similar movement can be observed in the allied iron and coal
industries. Fife Coal and Edinburgh Collieries in 1920-1 were dominant
not only in the East of Scotland but also in the Scottish coal industry
as a whole. Charles Carlow and his son Augustus ran Fife Coal as well as
Shotts Iron, and Carlow sat on the board of Edinburgh Collieries.

Similarly, members of the Nimmo family were represented on all three companies. By 1937-8 Sir Adam Nimmo, Sir James Lithgow and John Craig dominated the Colville board. Similarly, close links existed between Coltness, Wm Baird, and other Western coal interests. In 1935, Coltness purchased from Stewarts and Lloyds a controlling sharehold-ing in Wilsons and Clydes, which owned the collieries of Robert Addie and Sons. Coltness had previously been associated with Dalmellington Iron but sold its interest in the late 1920s, Dalmellington later being absorbed into Bairds and Dalmellington, a subsidiary of William Baird.

Figure 2.5: Interlocks in Coal, Iron, Steel and Electricity (1937-8)

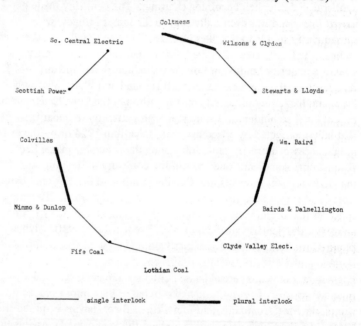

The break-up of the Tennant empire and the disappearance of the Scottish railway companies changed the structure of the heavy industry sector. By 1937-8, the sector was centred around the Nimmo, Lithgow and Craig companies, though separate groupings around Coltness (the Houldsworth and Wilson families) and Wm Baird (the McCosh family) were also of importance. Of 15 companies in the 1937-8 top 59 engaged in coal, iron, steel and electricity production, ten companies were divided between the three centres, two were linked to one another, and three had no interlocks in the sector. Figure 2.5 shows

that Baird, Coltness and Colville were each involved in plural interlocks
with close associates. The changes within heavy industry brought about
a number of changes in the whole structure of the west of Scotland
industrial sector. The dissolution of the Tennant empire and the loss of
the Caledonian Railway amounted to the disappearance of the companies which had been at the centre of Glasgow industrial life for more
than 50 years. Functional interlocks of horizontal and vertical integration continued and interlocks were still established through the
Glasgow banks and financial companies, yet the structure as a whole
broke down into more distinct sub-groups. Men such as Lithgow and
Craig rose to prominence in shipbuilding and steel and exercised
considerable power and influence throughout the economy. By the
1930s, the Lithgow-Colville group of companies had achieved a position
of dominance in Scottish heavy industry.

The major change in the textile sector was the formation of Jute
Industries in London in 1920. The company was based on the Cox jute
interests and acquired the firms of Gilroy, Walker, Bell and Kyd. The
original board of the company included Sir Alexander Roger of the
Commercial Bank of London, and G.L. Bevan, a stockbroker, but the
bulk of its membership was drawn from the families whose firms had
been acquired. By 1940 control rested with the Cox and Walker
families. For the whole of the inter-war period the Dundee textile
industry was effectively divided between Jute Industries and the firm
of Low and Bonar, though firms such as Prain and Caird had a minor
stake. In the west of Scotland Coats and Linen Thread continued to
grow, though they were no longer interlocked with one another. The
Coats family remained prominent on their company's board, but
members of the Clark family shared control with them. In 1920-1 the
board included seven Coats and two Clarks; by 1937-8 the families had
three members each. Coats was run on a day-to-day basis by its managing director A.E. Phillippi, who had engineered much of the firm's
growth, but ultimate control rested with the families who had both
shares and board representation. A study carried out in 1941 showed
that whilst Coats had 53,110 shareholders, eight of them held between
10 and 20 per cent of the shares. The list of top companies for 1920-1
also included Arthur and Co., a Glasgow-based firm of wholesale textile
distributors. The firm developed out of an earlier venture by James
Arthur and Hugh Fraser who set up a wholesale and retail drapery
business in 1849. In the 1860s disputes between the partners led to the
wholesale and retail side of the business being split up, each partner
going his own way. Hugh Fraser formed Fraser, Sons and Company,

and James Arthur formed Arthur and Company. From the 1880s the
firm had been run by Matthew Arthur who was created a Baronet in
1902 and a Baron in 1918 and who, like his father, was a director of
Young's Paraffin and the Glasgow and South Western Railway. Like
Coats, Arthur was very much a family concern, and it is significant that
the Coats and Arthur families were related through marriage.

The Distillers Company had continued to grow through mergers with
its competitors. Buchanan and Dewar merged into the London-based
holding company of Buchanan-Dewar in 1915, and in 1924 Distillers
acquired Walker and Buchanan-Dewar. The dominant figure in the
company for much of its existence, however, was William Ross, who
had joined the company in 1878 and had been made managing director
in 1900. After his death, and as a result of the substantial shareholdings
of the Dewar family, the board included three Dewars and the family
became a significant influence on company affairs. In brewing the firms
of William Younger and William McEwan merged in 1931 to form
Scottish Brewers. Whilst the holding company was supposed to permit
the autonomy of each of the two working companies, the dominance of
Harry Younger and his family was obvious from the beginning. The
only representative of the other Younger family on the holding company board was William McEwan Younger, the son of William Younger.
(See Chapter 1 for a discussion of these complex kinship relations.)

Finally, the James Finlay group of merchants and tea planters
remained a tightly-knit group. James Finlay had been formed into a
private company in 1909 as a way of parcelling-out the shares of the
late Sir John Muir to his family and some senior managers. In 1924, the
company went public and some of the shares still held by Muir's exe-
cutors were sold. Sir Kay Muir and J.F. Muir had both retired from the
board by 1937-8, though the Muir family were still represented on the
board: J.B. Muir was a brother of Sir Kay, and A.M. McGrigor was his
brother-in-law. The company was chaired by R.L. James who had spent
his whole career in the firm, and an important link to a Glasgow firm of
accountants and investment managers was present in the successive
board seats occupied by Peter Rintoul and John Tulloch from 1929 to
1943.

The Structure of the Business Network

We turn now to the overall structure of the business network as
exhibited in the general pattern of interlocking directorships. It is
necessary to move from the particular direct interlocks between
associated companies to the generalised network of communication

between companies which is generated through the cumulation of indirect interlocks.

In 1920-1, 94 of the 114 companies were interlocked and 20 had no interlocks with other top companies. A total of 14 of the interlocked companies had director links to smaller Scottish companies, and six (Acadia Sugar, Albion Motors, Allan Line, Barry Ostlere, Summerlee Iron, United Turkey Red) had links to no other Scottish companies. Although the proportion of companies which were interlocked fell from 85 per cent to 82 per cent over the period 1904-21, the proportion of companies with no Scottish connections also fell. In 1937-8, 87 of the 111 companies were interlocked, a further fall in the proportion of companies which were interlocked to 78 per cent. Of the 24 uninterlocked companies, ten had interlocks with smaller Scottish companies and 14 had no Scottish interlocks. The ten firms with links to smaller companies were Barry Ostlere, Donaldson Line, Federated Foundries, Fleming Reid, Inveresk, Jugra Land, Metal Industries, Moss Empires, Scottish Drapery and United Collieries. Two of the companies lacking Scottish links (Nobel's and Scottish Agricultural Industries) were constituent parts of Imperial Chemicals and so were linked through that concern.

Table 2.5 shows the company connections created by the multiple directors. The 118 multiple directors of 1920-1 generated 225 lines, 50 being plural lines; and the 132 multiple directors of 1937-8 generated 259 lines, of which 72 were plural. It can be seen that whilst the number of lines was slightly lower in 1937-8 than in 1904-5, the number of plural lines increased steadily over the period. In 1904-5, 16 per cent of all lines had been plural and this figure had risen to 28 per cent in 1937-8. Both the density and the connectivity of the network, as might be expected, showed a similar trend to that found for the total number of lines. Density fell to 3.49 per cent in 1920-1 and then rose to 4.24 per cent in 1937-8. Similarly, connectivity fell to 45.86 per cent and then rose to 53.12 per cent. The overall trend for the 30 year period since 1904 was, therefore, a slight downward movement in these variables. In 1920-1, the network comprised six components: one large component of 77 companies, an Aberdeen component, a group including the five Finlay companies and Scottish Equitable, and three pairs of companies (Jugra Land/Moss Empires, Dewar/Lowrie, Samnuggur/Titaghur). The Aberdeen component formed a mini-version of the whole network since it included the North of Scotland Bank, the Great North of Scotland Railway, Northern Assurance, Scottish Northern and North of Scotland

Table 2.5: Plural and Single Company Linkages (1920-38)

Value of Line	No. of Lines	
	1920-1	1937-8
1	175	188
2	33	35
3	4	13
4	4	6
5	1	6
6	2	1
7		7
8	6	
9		
10		1
11		1
12		1
TOTALS	225	258

Table 2.6: Distribution of Company Connections (1920-38)

No. of Companies Connected To	1920-1		1937-8	
	No. of Companies	No. of Connections	No. of Companies	No. of Connections
0	20	0	24	0
1	12	12	12	12
2	14	28	7	14
3	11	33	10	30
4	17	68	11	44
5	9	45	7	35
6	9	54	8	48
7	3	21	2	14
8	4	32	8	64
9	8	72	6	54
10	2	20	3	30
11	2	22	3	33
12			1	12
13	1	13	4	52
14	1	14		
15			4	60
16	1	16	1	16
TOTALS	114	450	111	518

Canadian, and had numerous local links to small industrials. In 1937-8, the network was similar to the 1904-5 pattern and comprised four components: one large component of 81 companies and three pairs (Dewar/Distillers, Samnuggur/Titaghur, Scottish Power/Scottish Central Electric). Taking all these measurements together certain conclusions can be drawn. The business boom of 1919-20 had generated a number of changes in the business network, but the subsequent slow-down and the depression of the 1930s led to a restructuring of the network which brought it nearer to the earlier pattern. Aberdeen business was incorporated into the national network, and although the proportion of companies which were interlocked had fallen, the network as a whole was more highly clustered into groups of companies with mutual plural links.

Tables 2.6 and 2.7 show more detail on the extent of company linking and on the centrality of companies in the network. The number of companies connected to more than 11 other companies dropped sharply in 1920-1, but rose to its 1904-5 level by the end of the inter-war period. Over the period as a whole there was a tendency for the number of companies with three or four connections to increase at the expense of the number with five or seven connections. The importance of the break-up of the Tennant empire is clear from Table 2.7, which shows that the Caledonian Railway lost almost a half of all its connections after Tennant's death. Similarly, the Clydesdale Bank had lost eight of its seventeen by 1920-1. The figures for 1920-1 also show the increasing centrality of investment companies, a tendency which became even more marked when the Scottish railway companies disappeared completely. The rise in centrality exhibited by the Bank of Scotland is largely due to its development of extensive links to investment companies. In line with the trends discussed earlier, it would seem that many of the features of the 1920-1 network must be explained in terms of the increase in the number of industrial companies without established interlocks. Over the following year, new links were forged and the network returned to its former pattern.

The network of plurally-connected companies for 1937-8 included a far higher proportion of the interlocked companies than was the case for either 1904-5 or 1920-1. However, the number of components in the plural network shows an interesting trend: a fall from 11 to seven by 1920-1, and a subsequent rise to 19. The clustering of the network had become more marked by the end of the inter-war period. Figures 2.6 and 2.7 show the largest components in the plural networks. In 1920-1 the 44 companies with plural links were divided as to 17

Table 2.7: Most Central Companies (1920-38)

1920-1		1937-8	
Company	No. of Connec-tions	Company	No. of Connec-tions
Bank of Scotland	16	Bank of Scotland	16
Union Bank	14	Investors' Mortgage	15
Caledonian Railway	13	Second Investors' Mortgage	15
Scottish Amicable	11	Edinburgh Investment	15
N.Z. & Australian Land	11	Second Edinburgh Investment	15
Investors' Mortgage	10	Commercial Bank	13
National Bank	10	National Bank	13
North British Railway	9	Scottish Widows	13
Glasgow and S.W. Railway	9	Scottish American Mortgage	13
Clydesdale Bank	9	Scottish Capital Investment	12
Scottish Widows Fund	9	Standard Life	11
Edinburgh Investment	9	Burmah Oil	11
Second Edinb. Investment	9	Scottish United Investors	11
Standard Life	9	Union Bank	10
Scottish Union	9	British Investment	10
		Edinb. and Dundee Invest.	10

Table 2.8: Distribution of Plural Linkages (1920-38)

No. of Plural Lines per Company	No. of Companies	
	1920-1	1937-8
0	50	22
1	15	32
2	15	12
3	8	7
4	6	7
5		4
6		3
TOTALS	94	87

Figure 2.6: Network of Plural Lines: Largest Component (1920-1)

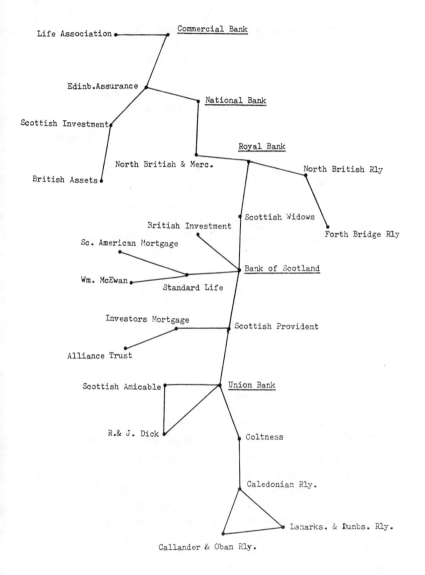

Figure 2.7: Network of Plural Lines: Two Largest Components (1937-8)

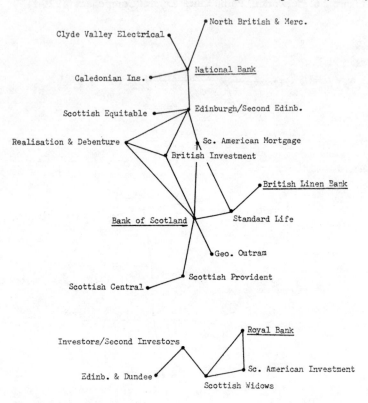

industrials and 27 financials, and the breakdown for 1937-8 was similar: 26 industrials and 39 financials. At the end of the period the industrial companies were predominantly involved in pair-wise relations with one another, whilst the largest components comprised mainly financial companies. It seems clear that there was an intensively-connected financial network and a number of smaller industrial groupings. The financial connections comprised the skeleton of the overall business network and the industrial groupings were embedded in this structure through their looser linkages to financial companies. In the model of the business network given in Figure 2.8 it is clear that the financial companies were dominant in determining the overall structure. Industrial interlocks were still both regional and functional, though to a lesser extent than in 1904-5.

Figure 2.8: The Structure of the Business Network (1937-8)

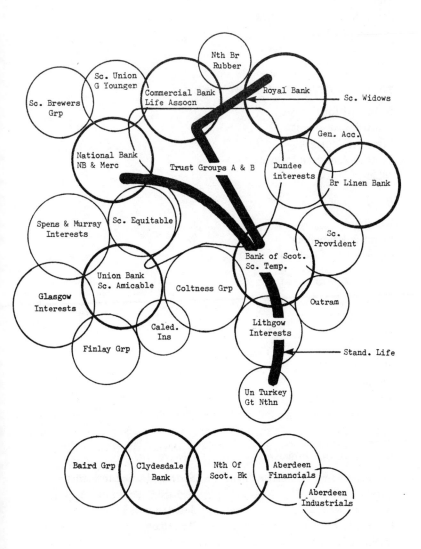

Key to Figure 2.8:

Trust Group A (linked to Standard Life)

Edinburgh Investment
Scottish American Mortgage
British Investment
Northern American Trusts
Ivory & Sime Trusts

Trust Group B (linked to Sc. Widows)

Baillie, Gifford Trusts
Scottish Investment
Investors' Mortgage
Scottish American Investment
Alliance Trust

Baird Group

Wm Baird
Bairds & Dalmellington
Clyde Valley Electrical

Coltness Group

Coltness Iron
Tharsis Sulphur
Stewarts & Lloyds

Lithgow Interests

Colvilles
Nimmo & Dunlop
Fife Coal
Lothian Coal

Spens & Murray Interests

Brown, Fleming & Murray Trusts
Burmah Oil
Scottish Oils
Irrawaddy Flotilla
British & Burmese
Hiram Walker
Hugh Baird

Glasgow Interests

Scottish United Investors
Scottish National Trust
J. & P. Coats
Wm Dixon

A striking feature of Figure 2.8 is that the Clydesdale Bank and the North of Scotland Bank had no strong links to the rest of the network. It is likely that these two banks were already operating 'in tandem' as the Glasgow and Aberdeen arms of the Midland Bank, albeit with a certain autonomy. These two banks had no interlocks with companies in the other sector of the network, though the Baird group had some links with the National Bank and the North British and Mercantile. By contrast with the network of 1904-5 (see Figure 1.5), the densest part of the system was that between the Bank of Scotland and the Union Bank. It is in this sector of the network that the industrial companies were concentrated, and it is here that Glasgow and Edinburgh interests were brought together. The Bank of Scotland lost some of its financial interlocks over the inter-war period but gained many industrial interlocks to replace these. Many of the industrial companies formerly linked to the Tennant empire and the Caledonian Railway, and so lying within the sphere of influence of the Clydesdale Bank, had come within the reach of the Bank of Scotland and the Union Bank. This movement can be explained partly by the growth of the Brown, Fleming and Murray trusts, which linked Burmah and other industrials firmly to the Union Bank, and partly by the rise of the Colville-Lithgow group.

The Men of Business

It can be seen from Table 2.9 that in 1920-1, 118 of the directors sat on two or more company boards and held a total of 321 directorships. In 1937-8, 132 multiple directors held 370 directorships. Thus, the figures for the end of the inter-war period were just slightly higher than those for 1904-5, with 23 per cent of directors holding 45 per cent of directorships. The figures for 1920-1, however, were considerably lower: 17 per cent of directors held 36 per cent of directorships. Whilst the proportion of directors with more than one directorship was low in 1920-1, mainly as a result of the business boom, 37 of the pre-war multiple directors (27 per cent) were still multiple directors in 1920-1, and these included many of the men with the largest numbers of directorships. A total of 21 of the 1920-1 multiple directors (18 per cent) were also directors in 1937-8 and three men (A. Wallace, Viscount Younger and H.G. Younger) were multiple directors throughout the period 1904-38. The continuity over the years was even greater if direct family relationships are taken into account. A comparison of multiple directors for 1904-5 and 1920-1 shows family continuity for the Duke of Buccleuch (father and son), Brown, Scott and Dundas, as well as

Table 2.9: Distribution of Directorships (1920-38)

No. of Directorships per Person	1920-1		1937-8	
	No. of People	No. of Directorships	No. of People	No. of Directorships
1	572	572	454	454
2	67	134	78	156
3	28	84	26	78
4	13	52	15	60
5	9	45	8	40
6	1	6	1	6
7			2	14
8			2	16
TOTALS	690	893	586	824

less obvious relationships. Similarly, families such as Dundas, Findlay, Houldsworth, Lawrie, Maitland, Murray, Warren and Younger all show continuity between 1920 and 1938.

Table 2.10 shows a substantial fall in the proportion of multiple directors with titles from 29 per cent to just 14 per cent. The number of earls and viscounts remained constant, but the number of dukes and marquesses fell, as did the number of knights. The number of baronets also fell, though this remained a large category. It is perhaps significant that there was a substantial increase in the number of barons. In fact, two-thirds of the titled multiple directors in 1937-8 were barons or baronets. It might be assumed that whilst a baronetcy was still a popular title for businessmen, many former baronets were being admitted to the lowest rungs of the nobility. The evidence, however, does not support this assumption. Only one of the 1937-8 barons can be regarded as originating in a 'promotion' (the second Lord Forteviot's father had been promoted from a baronetcy and had died in 1929). All the remaining titles were hereditary (or courtesy) and only one of these was of recent creation (the second Lord Kinross). The best interpretation would seem to be that the sons of the great magnates, rather than the higher nobles themselves, and the lower levels of the peerage were the most active elements of the nobility so far as Scottish business was concerned. The dukes and marquesses had withdrawn, or had been phased out, and the lesser nobility had become more active. Enoblement

Table 2.10: Multiple Directors and Their Titles (1920-38)

No. of People	2	3	4	5	6	TOTALS
			No. of Directorships per Person			
1920-1						
Knights	6	2				8
Baronets	6	4	2	2		14
Barons	2	1				3
Viscounts		1				1
Earls	3	1				4
Marquesses	2					2
Dukes	1	1				2
TOTALS	20	10	2	2		34
1937-8						
Knights	2					2
Baronets	3	1	1		1	6
Barons	6					6
Viscounts		1				1
Earls	2	2				4
Marquesses						
Dukes						
TOTALS	13	4	1		1	19

of manufacturers and financiers was not a significant phenomenon and seems to have occurred mainly when industrialists (such as Viscount Younger) were also active in politics.

In 1920-1, ten men held five or more directorships each. A half of these men held most of their directorships within the Finlay group of companies, two represented numerous Edinburgh financial interests, and three were active in Glasgow industrial and financial concerns. In 1937-8, 13 men held five or more directorships: eight were Edinburgh (and Dundee) financiers, three were from the Finlay group, and two were associated with the Brown, Fleming and Murray trusts and their associated Glasgow industrials. Table 2.11 goes beyond this basic measure of the number of directorships held to examine those directors who met the largest number of other directors in board meetings.

As might be expected, the directors who met the most other directors

Table 2.11: Central Directors in the Network (1920-38)

1920-1		1937-8	
Director	No. of Directors Met	Director	No. of Directors Met
A. Wallace	18	A. Wallace	23
W.S. Davidson	17	S.C. Hogarth	19
H.E. Gordon	17	H.A. Jamieson	19
W.J. Mure	17	T.J.C. Gifford	18
H.E. Richardson	17	W.H. Fraser	17
G. Dunlop	16	J. Craig	16
P. Rintoul	16	Lord Elphinstone	16
C.L. Dalziel	15	A.W. Robertson Durham	16
R.E. Findlay	15	J.T. Tulloch	16
Sir G. Younger	15	R.K. Blair	15

all sat on bank boards. In both years, about a half of the central directors sat on the Bank of Scotland board. In 1920-1, Union Bank directors were also prominent, though in 1937-8 the Commercial and Royal Banks were more important. Throughout the period, Edinburgh financial directors were well represented amongst central directors. In comparison with 1904-5, there was much more 'clustering' in the network of meetings, and this seems to correspond to the increased clustering apparent in the company network.

Kinship relations remained an important feature of the business network and resulted in continuing family representation on many boards. William Whitelaw, formerly of the Highland Railway, was chairman of the North British Railway in 1920-1 and was still associated with his kinsmen in the Baird family: Whitelaw and W.J. Baird both sat on the board of Glasgow Subway. Figure 2.9 shows the family connections of the Baird, Whitelaw and Disraeli families. The Coats family (Figure 1.7) remained a powerful influence in the 1920s. J. and P. Coats was still chaired by Sir Thomas Glen-Coats, and six other family members were on the board, including Lord Glentanar. Although Coats was no longer linked to the Linen Thread Company, run by the Barbour, Knox, Luke and Finlayson families, Coats family members were widely connected to other companies through kinship. Jane Glen had married James Arthur, and Elizabeth Coats had married

Thomas Arthur. The latter's brother, Sir Matthew Arthur, had become Lord Glenarthur and sat on the boards of Arthur and Co., the Glasgow and South Western Railway, and other companies. William Coats had married Sir Kay Muir's sister, Agnes, and Muir's second sister, Margaret, had married Alexander McGrigor (partner in solicitors McGrigor, Donald), whose sister was the wife of Lord Glenarthur. The McGrigor family were intermarried with the Denny and Muir families, and the daughter of Lord Glenarthur and Janet McGrigor was married to a descendant of Kirkman Finlay.

Finlay and Muir were families of former Glasgow colonial merchants, and the influence of the old merchant families was also apparent in the oil and shipping sectors. Sir John Cargill and his brother-in-law David McCowan both sat on the board of Burmah Oil, and McCowan also sat on Irrawaddy Flotilla where he was joined by Robert Findlay and J.M. Denny (later Sir Maurice Denny). Both Cargill and Findlay descended from colonial merchants (see Figure 2.10) and their families had numerous other connections: McCowan sat on the board of the Clydesdale Bank, and Findlay sat on the Union Bank and Scottish Amicable. The interests of the Cargill family in the Brown, Fleming and Murray trusts brought them into contact with the Murray and Spens families, both David Murray and J.A. Spens sitting on the Scottish Amicable, with Spens also sitting on the National Bank. Figure 2.11 shows the structure of these families.

The Edinburgh financial establishment of the 1920s continued to show a strong Dundas influence: R.W. Dundas, son of Ralph Dundas, sat on the Royal Bank as well as North British and Mercantile, and R.N. Dundas sat on Scottish Widows. The family was joined by other prominent families such as the Scott family of the Duke of Buccleuch, represented on the Bank of Scotland and the Royal Bank. In Aberdeen, the North of Scotland Bank was still dominated by the Ogston family, with three members on the board. Similarly, the investment trust sector of the 1920s still showed the preponderance of such familiar names as Cowan, Fleming, Dunlop, etc.

By the late 1930s, this pattern had changed a little. The Coats family were no longer so all pervasive, and only three members of the family sat on J. and P. Coats's board. Similarly, the deaths of Sir Kay Muir and J.F. Muir reduced their family influence, though the Finlay company boards included A.M. McGrigor and J.B. Muir, the remaining directors being faithful managers. Burmah Oil and the Brown, Fleming and Murray trusts were still presided over by Sir John Cargill, who was joined by the second generation of the Murray and Spens families.

Figure 2.9: The Baird and Whitelaw Families

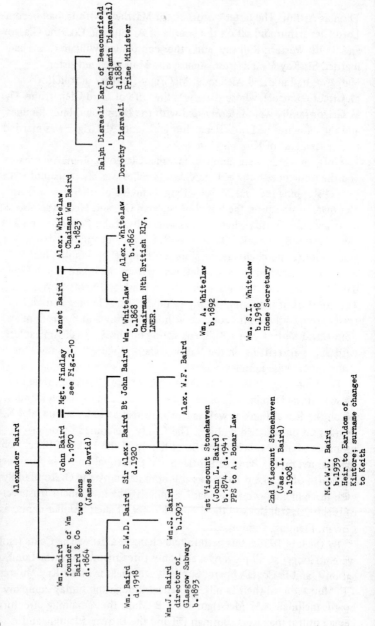

Figure 2.10: The Findlay and Dunlop Families

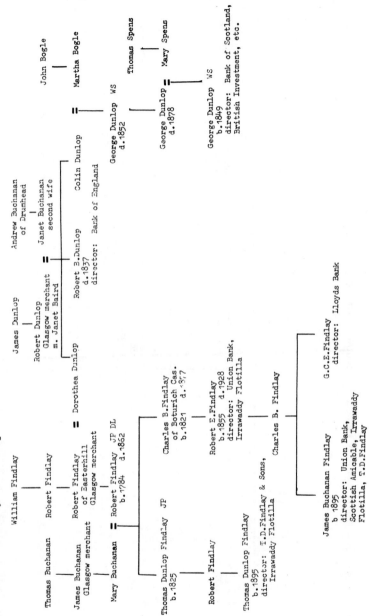

Figure 2.11: The Spens and Murray Families – Section A: The Spens Family

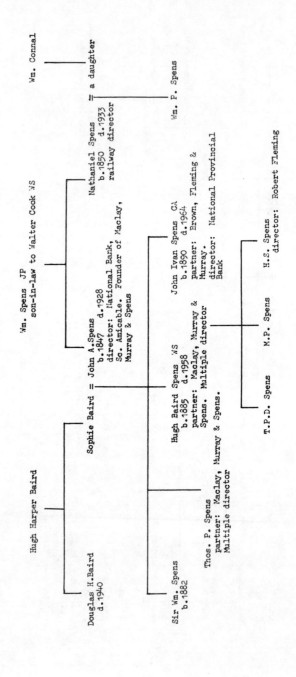

Figure 2.11: The Spens and Murray Families — Section B: The Murray Family

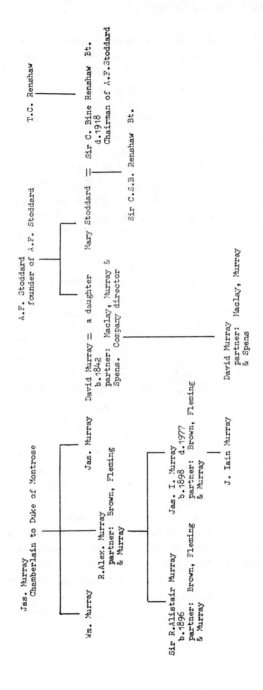

David McCowan had been knighted in 1928 and made a baronet in
1934. Though he died in 1937, his daughter's father-in-law, William
Bonnar of Edinburgh, sat on the board of New Zealand and Australian
Land along with T.P. Spens; McCowan and Bonnar having sat together
on this board in the 1920s. H.B. Spens sat on many of the group trusts
as well as the Union Bank (with Sir Maurice Denny and J.B. Findlay)
and Scottish Amicable (with J.B. Findlay). Denny was joined on the
boards of Irrawaddy Flotilla and British and Burmese by T.D. Findlay.

Heavy industry and the drinks industry showed both continuity and
change. The continued prominence of Sir Adam Nimmo and C.A.
Carlow (son of Charles Carlow) in the coal industry was countered by
the rise of Lithgow, Bilsland and Craig in steel, these steel men also
having directorships in the banking sector. Similarly, the dominance of
the Younger families in brewing was countered by the rise to
prominence of the Dewar family of Lord Forteviot in distilling. In
Edinburgh finance, Dundas remained a powerful name on the Royal
Bank and Scottish Widows, though the transfer of the North British
and Mercantile board to London meant that Dundas representation on
that company disappeared. The Bank of Scotland and Scottish Provident were both associated with the shipping interests of S.C. Hogarth,
and other shipping and shipbuilding families were represented on the
National Bank (J.G. Stephen, whose brother A.M. Stephen sat on Clyde
Valley Electrical), Clydesdale Bank (H.E. Yarrow), Union Bank (Sir
Maurice Denny), Scottish Investment (Harold K. Salvesen), Investors'
Mortgage (Noel G. Salvesen), and Scottish Temperance (Lord Maclay).
The board of Perth-based General Accident included the Norie-Miller
family as well as Ogilvys and William Low, the latter being related to
Sir John Leng of Dundee, Perth, and London Shipping. Dundee itself
was dominated by the textile interests of Cox, Walker, Bonar and
Prain. The North of Scotland Bank, though a subsidiary of the Midland
Bank, still included an Ogston on its board as well as Frank Fleming
(a member of the Aberdeen branch of Robert Fleming's family).
Fleming influence was still important in the investment trust sector,
not only through Cargill, Murray and Spens but also through M.V.
Fleming and W.H. Jamieson (from an Edinburgh family associated with
Fleming's bank). Further evidence on family connections in the financial
sector is considerable. A particularly important example is that J.M.
Balfour, a partner in Shepherd and Wedderburn and in London
merchant bankers Guiness, Mahon, sat on the boards of American Trust
and Scottish Eastern. His half-brother, the second Lord Kinross, sat on
Bank of Scotland and Scottish Widows. This family was important in
Edinburgh legal circles: their father had been Lord Justice General,

Balfour's maternal grandfather had been Lord Advocate, and Lord Kinross's maternal grandfather had been a Lord of Session.

Conclusion

The inter-war period seems to have been a phase of consolidation. Many of the amalgamations of the previous period were restructured and established prominent positions in their markets. Expansion of these companies tended to occur through the direct acquisition of other companies rather than through the older holding company form. Monopolisation in each of the major industrial sectors was producing the large corporations of the modern period. This does not seem to have resulted in any straightforward separation of ownership from control. Companies still seem to have been controlled through ownership of a substantial shareholding, and family control remained a reality. There is some evidence of the rise of internal managers to prominent positions, though these were often due to family patronage and occurred because the heir was not yet old enough to take over the firm himself. Those managers who did rise do not seem to have had distinct interests from the family controllers, and they not only bought into the company but also secured the recruitment of their own sons. This was probably not, in any case, a recent phenomenon. It seems to have been fairly common for trusted managers to be taken into partnership right back to the early stages of capitalist development, and many of the dominant families of the inter-war period built up their own firms in exactly this way. Without further evidence it is impossible to assess whether the promotion of internal managers was any greater in this period than in the past.

The decline and restructuring of the old industrial base was matched by a massive expansion of the financial sector, particularly the investment sector. Scottish capital flowed into investment trusts, old and new, which invested in stable companies, and government and foreign stock. At the same time as the financial sector was expanding it was also growing closer to the industrial sector. Whilst companies could still be classified as 'industrial' or 'financial', the men who controlled them moved with ease between the two sectors. This perhaps symbolised the ease of movement of capital between the sectors and, in particular, the growing role of the banks in all aspects of industrial finance. This relationship was particularly clear in the steel and shipbuilding industries, both of which showed also the increased involvement of the state in the affairs of big business. A further development in this period is the rapid increase in the number of firms which moved their headquarters to England or became subsidiaries of English companies, as well as the direct establishment of English companies in Scotland. Figure 2.8 brings out the impossibility of giving a complete description of the Scottish economy independently of the English. By the 1930s the two economies were greatly interdependent, with English capital taking the dominant part. As we shall see, all these features were to become even more marked in the post-war period.

Table 2A: Scotland's Top Companies (1920-1)

Section A: Non-Financial Companies

Rank	Company	Industry	Capital (£000)	Multiple Directors
1	North British Railway	Railways	49,155	W. Whitelaw (C), Duke of Buccleuch (DC), C. Carlow, Earl of Elgin, H.G. Younger
2	Caledonian Railway	Railways	45,045	H. Allan (C), W. Younger (DC), Marquess of Breadalbane, J.M. Denny, H.E. Gordon, J.H. Houldsworth, F.B. Sharp, J.G. Stewart
3	J. & P. Coats	Textiles	20,250	R. Clark
4	Glasgow & South Western Railway	Railways	14,303	Lord Glenarthur (C), C. Ker (DC), Sir J. Bell, Sir W. Lorimer, Sir H.E. Maxwell, A. Walker
5	Burmah Oil	Oil	9,151	Sir J.T. Cargill (C), D.W.T. Cargill, R.A. Murray, D. McCowan, R.I. Watson (MD)
6	Great North of Scotland Railway	Railways	5,211	G.A. Duff (DC), J.M. Henderson
7	Highland Railway	Railways	4,923	Duke of Atholl, R.M. Wilson
8	Stewarts and Lloyds	Iron and steel	4,030	J.G. Stewart (C), G.A. Mitchell, R.M. Wilson
9	Scottish Oils	Oil	3,963	R.I. Watson
10	Linen Thread	Textiles	3,850	Sir J. Knox (VC)
11	Clan Line Steamers	Shipping	3,700	–
12	David Colville & Sons	Iron and steel	3,669	T.G. Hardie, Viscount Pirrie, R. Crichton
13	Distillers	Whisky distillers	3,243	J. Duff, A. Walker
14	Nobel's Explosives	Explosives	2,793	Sir R.W. Anstruther (C)

Table 2A: Section A—cont.

Rank	Company	Industry	Capital (£000)	Multiple Directors
15	Forth Bridge Railway	Railways	2,325	W. Whitelaw, Duke of Buccleuch
16 =	Consolidated Tea and Lands	Tea merchants	2,000	Sir A.K. Muir (C), Sir R.D. Moncrieffe, R.H. Sinclair, D.M. Hannay, J.F. Muir, R.H.M. Scott, Sir J.D. Rees, W. Brown
16 =	North British Locomotive	Engineering	2,000	Sir W. Lorimer (C), Sir H. Reid (DC & MD)
18	Clyde Valley Electrical Power	Electricity production	1,900	C. Ker (DC), R.T. Moore
19	United Collieries	Coal mining	1,801	–
20	Fife Coal	Coal mining	1,642	C. Carlow
21	United Turkey Red	Printers & dyers	1,606	–
22 =	Arthur & Co.	Retail stores	1,500	Lord Glenarthur (C)
22 =	James Finlay	Tea merchants	1,500	Sir A.K. Muir (C), J.F. Muir, W. Brown, R.H. Sinclair
24	Irrawaddy Flotilla	Shipping	1,440	J.M. Denny (C), R. Findlay (VC), D. McCowan
25	Jugra Land & Carey	Rubber planters	1,436	J. Wishart (C)
26	Scottish Co-operative Wholesale	Wholesale distribution	1,328	–
27 =	Glasgow Subway Railway	Railways	1,300	W. Whitelaw (C)
27 =	Kanan Devan Hills Produce	Tea merchants	1,300	Sir A.K. Muir (C), Sir R.D. Moncrieffe, R.H. Sinclair, J.F. Muir, D.M. Hannay, R.H.M. Scott, Sir J.D. Rees, W. Brown
29	Tharsis Sulphur & Copper	Copper mining	1,250	T.G. Hardie, Sir H.E. Maxwell
30	Summerlee Iron	Iron and coal	1,200	–

Table 2A: Section A—cont.

Rank	Company	Industry	Capital (£000)	Multiple Directors
31	Donaldson Line	Shipping	1,104	–
32	Alex Pirie & Sons	Paper makers	1,100	–
33	'Moss' Empires	Theatre management	1,039	J. Wishart
34	Coltness Iron	Iron and coal	1,025	H.E. Gordon, J.H. Houldsworth, P. Rintoul
35=	Barry, Ostlere & Shepherd	Linoleum manufacturers	1,000	–
35=	William Denny & Brothers	Shipbuilding	1,000	J.M. Denny (C)
35=	William McEwan	Brewers	1,000	W. Younger (C & MD), E.M. Beilby
35=	William Younger	Brewers	1,000	H.G. Younger (C)
39	Callander & Oban Railway	Railways	968	H. Allan (C), Marquess of Breadalbane, J.M. Denny, H.E. Gordon, J.H. Houldsworth, J.G. Stewart
40	William Dixon	Coal mining	956	T. Warren (C), R.T. Moore
41	Anglo-American Direct Tea Trading	Tea merchants	910	Sir A.K. Muir (C), Sir R.D. Moncrieffe, R.H. Sinclair, J.F. Muir, D.M. Hannay, R.H.M. Scott, Sir J.D. Rees, W. Brown
42	G. & J. Maclachlan	Distillers	900	–
43	Amalgamated Tea Estates	Tea merchants	898	Sir A.K. Muir (C), Sir R.D. Moncrieffe, R.H. Sinclair, J.F. Muir, D.M. Hannay, R.H.M. Scott, Sir J.D. Rees, W. Brown
44	Stewart and McDonald	Warehousemen	885	–

Table 2A: Section A—cont.

Rank	Company	Industry	Capital (£000)	Multiple Directors
45	R. and J. Dick	Shoe and leather goods man.	813	J.P. Smith (C), Sir J.U. Primrose, P. Rintoul, J.T. Tulloch
46=	Scottish Iron and Steel	Iron and steel	750	R. Crichton (VC), P. Rintoul
46=	George Younger	Brewers	750	Sir G. Younger (C), Earl of Mar and Kellie
48	Arizona Copper	Copper mining	737	G. Readman, Sir D. Paulin
49	Sir William Arrol	Engineering	726	Sir T. Mason (C), Sir J. Hunter (MD), A. Hunter
50	North British Rubber	Rubber man.	725	T.W. Tod, Sir J.H. Warrack
51	Fife Tramway, Light and Power	Electricity	720	W. Low
52	Rivet, Bolt and Nut	Engineering	688	Sir J. Hunter (C)
53	Scottish Gympie Gold Mines	Gold mining	660	–
54	Scottish Tube	Iron and steel	623	Sir T. Mason (C)
55	Allan Line Steamship	Shipping	606	–
56=	John Dewar and Sons	Whisky distillers	600	J. Dewar
56=	David and William Henderson	Shipbuilding	600	Viscount Pirrie
56=	Samnuggur Jute Factory	Jute spinners	600	J. Nicoll (C), W.W. Duff, G.N. Nairn, C.B. Ovenstone, D. Stewart, A. Wighton
56=	Titaghur Jute Factory	Jute spinners	600	J. Nicoll (C), G.N. Nairn, W.W. Duff, C.B. Ovenstone, D. Stewart, A. Wighton
60	Anchor Line (Henderson Bros)	Shipping	575	R. Clark
61	Wallace (Glasgow)	Agricultural eng.	564	D.W.T. Cargill

Table 2A: Section A –cont.

Rank	Company	Industry	Capital (£000)	Multiple Directors
62=	Acadia Sugar Refining	Sugar refiners	560	–
62=	Lochgelly Iron & Coal	Iron and coal	560	Lord Glenarthur (C), G.A. Mitchell, G. Readman
64	James Dunlop	Iron, coal & steel	550	R.T. Moore
65	Lanarkshire & Ayrshire Railway	Railways	535	H.E. Gordon (C), H. Allan, Sir J. Knox
66	Carron Grove Paper	Paper makers	530	–
67=	Fleming, Reid	Textiles	525	Sir D. Paulin
67=	Redpath, Brown	Iron & steel merch.	525	–
69	Greenlees & Sons ('Easiphit' Footwear)	Shoe retailers	520	–
70	Edinburgh Collieries	Coal mining	510	C. Carlow, R.T. Moore
71	Albion Motor Car	Vehicles	502	–
72=	G. & J. Burns	Shipping	500	Viscount Pirrie
72=	Fairfield Shipbuilding & Engineering	Shipbuilding	500	–
72=	W.P. Lowrie	Distillers	500	J. Dewar
72=	Steel Company of Scotland	Iron & steel	500	–
72=	Wemyss Collieries Trust	Coal mining	500	A. Drysdale

Table 2A—cont.

Section B: Banking Companies

Rank	Company	Deposits (£000)	Multiple Directors
1	Commercial Bank of Scotland	43,712	Earl of Mar & Kellie (G), J.M. Howden, Sir J.A. Hope, Sir J. Rankine, W. Thomson, J.W. Tod, T. Warren
2	Royal Bank of Scotland	40,740	Duke of Buccleuch (G), Earl of Strathmore (DG), C. Carlow, Sir H. Cook, R.W. Dundas, J.A. Fleming, C.C. Maconochie
3	National Bank of Scotland	38,591	Marquess of Zetland (DG), J. Cowan, Sir G. Younger, C. Ker (C), C.H.S. Plummer, W.S. Davidson, J.A. Spens, J. Mylne, Sir J. Guthrie
4	Clydesdale Bank	37,834	Sir J. Bell (C), H. Allan (DC), D. McCowan, Sir H. Reid, A. Walker
5	Bank of Scotland	37,687	W.J. Mure (G), Lord Elphinstone (DG), A. Wallace, Sir J.H. Warrack, Lord Henry Scott, Sir R. Anstruther, J.M. Trotter, W. Whitelaw, G. Dunlop, J. Rae, H.E. Richardson
6	Union Bank of Scotland	32,702	Duke of Atholl (C), R. Clark, C.L. Dalziel, R.E. Findlay, H.E. Gordon, J.M. Graham, Sir L.J. Grant, A.R.C. Pitman, P. Rintoul, J.P. Smith
7	British Linen Bank	30,187	Earl of Rosebery (G), A.L. McClure, Sir J.U. Primrose
8	North of Scotland and Town and County Bank	24,359	Sir T. Burnett, J.M. Henderson, D.M.M. Milligan, A.M. Ogston

Table 2A—cont.

Section C: Insurance Companies

Rank	Company	Life and General Funds (£000)	Multiple Directors
1	Scottish Widows Fund Life Assurance	22,521	Earl of Roseberry (P), Earl of Strathmore (VP), Sir H. Cook, A.W.R. Durham, J.A. Fleming, T.J.C. Gifford, Sir H.E. Maxwell, W.J. Mure, H.E. Richardson
2	North British & Mercantile Insurance	21,343	Marquess of Zetland (VP), C.L. Dalziel, R.W. Dundas, C.C. Maconochie, Sir J.U. Primrose, J. Rae, Sir G. Younger
3	Scottish Provident Institution	16,081	Sir L.G. Grant, J.M. Trotter, G. Dunlop, J.M. Graham, F.B. Sharp, Lord Elphinstone
4	Standard Life Assurance	13,311	Sir R.W. Anstruther, E.M. Beilby, A.R.C. Pitman, A. Wallace, W. Younger
5	Northern Assurance	10,851	D.M.M. Milligan (C), Sir T. Burnett (DC), G.M. Cook, G.A. Duff
6	Scottish Union & National Insurance	10,095	T.M. Murray (C), W.S. Davidson, Earl of Mar and Kellie, Sir T. Mason, H.G. Younger
7	Scottish Amicable Life Assurance	7,105	D. Murray (VP), Earl of Elgin (VP), J.A. Spens, R.E. Findlay, J.T. Tulloch, P. Rintoul
8	Scottish Equitable Life Assurance	6,477	Sir R.D. Moncrieffe
9	Life Association of Scotland	5,466	Lord Henry Scott (C), Sir J.A. Hope, W. Thomson
10	Edinburgh Assurance (formerly Edinburgh Life)	Not known	A.L. McClure, Sir J. Guthrie, J.M. Howden, C. Munro, I. McIntyre, J.W. Tod, Sir J. Rankine, J. Mylne
11	Caledonian Insurance	5,186	Sir J.H. Warrack (C), E. Berry, C.H.S. Plummer
12	General Accident, Fire & Life Assurance	2,325	W. Low (C), J. Duff
13	Scottish Legal Life Assurance	1,796	—

Table 2A—cont.

Section D: Investment and Property Companies

Rank	Company	Capital (£000)	Multiple Directors
1	New Zealand & Australian Land	3,000	D. Murray (C), E. Berry, W.S. Davidson, A. Drysdale, D. McCowan, R.A. Murray
2	Scottish American Investment	2,100	A.W.R. Durham, T. Maitland, T.M. Murray
3	British Investment Trust	2,000	J. Cowan (C), G. Dunlop, A. Wallace
4	Alliance Trust	1,700	F.B. Sharp (C), T. Maitland
5	Scottish American Mortgage	1,500	A. Wallace (C), E.M. Beilby
6	North of Scotland Canadian Mortgage	1,380	A.M. Ogston (C), G.A. Duff
7=	Investors' Mortgage Security	1,000	G. Dunlop, T.J.C. Gifford, T. Maitland, F.B. Sharp
7=	Northern American Trust	1,000	A. Hunter, W. Low
7=	Scottish Western Investment	1,000	D. Murray (C), Sir J.T. Cargill, R.A. Murray
10	Edinburgh Investment Trust	840	W.H. Cook, W.B. Dunlop, H.D. Lawrie, T. Maitland, A. Wallace
11	British Assets Trust	700	J.W. Bowhill, C. Munro
12	Scottish Reversionary	550	J.A. Fleming (C), H.D. Lawrie
13=	Caledonian Trust	500	D. Murray (C), Sir J.T. Cargill
13=	Clydesdale Investment	500	D. Murray (C), Sir J.T. Cargill, R.A. Murray
13=	Scottish Investment Trust	500	J.W. Bowhill (C), T.J.C. Gifford, I. McIntyre, C. Munro
13=	Scottish Northern Investment Trust	500	G.M. Cook (C), A.M. Ogston
13=	Second Edinburgh Investment Trust	500	W.H. Cook, W.B. Dunlop, H.D. Lawrie, T. Maitland, A. Wallace

Table 2B: Scotland's Top Companies (1937-8)

Section A: Non-Financial Companies

Rank	Company	Industry	Capital (£000)	Multiple Directors
1	J. & P. Coats	Textiles	20,250	J.O.M. Clark (C), C.H. Mackenzie
2	Burmah Oil	Oil	17,737	Sir John T. Cargill (C), R.I. Watson (MD), D.W.T. Cargill, Col. H.B. Spens
3	Distillers	Whisky distillers	12,891	Lord Forteviot (C), P.M. Dewar, J.A. Dewar
4	Stewarts & Lloyds	Iron and steel	7,881	A.C. Macdiarmid (C)
5	Scottish Power	Electricity	7,500	A.H. Bowhill, I.C.A. Murray, K. Sanderson
6	Colvilles	Iron and steel	5,920	J. Craig (C & MD), Sir James Lithgow, Henry Lithgow, P. Baxter, Sir A.S. Bilsland
7	Nobel's Explosives	Explosives	4,000	– (No independent board)
8	Scottish Oils	Oil	3,963	Sir John T. Cargill (C), R.I. Watson
9	Clyde Valley Electrical Power	Electricity	3,950	C. Ker (C), J.H.M. Clark
10	Linen Thread	Textiles	3,850	–
11	Inveresk Paper	Paper production	2,705	–
12	Metal Industries	Ship salvers, etc.	2,650	–
13	Consolidated Tea and Lands	Tea merchants	2,600	R.L. James (C), R.H.M. Scott, A.M. McGrigor, W.B. Bruce, J.D. Gatheral, H.L. Pinches, G. Fellowes

Table 2B: Section A—cont.

Rank	Company	Industry	Capital (£000)	Multiple Directors
14	Scottish Brewers	Brewing	2,520	H.G. Younger (C), J.A.C. Younger (DC), J.W.H.B. Younger, R. Bruce, H.C. Wilson, J.S. Ford, J.T. Eadie, H.J. Younger, A.P. Williams, S.E.A. Landale, W.McE. Younger, P.C.M. Beilby, O.H. Shennan
15	Irrawaddy Flotilla	Shipping	2,160	J.S. Spencer (C), R. Galloway (DC & MD), R.J. Wilkinson, Sir Maurice Denny, D.W.T. Cargill, J.C. Graham, R.D. Findlay
16	Scottish Motor Traction	Transport	2,073	–
17	Clan Line Steamers	Shipping	2,050	–
18=	James Finlay	Tea merchants	2,000	R.L. James (C), A.M. McGrigor, J.D. Gatheral, J.T. Tulloch
18=	North British Locomotive	Engineering	2,000	–
18=	Singer Manufacturing	Engineering	2,000	–
21	Scottish Cooperative Wholesale	Wholesale distrib.	1,896	–
22	William Baird	Coal and iron	1,858	R.L. Angus (C), A.K. McCosh (VC), J. Morton, M. Brand, J.W. Tweedie
23	Scottish Agricultural Industries	Feedstuffs & fertilisers	1,652	–
24	Fife Coal	Collieries	1,642	Sir Adam Nimmo (C), J.A. Hood, A. Wallace
25	Bairds & Dalmellington	Collieries	1,629	R.L. Angus (C), C. Ker (VC), M. Brand, A.K. McCosh, J. Morton, J.W. Tweedie
26	United Turkey Red	Textile dyers	1,606	G.H. Christie, J.C. Campbell

Table 2B: Section A—cont.

Rank	Company	Industry	Capital (£000)	Multiple Directors
27	John Dewar & Sons	Whisky distillers	1,600	P.M. Dewar (C), J.A. Dewar, Lord Forteviot
28	Hiram Walker & Sons (Scotland)	Maltsters	1,500	Col. H.B. Spens
29	Jugra Land & Carey	Rubber planters	1,436	–
30	Scottish Drapery	Retail drapers	1,400	–
31	Amalgamated Tea Estates	Tea merchants	1,377	R.L. James (C), R.H.M. Scott, A.M. McGrigor, W.B. Bruce, J.D. Gatheral, H.L. Pinches, G. Fellowes
32	Moss Empires	Theatre management	1,340	–
33	Kanan Devan Hills Produce	Tea merchants	1,300	R.L. James (C), R.H.M. Scott, A.M. McGrigor, J.D. Gatheral, H.L. Pinches, W.B. Bruce, G. Fellowes
34	Tharsis Sulphur & Copper	Sulphur mining	1,250	S.C. Hogarth, Maj. Gen. Sir Walter Maxwell-Scott, W.A. Wilson
35	Federated Foundries	Iron founders	1,213	–
36	Anglo-American Direct Tea Trading	Tea merchants	1,162	R.L. James (C), R.H.M. Scott, A.M. McGrigor, J.D. Gatheral, H.L. Pinches, W.B. Bruce, G. Fellowes
37	Donaldson Line	Shipping	1,114	–
38	Alex Pirie & Sons	Paper production	1,100	–
39	Coltness Iron	Iron and coal	1,091	W.H. Telfer (VC), D.J. Barr (MD), W.A. Wilson, Capt. J.F.H. Houldsworth
40	Fleming, Reid	Textiles	1,050	–
41=	Barry, Ostlere & Shepherd	Linoleum prodn.	1,000	–

Table 2B: Section A—cont.

Rank	Company	Industry	Capital (£000)	Multiple Directors
41=	William McEwan	Brewing	1,000	H.G. Younger (C), J.T. Eadie, W.McE. Younger, H.C. Wilson, J.A.C. Younger, R. Bruce, J.S. Ford, J.W.H.B. Younger, H.J. Younger, A.P. Williams, P.C.M. Beilby
41=	United Collieries	Collieries	1,000	—
41=	William Younger	Brewing	1,000	H.G. Younger (C), J.A.C. Younger (DC), J.S. Ford, H.J. Younger, J.T. Eadie, W.McE. Younger, J.W.H.B. Younger, R. Bruce, A.P. Williams, S.E.A. Landale, P.C.M. Beilby, O.H. Shennan
45	William Dixon	Iron and coal	956	D.B. Warren (C)
46	Saxone Shoe	Shoe manufacturers	950	—
47	British & Burmese Steam Navigation	Shipping	913	J.S. Spencer (C), R. Galloway (DC & MD), R.J. Wilkinson, Sir Maurice Denny, D.W.T. Cargill, J.C. Graham, T.D. Findlay
48	George Outram	Newspaper proprietors	876	J. Gourlay (C), Col. N. Kennedy
49	Bank Line	Shipping	875	—
50	Lothian Coal	Collieries	809	J.A. Hood (C & MD)
51	Cooper & Co.'s Stores	Retail grocers	800	—
52	Scottish Iron & Steel	Iron and steel	780	—
53=	Samnuggur Jute Factory	Jute spinners	750	J. Robertson (C), R.N. Band, Sir Alexander R. Murray, A. Wighton
53=	Titaghur Jute Factory	Jute spinners	750	J. Robertson (C), R.N. Band, Sir Alexander R. Murray, A. Wighton

Table 2B: Section A—cont.

Rank	Company	Industry	Capital (£000)	Multiple Directors
53=	George Younger & Son	Brewers	750	Viscount Younger of Leckie (C), Earl of Mar & Kellie
53=	Scottish Central Electric Power	Electricity	750	A.H. Bowhill (C), I.C.A. Murray, K. Sanderson
57	Nimmo & Dunlop	Iron and steel	741	Sir Adam Nimmo (C), H. Lithgow (VC), Sir James Lithgow, J. Craig, P. Baxter
58=	North British Rubber	Rubber man.	725	W. Thomson
58=	Wilsons & Clyde Coal	Collieries	725	W.H. Telfer (VC), D.J. Barr (MD), A.C. Macdiarmid, W.A. Wilson, Capt. J.F.H. Houldsworth

Table 2B—cont.

Section B: Banking Companies

Rank	Company	Deposits (£000)	Multiple Directors
1	Royal Bank of Scotland	69,922	H.W. Haldane, G.J. Lidstone, R.N. Dundas, A. Maitland, J.T. Tulloch, K. Murray, Sir Iain Colquhoun
2	Commercial Bank of Scotland	44,739	Earl of Mar & Kellie (G), W. Thomson, A.W.R. Durham, D.J. Smith, G. Archer
3	Bank of Scotland	39,298	Lord Elphinstone (G), Lord Henry Scott (DG), W. Brodie, J. Craig, J. Gourlay, S.C. Hogarth, H.A. Jamieson, Col. N. Kennedy, Lord Kinross, A. Wallace, J.P. Watson
4	National Bank of Scotland	38,282	C.M. Black, R.K. Blair, J.H.M. Clark, W.H. Fraser, C. Ker, C.H.S. Plummer, Viscount Younger of Leckie
5	British Linen Bank	38,153	Earl of Home (G), Earl of Airlie (DG), E.M. Beilby, Lord Kinnaird
6	Clydesdale Bank	35,645	R.L. Angus, R. McKenna
7	Union Bank of Scotland	33,437	Sir A.S. Bilsland (C), J.O.M. Clark, Sir Maurice E. Denny, J.B. Findlay, Lord George Douglas-Hamilton, Col. H.B. Spens, N.L. Hird (GM)
8	North of Scotland Bank	29,124	A.S.R. Bruce, Earl of Caithness, R. McKenna

Table 2B—cont.

Section C: Insurance Companies

Rank	Company	Life & General Funds (£000)	Multiple Directors
1	North British & Mercantile Insurance	44,321	C. Ker, Viscount Younger of Leckie
2	Scottish Widows Fund & Life Assurance	33,470	R.N. Dundas, A.W.R. Durham, T.J.C. Gifford, Lord Kinross, G.J. Lidstone, K. Murray
3	Standard Life Assurance	26,533	E.M. Bellby, J.C. Campbell, J. Ivory, H.A. Jamieson, Lord Kinnaird, J.H. Richardson, A. Wallace
4	Scottish Provident Institution	24,315	J. Maxstone Graham, A. Maitland, D. Smith, Earl of Home, S.C. Hogarth, A. Shepherd, Lord Elphinstone, W.H. Askew-Robertson
5	Scottish Union & National Insurance	13,733	G. Archer, C.M. Black, Earl of Mar & Kellie, J.L. Mounsey, H.G. Younger
6	General Accident, Fire & Life Assurance	13,418	Earl of Airlie
7	Scottish Amicable Life Assurance	12,509	J.B. Findlay (C), Col. H.B. Spens, N.L. Hird, D.B. Warren, Sir A. Steven Bilsland, J.T. Tulloch
8	Northern Assurance	12,005	A.S.R. Bruce, Earl of Caithness
9	Scottish Equitable Life Assurance	11,218	R.K. Blair, Lord Nigel Douglas-Hamilton, A.A. Lawrie
10	Caledonian Insurance	9,687	C.H.S. Plummer (C), Sir Walter Maxwell-Scott, W. Blair, W.H. Fraser, W. Brodie
11	Scottish Life Assurance	8,587	W. Lawson, J.H. Guild, Sir Iain Colquhoun
12	Scottish Temperance & General Insurance	8,246	A.K. Rodger (C), J. Craig
13	Life Association of Scotland	8,129	Lord Henry Scott (C), J.L. Mounsey, W. Thomson
14	Scottish Legal Life Assurance	7,802	—

Table 2B—cont.

Section D: Investment & Property Companies

Rank	Company	Capital (£000)	Multiple Directors
1	Scottish American Investment	3,400	A.W.R. Durham (C), A. Maitland, K. Murray
2	Alliance Trust	3,250	J. Prain (C), D. Pirie, W.D. MacDougall (M), H.S. Sharp
3	British Assets Trust	3,094	A.W.R. Durham (C), J. Ivory, C. Munro, H.G. Sharp
4	New Zealand & Australian Land	3,000	T.P. Spens (C), W.H. Fraser
5	British Investment Trust	2,500	H.A. Jamieson (C), R.K. Blair, W. Lawson, J.H. Richardson, A. Wallace
6	Second Scottish Investment Trust	2,250	T.J.C. Gifford (C), I. McIntyre, R.G. Simpson, A. Hutchison, H.K. Salvesen
7	Investors' Mortgage Security	1,815	T.J.C. Gifford (C), J.H. Guild, A.W.R. Durham, J. Prain, N.G. Salvesen
8	Scottish Mortgage & Trust	1,650	J. Maxstone Graham (C), W.D. MacDougall, J.H. Guild
9=	Great Northern Investment Trust	1,500	A.K. Rodger (C), G.H. Christie
9=	Northern American Trust	1,500	W.H. Fraser
9=	Scottish American Mortgage	1,500	E.M. Beilby (C), A. Wallace, J.P. Watson, Hon. R.B. Watson, W.H. Fraser
9=	Scottish Investment Trust	1,500	T.J.C. Gifford (C), I. McIntyre, R.G. Simpson, A. Hutchison, H.K. Salvesen
13	North of Scotland Canadian Mortgage and General Investment Trust	1,373	Earl of Caithness

Table 2B: Section D—cont.

Rank	Company	Capital (£000)	Multiple Directors
14	Second Investors' Mortgage Security	1,250	T.J.C. Gifford (C), J.H. Guild, A.W.R. Durham, J. Prain, N.G. Salvesen
15	Edinburgh Investment Trust	1,240	W.H. Fraser (C), R.K. Blair, W.B. Dunlop, A.A. Lawrie, W. Thomson, A. Wallace
16=	Scottish United Investors	1,200	J.T. Tulloch (C), C.H. Mackenzie, R.G. Simpson, Col. H.B. Spens
16=	Second Alliance Trust	1,200	J. Prain (C), D. Pirie, W.D. MacDougall (M), H.S. Sharp
18	Edinburgh & Dundee Investment	1,188	J. Prain (C), W. Blair, T.J.C. Gifford
19=	Caledonian Trust	1,100	Sir John T. Cargill (C), R.F. Barclay, M.V. Fleming
19=	Scottish Western Investment	1,100	Sir John T. Cargill (C), R.F. Barclay, R.A. Murray, M.V. Fleming, T.P. Spens
21=	Clydesdale Investment	1,000	Sir John T. Cargill (C), R.F. Barclay, R.A. Murray, M.V. Fleming, T.P. Spens
21=	Realisation & Debenture Corporation of Scotland	1,000	H.A. Jamieson (C), A. Wallace, W.B. Dunlop, A.A. Lawrie
21=	Scottish Capital Investment	1,000	T.J.C. Gifford (C), H.W. Haldane, C. Munro, R.G. Simpson
21=	Scottish Central Investment Trust	1,000	A. Shepherd (C), W.H. Askew-Robertson, T.J.C. Gifford
21=	Scottish National Trust	1,000	R.G. Simpson (C), J.O.M. Clark, Sir A. Steven Bilsland
21=	Second Scottish Western Investment	1,000	Sir John T. Cargill (C), R.A. Murray, M.V. Fleming, R.F. Barclay, T.P. Spens
27	Second Edinburgh Investment Trust	900	W.H. Fraser (C), R.K. Blair, W.B. Dunlop, A.A. Lawrie, W. Thomson, A. Wallace
28	Second British Assets Trust	874	A.W.R. Durham (C), J. Ivory, C. Munro, H.G. Sharp
29=	American Trust	800	Hon. J.M. Balfour, Hon. R.B. Watson
29=	Scottish Eastern Investment Trust	800	Hon. J.M. Balfour

3 CONSOLIDATION AND GROWTH IN THE POST-WAR YEARS

Preparation for war and the actual waging of war buttressed heavy industry and so ensured that the long-term problems of decline were obscured. In the post-war years they continued to be obscured. The international environment was far more favourable than before since the growth of world trade masked the British lack of competitiveness. Allied with growing consumer demand, this ensured that the 15 years following the war were a period of relative prosperity and low unemployment. Steady economic growth was punctuated only by the periodic credit squeezes of a 'stop-go' economic policy. This situation allowed the large scale enterprises to consolidate their position as the dominant economic form, whilst allowing business in property and retail distribution to grow in size.

Perhaps the most important events of the period were the nationalisations which occurred immediately after the war. In 1947 the Labour Government nationalised the coal industry and instigated its reorganisation on a geographical, coalfield basis; as a result, the Scottish collieries were grouped under a Scottish board. In 1948 the railways, buses and electricity were nationalised, again along regional lines. The Scottish railways had already been incorporated into the British companies and so the formation of the British Transport Commission had little impact, though road transport was reorganised. Electricity nationalisation involved the creation of a Central Electricity Generating Board, to deal with generation and transmission and a number of Area Boards to deal with supply. In Scotland the South of Scotland Electricity Board combined all these functions. The final act of nationalisation involved the iron and steel industry, though the old company structure was not dismantled and the industry was denationalised by a Conservative Government in 1952. Government impact on the economy, however, went beyond nationalisation, since the government encouraged and supported restructuring in the cotton, shipbuilding and aircraft industries. This extension of public involvement in the traditional industries had a considerable impact upon Scotland, in which many of these industries were concentrated.

126

The period was marked not only by a growth in governmental involvement but also by an increase in 'external control' generally. The extent of Scottish ownership of Scottish economic activity declined considerably in the face of the expansion of English and American firms in Scotland, particularly in the growth industries. After 1960, the problems of an unbalanced industrial mix — a concentration of slow growth or declining industries, and control over growth industries by 'external' forces — were to become the key to understanding Scottish economic development. In this chapter we shall attempt to illustrate these processes through an analysis of data relating to 1955-6.

Scotland's Top Companies 1955-6

The list of top Scottish companies for 1955-6 (Table 3.A) shows a total of 109 enterprises: 55 non-financial companies, six banks, 14 insurance companies, and 34 investment and property companies. Table 3.1 gives the size distribution of the non-financial companies. The total capital of these companies had risen from its low point in 1938-9 to a level £40m above its 1920-21 level. The ten largest companies accounted for 69 per cent of the total capital, most of this being the capital of the five largest companies. In terms of asset value, the company rankings differed a little. A Board of Trade analysis of the top 100 British manufacturing and retailing companies in 1957 included only five Scottish companies: Distillers (ranked 7th), Stewarts and Lloyds (16th), Coats (19th), Colvilles (35th), and House of Fraser (82nd).

Table 3.1: Size Distribution of Non-Financial Companies (1955-6)

Companies by Rank	Total Share Capital (£)	Cumulative Total (£)
Top 10	187,904,391	187,904,391
11-20	34,889,139	222,793,530
21-30	19,656,927	242,450,457
31-40	13,930,561	256,381,018
41-55	15,988,187	272,369,205
TOTALS	272,369,205 (N = 55)	

Table 3.2 shows the industrial distribution of the non-financial companies. There are certain problems in this industrial classification in

Table 3.2: Industrial Distribution of Non-Financial Companies (1955-6)

Industrial Sector	Number of Companies		
	Top 30	Top 49	All
Tea and rubber	2	6	6
Food and drink	5	6	8
Oil	1	1	1
Chemicals	1	1	1
Dyeing	1	1	1
Textiles	5	8	8
Non-coal mining		1	1
Brickworks, etc.			1
Iron and steel	3	3	3
Metal and engineering	5	9	9
Paper and publishing, etc.	2	4	5
Shipping	2	3	4
Distribution	3	5	6
Theatres		1	1
TOTAL			55

relation to the coal companies, whose assets had been nationalised. United Collieries, for example, appears merely as a brickworks, whilst William Baird classified itself as a textile firm (since this was the area in which it had begun to diversify). This problem is clear from Table 3.3, in which Baird was allocated to the brickworks category. Nevertheless, this table gives some indication of the importance of Scottish companies in the British economy. A total of 15 Scottish companies were to be found amongst the largest companies in their sector, 13 of these being included in the present analysis.

The six Scottish banks had total deposits of £971m, and insurance funds amounted to £623m. By far the biggest bank was the Royal, with the other banks being similar in size to one another. Standard Life was much larger than its competitors, and was one of the five largest British life insurance companies. The total capital of the investment companies was £71m, equivalent to just over a quarter of the capital of non-financial companies and almost as large as the textile and steel sectors together.

The average size of company boards had increased since 1938 to 7.8 members. Bank boards rose considerably to 15.2, though insurance and

Table 3.3: Scottish Companies in the Top 20 of their Industrial Sector (1957)

Industrial Sector	Company	Rank in Sector	Assets (£m)
Food	United Biscuits	16	9.04
Drink	Distillers	1	125.37
	Scottish Brewers	14	13.88
Metal Man.	Stewarts & Lloyds	3	84.93
	Colvilles	8	49.32
Textiles	Coats	2	76.16
	Linen Thread	10	13.34
Clothing, etc.	Saxone	3	10.12
Leather, rubber	North British Rubber	15	3.40
Brickworks, etc.	Wm Baird	11	7.61
Paper, etc.	Inveresk	8	16.75
Retail distribn.	House of Fraser	9	22.92
Entertainment	Moss Empires	4	3.44
	Caledonian Ass. Cinemas*	12	1.23
	Howard & Wyndham*	14	0.83

NOTE:
Companies marked with an asterisk are not included in Table 3.A. The 20 largest British companies in each industrial sector were analysed and the Scottish companies were identified. The analysis did not cover all oil, shipping and trading companies. Sectors in which no Scottish companies appeared in the top 20 are not listed.
SOURCE: *Company Assets and Income in 1957*, Board of Trade HMSO, (London, 1960).

investment boards were comparable to their earlier levels (insurance boards averaged 10.3 and investment boards averaged 5.0). The increased size of the banking boards was parallel to a movement in the ten largest industrial companies, where board size increased to 11.7. A total of 620 men held 848 directorships, with 119 multiple directors holding 41 per cent of directorships. Whilst 48 per cent of all directorships were in the financial sector, 73 per cent of the directorships held by multiple directors were in the financial sector. This is in line with the trend identified in Chapter 2: multiple directors held an increased proportion of the financial directorships, and these financial interests were of considerable significance in the Scottish economy as a whole.

The average number of multiple directors sitting on each inter-locked company in 1955-6 had fallen slightly to 4.0, resulting from

Table 3.4: Multiple Directors on the Board (1955-6)

No. of Multiple Directors on Board	Number of Companies		
	Non-financial	Financial	TOTAL
0	21	1	22
1	17	3	20
2	4	4	8
3	3	10	13
4	3	14	17
5	1	6	7
6	2	3	5
7		6	6
8	4	5	9
9		1	1
16		1	1
TOTALS	55	54	109

the reduction in the number of companies with two or five multiple directors and a parallel increase in the number with just one. Whilst the number of companies with seven or more multiple directors increased, largely as a result of changes in the banking sector, the fall in the middle range was greater. The companies with the most multiple directors were Bank of Scotland (16), Royal Bank (9), Commercial Bank (8), National Bank (8), Scottish Widows (8), Standard Life (8), Scottish Union (8), and four of the Finlay tea companies (8 each). These figures show that the number of widely connected companies had returned to the same level as in the 1920s.

The Financial Sector

(i) The Banking and Insurance Sector

The early 1950s saw a reduction in the number of Scottish banks from eight to six. In 1950 the Clydesdale and the North of Scotland, both owned by the Midland Bank, were merged. The consequence of this change for the directorate of the new Clydesdale and North of Scotland Bank was that there were four common directors with the Midland: Sir Harold Yarrow (former chairman of the Clydesdale), Lord Harlech (chairman of the Midland), Sir A.G. Stern, and the Earl of Faversham. In 1954 the Bank of Scotland acquired the Union Bank, resulting in a considerably enlarged bank and a considerably enlarged board. Of the pre-war directors, the new Bank of Scotland board still included Sir John Craig, Lord Elphinstone and Norman Kennedy (all from the old Bank of Scotland), and Lord Bilsland, Sir Samuel Beale, Sir Hugh Rose, and H.B Spens (all from the Union Bank). The Royal Bank too had grown, but through the acquisition of two of the smaller English banks. As a result, its board included Sir Francis Glyn of Glyn Mills, and Sir Eric Carpenter of Williams Deacons. Whilst the Commercial Bank was still independent, it was to merge with the National Bank in 1959, Lloyds Bank having 37 per cent of the new National Commercial Bank.

This restructuring of bank capital consolidated the top position of the Royal Bank in terms of deposits, and resulted in the Bank of Scotland rising to second position. As a consequence, the Commercial and the National fell to fourth and fifth place, and British Linen fell to sixth place. There had been few important changes within the insurance sector, though Scottish Temperance had changed its name to Scottish Mutual in 1951. In 1957, however, Caledonian Insurance was bought by Guardian Assurance; and in 1959 North British and Mercantile was bought by Commercial Union and Scottish Union was bought by Norwich Union.

Capital restructuring was associated with changes in the pattern of interlocking directorships. Interlocks between banking and insurance companies became more diffuse. A smaller number of lines were plural lines, and both the Commercial Bank and Scottish Union had no plural lines. Figure 3.1 shows the strongest lines in the sector — those which were plural or which involved office holders — and it can be seen that the Clydesdale Bank continued to have no insurance connections, and that the Bank of Scotland had inherited the Union Bank's link with Scottish Amicable. The Bank of Scotland was most closely connected to the insurance sector, having two Glasgow links and two Edinburgh links. The Aberdeen-based Northern Assurance, which was formerly linked to the North of Scotland Bank, was connected to the Royal Bank (through the chairman, D.F. Landale) rather than to the enlarged Clydesdale Bank.

(ii)   The Investment and Property Sector

The internal structure of the investment company sector was very similar to that of the inter-war period. Table 3.5 shows the relative size of the trusts measured in terms of their asset value. The largest group was Baillie, Gifford with total assets of £43.9m, though the largest single trust was the Alliance with assets of £30.7m. Each of

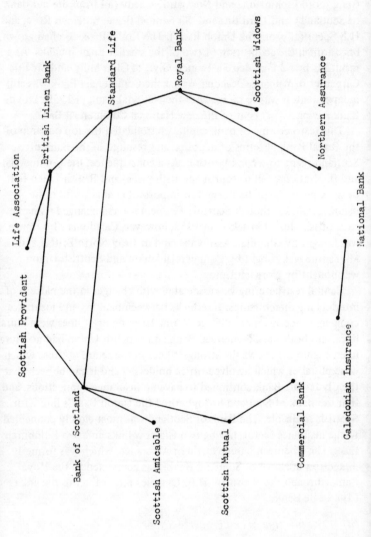

Figure 3.1: Strong Links Between Banks and Insurance Companies (1955-6)

the Baillie, Gifford companies was chaired by T.J.C Gifford, and their boards included various partners in Baillie, Gifford as well as other lawyers and accountants. The boards of the two Alliance trusts included the managers together with Gifford and James Prain, whose jute firm had been absorbed by Caird (Dundee). Also on the Alliance boards was Hugh Spens, so linking the three great Edinburgh, Dundee and Glasgow groupings together. Spens was a partner in Maclay, Murray and Spens and was chairman of the two Moores, Carson and Watson trusts. His brother, T.P Spens, was chairman of the Brown, Fleming and Murray trusts, which were managed by R.A Murray and his brother J.I Murray. Hugh Cowan-Douglas, a partner in Brown, Fleming and Murray, was a director of the Moores, Carson and Watson trusts.

The Baillie, Gifford group was closely connected with the Alliance trusts, Investors' Mortgage Security, and the Scottish Investment Trusts. The main outside links of these trusts were to the Royal Bank and to Scottish Widows. Edinburgh Investment was linked to Standard Life and British Linen Bank, the latter being closely linked with Northern American Trust and Scottish Northern. British Investment connected closely with Royal Bank, Standard Life and Scottish Provident, and so bridged the distinct spheres. Similarly, the Ivory and Sime trusts were connected to both Scottish Widows and Bank of Scotland. The Brown, Fleming and Murray trusts were closely linked to Clydesdale Bank and Scottish Amicable, though their close association with the Moores, Carson and Watson trusts joined them also to the Bank of Scotland. It would seem that the division between Glasgow and Edinburgh spheres of influence was still important, and that Dundee was connected primarily with Edinburgh interests. Similarly, Aberdeen investment interests were allied with Edinburgh: Aberdeen and Canadian was linked to Standard Life through its association with Chiene and Tait (East of Scotland Trust), and Scottish Northern was linked to British Linen Bank through its connection to Northern American Trust.

The Industrial Sector

Of the 59 large non-financial companies of 1937-8, 36 were still to be found amongst the top 55 of 1955-6. Amongst the 23 companies 'lost' over the period, four were too small to appear in the list (Titaghur Jute, Coltness, Outram, Geo. Younger), three had been put into liquidation (Hiram Walker, Scottish Drapery and Irrawaddy Flotilla), eight had been merged or incorporated into other companies, and eight had been liquidated following nationalisation of their assets. The 1948

Table 3.5: Scottish Investment Trust Assets (1957)

Group	No. of Trusts	Group Assets (£m)	Trusts Included in Present Analysis	Assets (£m)
Baillie, Gifford	6	43.9	Scottish Mortgage and Trust	13.8
			Edinburgh & Dundee	9.1
			Scottish Capital	6.4
			Scottish Central	5.7
Alliance	2	42.0	Alliance	30.7
			Second Alliance	11.3
Brown, Fleming & Murray	9	31.5	Scottish Western	5.1
			Second Scottish Western	4.9
			Caledonian	4.4
			Clydesdale	4.2
Ivory & Sime	2	27.7	British Assets	20.7
			Second British Assets	7.0
Robertson	2	26.3	British Investment	18.3
			Realisation & Debenture	8.0
Ball, Macgregor	3	23.3	Scottish Investment	8.2
			Second Scottish Inv.	11.5
Friarfield House	5	22.6	Northern American	7.8
McGregor	3	19.9	Edinburgh Investment	8.2
			Second Edinburgh Inv.	6.8
Grahams Rintoul	4	17.3	Scottish National	5.7
Carnegie	2	16.9	Investors' Mortgage	9.4
			Second Investors	7.5
– –	1	–	Scottish American Investment	16.6
Paull and Williamson	3	12.4	Scottish Northern	5.3
Moores, Carson & Watson	2	9.2	Scottish United	6.2
			Scottish Consolidated	3.0
–	1	–	Great Northern	7.8
–	1	–	Scottish American Mortgage	6.6
–	1	–	Scottish Eastern	6.0
–	1	–	Aberdeen & Canadian	5.8
–	1	–	Clyde and Mersey	5.1
–	1	–	American Trust	4.8
–	1	–	East of Scotland Trust	3.3

Note: This table lists all investment companies included in the present analysis (except New Zealand & Australian Land). Where two or more of these companies are commonly managed, further details are given for the group as a whole. Where the trust is not grouped with other companies in the analysis details of its management group are not given. Figures for NZ & Australian Land were not given by Bullock since the company still operated as an agricultural mortgage company.
Source: Adapted from H. Bullock, *The Story of Investment Trust Companies* (Columbia University Press, New York, 1959).

nationalisation of the electricity supply industry resulted in the
disappearance of Scottish Power, Clyde Valley Electrical and Scottish
Central Electric. Similarly, nationalisation of the coal industry led to
the liquidation of Fife Coal, Dixons (whose iron interests were acquired
by Colvilles in 1954), Lothian Coal, Nimmo and Dunlop, and Wilsons
and Clyde. Coal nationalisation, as we have already pointed out, had an
impact on Wm Baird; and Coltness Iron also took nationalisation as the
opportunity to begin a period of industrial diversification. Six of the
companies disappearing through merger were simply absorbed completely into their parent group: Nobel's into ICI, Scottish Oils into BP,
Barry Ostlere into Barry and Staines, and McEwan and William Younger
into Scottish Brewers. Samnuggur Jute had merged with its sister firm
Titaghur Jute, Scottish Iron and Steel was part of Bairds and Scottish,
and British and Burmese Shipping had been acquired by Ocean Steamship (now Ocean Transport and Trading).

A total of 65 per cent of the 1955-6 non-financial companies had
been on the 1937-8 list, and 40 per cent had been on the 1920-1 list.
Of the 19 companies new to the list in 1955-6, eight had been too small
to appear in the 1937-8 list: Rivet Bolt and Nut, Arrol, Lawsons,
Glenfield and Kennedy, G. and J. Weir, Wm Teacher, Collins and
A.B. Fleming. The 11 new flotations included several established
firms, such as Alex Cowan, Low and Bonar, House of Fraser and Lyle
Shipping, but included only one holding company (United Biscuits —
formed to amalgamate McFarlane Lang, McVitie, and other firms).

**Figure 3.2: English and American Ownership of Scottish Industrial
Companies (1955-6)**

Company	Status	Parent
English-owned		
Clan Line	Subsidiary	British and Commonwealth Shipping
Jugra Land & Carey	Subsidiary	Pataling Rubber Estates
Moss Empires	Associate	Stoll Theatre Corporation
Alex Pirie	Subsidiary	Wiggins, Teape
Scottish Agricultural Industries	Subsidiary	Imperial Chemical Industries
Scottish Motor Traction	Subsidiary	Sears Holdings
American-owned		
Singer Manufacturing	Subsidiary	Singer Manufacturing
North British Rubber	Subsidiary	United States Rubber

English and American ownership of Scottish companies had become an important feature of the Scottish economy in the 1950s. Figure 3.2 shows that five of the top Scottish industrial companies were subsidiaries of English concerns, one was an associate of an English firm, and two were subsidiaries of American corporations. Some of these, such as Singer, were long-established links, but others were new, such as Scottish Motor Traction. Another recent amalgamation involved the reconstruction of Clan Line. In 1956 the Cayzer family who dominated Clan Line, consistently amongst the top companies, engineered a merger between their company and Union-Castle Line. The resulting company was named British and Commonwealth Shipping and became the London-based holding company for Clan Line. This trend towards English ownership was to continue, but it was not a one-way process: in 1958-9 Fleming, Reid was taken over by Patons and Baldwins, this joining Coats in 1961 to form Coats Patons. But English influence was not limited to these subsidiary or associate companies. Many of the Scottish companies which had 'disappeared' over the period studied had become subsidiaries of English concerns and operated merely as 'branch plants' of the parent company. Branch plants with no separate legal existence had also been set up, the Ferranti factory in Edinburgh being perhaps the best known. The formation of branch plants was the favoured strategy for American multinationals, and Scotland was 'host' to the plants of companies such as National Cash Registers and Hoover, though some of these were, strictly, branch plants of the English subsidiaries of the American firms. Furthermore, many of the largest Scottish companies were on the receiving end of the growth of 'institutional' shareholding. The large insurance companies had become important owners of company shares and so were rivalling the family directors who continued to run their firms. Growing English ownership in this area, however, was not to reach its full significance until the 1970s.

The network of lines between industrial companies was far less dense than in earlier years. A total of 34 of the industrial companies were interlocked, most of their interlocks being with financial companies. However, 21 had interlocks with other industrial companies. These 21 companies formed five components, as shown in Figure 3.3. Many of these interlocks were, at least in part, the consequence of financial interlocks. Thus Lord Bilsland linked Burmah to Colvilles because he sat on the board of the Bank of Scotland, which was Burmah's banker. Similarly, Hugh Cowan-Douglas, a partner in Brown, Fleming and Murray, linked Glenfield and Kennedy with

Figure 3.3: Industrial Interlocks (1955-6)

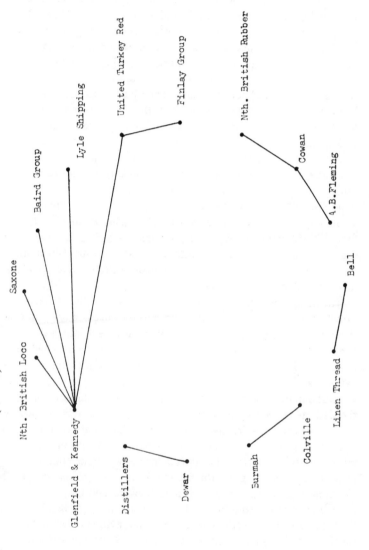

United Turkey Red because of his many financial directorships. There were relatively few obvious functional interlocks. The hydraulic engineers Glenfield and Kennedy were interlocked with North British Loco and the Baird companies, the link between Glenfield and Baird being generated by H.R Neilson, formerly of North British Loco. The only other possible functional interlock, rather a marginal case, was between Cowan the paper manufacturers, Fleming the ink manufacturers, and North British Rubber. These links were generated through the financial network: Sir William Wallace (of Cowan and North British Rubber) was a director of British Linen Bank, and Sir Hugh Rose (of Cowan and Fleming) was a director of the Bank of Scotland, though it should be noted that a Hugh Rose sat on the board of North British Rubber. It would appear that the larger integrated concerns had less need for interlocking directorships with other industrial companies. They had already merged with their most important associates. At the same time, some industrial companies would have been directly interlocked with English industrials. The break-up of functionally integrated groupings which we noted for the 1930s had proceeded even further than at that time. Direct links between industrial companies and the financial sector were becoming more important.

The dominant force in Scottish heavy industry in the 1930s was the Colville-Lithgow-Nimmo group, but this dominance had been upset by the post-war nationalisations. The heavy industries to which the Scottish economy was heavily committed were those which had been most affected by nationalisation. In 1940 the Labour Government had nationalised the steel companies and set up the Iron and Steel Corporation of Great Britain, which operated as a holding company for the separate concerns. Since strategic control was not relinquished by the operating companies, nationalisation had little impact on patterns of control. In consequences the 1952 denationalisation could proceed fairly smoothly. Ownership of the companies was transferred to the Iron and Steel Holding and Realization Agency, whose job was to sell the firms back to their original owners. Stewarts and Lloyds was returned to private hands in 1954 and Colvilles in 1955. Bairds and Scottish Steel, though still having five common directors with William Baird, remained in public ownership until 1963, when it was sold to Iron and Steel Investments (a consortium of steel companies, one of which was Colvilles'. Colvilles remained the major Scottish steel producer, and the industry as a whole was much concerned with financing the de-nationalisation plans.

The coal industry had been nationalised in 1947, but this extension of public ownership involved nationalisation of *assets* rather than *companies*. Many companies had taken on lawyers and accountants to help them in the fight against nationalisation and, subsequently, to ensure a smooth passage into liquidation. Coltness recruited Sir Ian Bolton of McClelland, Ker as their adviser, whilst Fife Coal appointed T.J.C. Gifford and W.H. Fraser to help with the liquidation. There is here an interesting divergence in response to nationalisation: nationalisation of the assets resulted, in each case, in a 'shell company' with considerable financial resources, yet Fife Coal distributed its funds to its shareholders and Coltness used its funds to diversify. The nationalised coal industry itself was reorganised along geographical lines and the Earl of Balfour became head of the Scottish board of the National Coal Board.

The remaining important development of this period was the popularisation of the 'take-over bid', in which one company acquired another by means of a competitive bid for its shares. In the forefront of this development was Hugh Fraser, who built up a large organisation through the technique of sale and lease-back. Hugh Fraser (later Lord Fraser of Allender) was the grandson of the man who had entered into partnership with James Arthur, and it was the family store of Fraser, Sons and Co., which became House of Fraser. Hugh Fraser became managing director of the firm in 1924 and, with the backing of the National Bank and Glasgow Industrial Finance, converted it into a public company in 1948. The Fraser family stake in House of Fraser was partly direct and partly through Scottish and Universal Investments, a private family investment company. Fraser acquired department stores such as John Barkers, Binn's, and the Scottish Drapery Corporation chain. These acquisitions were financed in a way that became Fraser's hallmark. A company was bought and the freeholds of the stores were sold to an insurance company in return for a long lease. In this way, the capital value of the site was released and could be used to finance the next acquisition. Many of Fraser's sale and lease-back arrangements were with Legal and General Assurance, in which Fraser built up a large holding. Although the high point of this process was Fraser's acquisition of Harrod's in 1959, a minor irony was that he took over Arthur & Co. in 1958. But Fraser did not have everything his own way. Scottish Motor Traction, which was the distributor for Vauxhall cars and Bedford trucks and which carried out some engineering, was the object of an unwelcome take-over bid from Charles Clore in 1956 and invited Fraser onto its board to help fight the Clore offer. Instead Fraser put in an offer of his own for SMT but, after a minor skirmish, was beaten by Clore and SMT became a subsidiary of Sears Holdings.

The Structure of the Business Network

Of the 109 companies 87 were interlocked with one another and 12 of the uninterlocked companies had links with smaller Scottish firms, ten having no Scottish interlocks at all (Metal Industries, Alex Pirie, Stewarts and Lloyds, Blackwood Morton, Angus Milling, Arrol, Lawsons, Cooper, United Collieries and Scottish Legal Life).

T'ble 3.6: Plural and Single Company Linkages (1955-6)

Value of Line	No. of Lines
1	266
2	49
3	0
4	3
5	7
6	0
7	5
8	3
TOTAL	333

It can be seen from Table 3.6 that whilst the number of lines had risen to above the level for 1937-8, the number of plural lines had fallen slightly. The density of the network rose to 5.66 per cent and the connectivity rose to 57.8 per cent. The network comprised just two components: one large component of 83 companies and the pair formed by Bell and Linen Thread. These facts together indicate that the Scottish business network had become less intensively clustered, but more densely connected.

Table 3.7 shows that the distribution of company connections in 1955-6 was similar to that for 1937-8, except in the higher reaches. Exactly twice as many companies had ten or more connections than in the earlier period. Both the Bank of Scotland and Scottish Widows increased their centrality scores, the Bank of Scotland being directly connected to almost a third of the top companies (Table 3.8). This is no doubt partly due to the merger between this bank and the Union

Table 3.7: Distribution of Company Connections (1955-6)

No. of Companies Connected To	No. of Companies	No. of Connections
0	22	0
1	15	15
2	5	10
3	6	18
4	6	24
5	5	25
6	9	54
7	2	14
8	6	48
9	1	9
10	4	40
11	4	44
12	5	60
13	5	65
14	2	28
15	4	60
16	4	64
17	2	34
20	1	20
34	1	34
TOTALS	109	666

Bank which brought together the financial links of the Bank of Scotland and the industrial links of the Union Bank. Of the Bank of Scotland's links to other companies, 20 were with financial companies and 14 were with industrials. This would seem to confirm the view that industrial companies were still tied into the network at the same level as in the inter-war period, but they were now far more likely to be linked to a financial company than to other industrials.

Table 3.9 shows that 48 of the interlocked companies were involved in the network of plural lines, a fall from the level of 1937-8. Similarly, the number of components in the plural network had fallen to eight. This again confirms the post-war trend from intensive clustering to dense connection. Only ten of the 48 companies were industrial: the Finlay group, the Baird companies, and three industrials with banking

Table 3.8: Most Central Companies (1955-6)

Company	No. of Connections
Bank of Scotland	34
Scottish Widows	20
Alliance Trust	17
Second Alliance Trust	17
Scottish Central Investment	16
Scottish Consolidated	16
Scottish Investment	16
Second Scottish Investment	16
Investors' Mortgage	15
Second Investors' Mortgage	15
Scottish United Investors	15
National Bank	15
Commercial Bank	14
Royal Bank	14

Table 3.9: Distribution of Plural Linkages (1955-6)

No. of Plural Lines per Company	No. of Companies
0	39
1	14
2	7
3	14
4	6
5	6
8	1
TOTAL	87

links. Thus the main form of interlocking for industrial companies was single interlocks with financial companies. Figure 3.4 shows the largest component in the plural network and it can be seen that only three industrial companies were included in this component.

As in the inter-war period, links between financial companies constituted the skeleton of the business network as a whole, with industrial companies being tied into this network through their financial linkages.

Figure 3.4: Network of Plural Lines: Largest Component (1955-6)

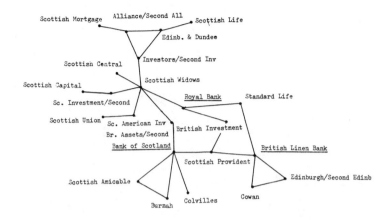

Figure 3.5 makes this point very clearly. The major banking centres were closely connected to one another through investment trust groups and insurance companies, but the industrial companies had specialised linkages to particular banks or trust groups. The regional pattern of interlocks was still present, but this was far weaker than during the inter-war years: Glasgow-based companies such as Weir and House of Fraser lying within the sphere of influence of the National Bank. Nevertheless, the regional pattern predominated. An important feature is that the Bank of Scotland was a definite area of intersection for Edinburgh and Glasgow interests, a role which had been strengthened by its merger with the Union Bank. Whilst connections with the English business network have not been investigated systematically, certain important links can be pointed to. Three of the banking centres in Figure 3.5 had English parents – but other English banks played an important role as well. Lloyds Bank had close links with merchant bankers Robert Benson and Lazards, Benson being financial adviser to House of Fraser and Lazards being linked to Rivet, Bolt and Nut. The National Provincial Bank and Robert Fleming's merchant bank, both linked with Prudential Assurance, had a number of links with Burmah Oil and the North British and Mercantile. Of the 'Big 5' London clearing banks, only the Westminster seems to have been separated from the Scottish network.

Figure 3.5: The Structure of the Business Network (1955-6)

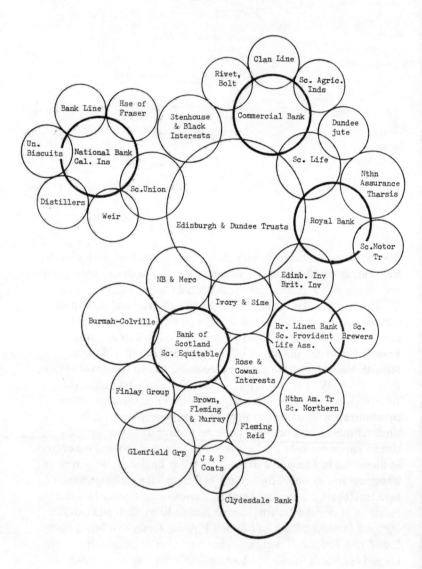

Edinburgh & Dundee Trusts

Baillie, Gifford Trusts
Scottish American Investment
Scottish American Mortgage
Alliance Trust
Investors' Mortgage
Scottish Investment
Chiene & Tait Trusts
Brander & Cruickshank Trusts

Stenhouse & Black Interests

General Accident
Donaldson Line
Great Northern Inv.
Clyde and Mersey

Brown, Fleming & Murray Interests

Brown, Fleming & Murray Trusts
Scottish Amicable
Moores, Carson & Watson Trusts
N.Z. & Australian Land

Burmah-Colville

Burmah Oil
Colvilles
Scottish Mutual
Scottish National Trust

Glenfield Group

Glenfield and Kennedy
North British Locomotive
United Turkey Red
Saxone, Lilley & Skinner
Wm Baird
Lyle Shipping

Rose & Cowan Interests

Alex. Cowan
North British Rubber
A.B. Fleming

Bridges not shown in network:

Scottish Widows – links
    Commercial Bank, Royal
    Bank and Bank of Scotland
Standard Life – links
    Bank of Scotland, Linen
    Bank and Royal Bank

The Men of Business

From Table 3.10 it can be seen that 118 multiple directors held a total of 347 directorships in the top companies. That is, 19 per cent of the directors held 41 per cent of the directorships. Of those who had been multiple directors in 1937-8, 25 were to be found on the list for 1955-6. The survival rate of the post-war multiple directors was, therefore, similar to that for the inter-war period.

As shown in Table 3.11, 29 of the multiple directors (25 per cent) had titles, compared with only 19 in 1937-8. There was a further drop in the representation of higher titles: only two men had titles above the rank of baron, both being earls. The number of barons increased steadily, but the largest increase was in the number of knights. In 1937-8 there had been only two knights, but by 1955-6 this number had risen to 12. In fact, two of the men who had 'survived' from the inter-war period had received knighthoods: Sir James Campbell and Sir John Craig. The majority of the titled men held just two directorships, though the nine men with three or more directorships were spread evenly across all ranks. The educational background of the multiple directors was predominantly law or accountancy: 30 men had legal degrees or qualifications (18 being Writers to the Signet) and 27 men were qualified accountants, a further four being actuaries. Men with degrees other than Law, or equivalent technical qualifications, numbered just ten, of which one was a company secretary, two were engineers, and seven held degrees in arts or commerce. The multiple directors retained their positions of high social status since, in addition to the possession of titles, their ranks included 20 men who were JPs or Deputy Lieutenants for their County and a great many ex-MPs, though only one was currently an MP.

It can be seen from Table 3.10 that 18 men held five or more directorships each, and that seven men held six or more. Of these seven men, three were associated with the Brown, Fleming and Murray trusts (H.B. Spens, H. Cowan-Douglas, T.P. Spens), one was part of the Finlay group (Sir James Jones), one had numerous Glasgow interests in both the Finlay and Brown, Fleming and Murray spheres (W.H. Marr) and two were Edinburgh financiers (T.J.C. Gifford and A.C. Blair). These findings correspond to the high density of the network around the Bank of Scotland (see Figure 3.5). Table 3.12 again confirms this picture, this time through an analysis of the directors who meet the largest number of other multiple directors. No fewer than nine of the men listed in Table 3.12 were directors of the Bank of Scotland. The two men without a bank directorship, Gifford and Cowan-Douglas,

Table 3.10: **Distribution of Directorships (1955-6)**

No. of Directorships per Person	No. of People	No. of Directorships
1	501	501
2	67	134
3	24	72
4	9	36
5	11	55
6	4	24
7	1	7
8	1	8
11	1	11
TOTALS	619	848

Table 3.11: **Multiple Directors and their Titles (1955-6)**

No. of Directorships per Person	Knights	Baronets	No. of People Barons	Earls	TOTALS
2	9	4	7		20
3	1		1	2	4
4		1			1
5	1	1	1		3
6	1				1
TOTALS	12	6	9	2	29

both participated in major investment groups.

It is possible to analyse the part played by kinship in maintaining this structure by describing the various spheres of influence depicted in Figure 3.5. The directors of the Edinburgh trusts which constituted the heart of the network were very much a financial establishment. Familiar names from the history of the investment trust movement were still to be found amongst the trust directors of the 1950s: Guild, Blair, Watson, Ivory, Fraser and McClure. These men joined those who had been important in the inter-war period and those who played a key integrative role in post-war investment: Gifford, McCurrach, Chiene and Oliphant. W.H. Fraser, the son of W.S. Fraser and related by marriage

Table 3.12: Central Directors in the Network (1955-6)

Director	No. of Directors Met
H.B. Spens	28
W.H. Marr	27
A.C. Blair	26
T.J.C. Gifford	23
Lord Bilsland	22
Sir Hugh Rose	22
W. Watson	22
D.M. Wood	22
Sir D. Thomson	21
T.H. Thorneycroft	21
J.T. Dowling	20
W.H. Fraser	20
A. Harrison	20

to the Inglis family, married a daughter of John James Cowan and was for some time a director of the Cowan paper firm. He was a partner in Fraser, Stodart, and Ballinghall WS, and his directorships included Lloyds Bank and the Industrial and Commercial Finance Corporation. Similarly, as we have shown in Figure 1.8, R.M. Guild's two grandfathers were John Guild and Edward Cox.

W.H. Fraser and P.J. Oliphant linked the Edinburgh trusts to the National Bank sphere. The National Bank board included many Edinburgh financiers and representatives of the steel industry: Sir Andrew McCance of Colvilles and Harald Peake of the Steel Company of Wales. But many members of the National Bank board were representatives of numerous non-financial companies: Hugh Fraser of House of Fraser, Lord Teviot of Bank Line and J.K. Weir of the Weir Engineering firm. Sir Henry Ross of Distillers, son of William Ross, and Peter MacDonald of United Biscuits linked their companies to Caledonian Insurance. House of Fraser was very much a tycoon-controlled firm, the board comprising Hugh Fraser and his senior managers. By contrast, Distillers was an alliance of family interests (Dewar), top managers (Ross), and financial interests (Sir Percy Grigg of Prudential Assurance and the National Provincial). Weir, Bank Line and United Biscuits were all, to varying degrees, family firms. Though chaired by Peter MacDonald (a partner in the company's solicitors),

United Biscuits included three MacFarlanes on its board. Bank Line included three members of the Weir family of Lord Inverforth and was linked to the National Bank through Lord Teviot (Charles I. Kerr), a Liberal politician and former director of General Accident. G. and J. Weir was the marine engineering firm of another Weir family: its board included two sons of Viscount Weir together with the managing director Sir Charles Connell, who came from the shipbuilding family and who was related by marriage to the Weirs. Weir was linked to Scottish Union through James Lumsden, a partner in Maclay, Murray and Spens. Lumsden's great, great grandfather had been a founder of both the Clydesdale Bank and Glasgow and South Western Railway, and his great grandfather, Sir James Lumsden, had also been connected with these companies. Lumsden himself was the son of Sir James Robert Lumsden and was shortly to become a key figure in the Brown, Fleming and Murray group of trusts. Scottish Union's board also included Hugh Cowan-Douglas and many members of the Edinburgh financial establishment, the chairman being C.F.J. Younger of Scottish Brewers.

Centred around General Accident was a small insurance, investment and shipping group, the key figures being Sir Stanley Norie-Miller, I.H.S. Black, and J.G. Stenhouse. Donaldson Line had for some time been run by the Donaldson and Black families, executive power lying with the Blacks. In the 1950s the company board included two Donaldsons and two Blacks (father and son). Hervey Black sat as a non-executive member of the General Accident board, the deputy chairman of this company, R.G. Simpson, being a partner in Chiene & Tait and a director of numerous Edinburgh trusts. Norie-Miller linked General Accident to the investment interests of J.G. Stenhouse, a member of the Dumbarton shipbuilding family. Through Simpson, this grouping connected to the trusts managed by Chiene and Tait in Edinburgh and Brander and Cruickshank in Aberdeen. Apart from Brander and Cruickshank themselves, an important director of these trusts was G.P.S. Macpherson of merchant bankers Robert Benson and Lonsdale.

The Commercial Bank also had a strong shipping representation: Lord Rotherwick (Herbert Cayzer) was the chairman, and the board included Noel Salvesen of Christian Salvesen. Also represented on the board were I.W. MacDonald, the general manager, and Edinburgh lawyers and accountants such as R.Y. Weir and G.T. Chiene. The board of Clan Line included six Cayzers, with Lord Rotherwick as chairman and Sir Nicholas Cayzer, his brother, as vice chairman. By contrast, the board of Scottish Agricultural Industries seemed to have included

mainly internal managers, with E.P. Hudson linking the company with
the Commercial Bank. Rivet, Bolt and Nut retained some family
representation, with two Croshers and one Macouat on the board,
though its interlock with the Commercial Bank involved James
Gilchrist. The main insurance link of the Commercial Bank was with
Scottish Life, the board of which closely overlapped with the
directorates of the Edinburgh and Dundee trusts: George Chiene,
R.M. Guild, W.L. Milligan and James Prain.

The Royal Bank retained the Duke of Buccleuch as its governor,
though the chairman was D.F. Landale. The board also included the
Earl of Elgin, who chaired Scottish Motor Traction and whose family
had long been a part of Scottish business. Northern Assurance and
Tharsis were linked through Lord Glenconner (grandson of Sir Charles
Tennant) and were tied to the Royal Bank through D.F. Landale.
Northern Assurance was based in Aberdeen but was associated with
London and Scottish Assurance Corporation, two directors of which
(Viscount Hinchingbroke and Victor Agar-Robartes) sat on its board.
The company was probably associated with Hambros merchant
bank, of which Lord Glenconner was a director (as well as retaining
the family seat on the ICI board). The board of Tharsis itself included
Hugh Hogarth of the shipping firm, and three members of the Ruther-
ford family which had provided the top management of the firm for
50 years. The boards of Edinburgh Investment and British Investment
were an important link between the Royal Bank and the British Linen
Bank. British Investment included Landale, I.R. Pitman, R.Y. Weir
and David Robarts (a director of Robert Fleming and chairman of the
National Provincial Bank). The Edinburgh Investment board included
Sir William Wallace, I.M. Stewart and John Chiene (brother of George
Chiene).

The British Linen Bank brought together a number of important
interests. The Earl of Airlie, related by marriage to the Tennants,
was governor and represented the company on Barclays board (T.D.
Barclay sitting on the British Linen board) and linked the bank with
the Northern American Trust of Dundee. The board of the latter
included William G.N. Walker of Jute Industries and Sir George
Williamson, a partner in Paull and Williamson of Aberdeen. The British
Linen board itself included Lord Clydesmuir (R.J.B. Colville) and
William McEwan Younger, of Scottish Brewers and Scottish Investment.
Scottish Brewers directorate included two grandsons of H.J. Younger
(C.F.J. Younger and J.W.H.B. Younger) as well as E.H.M. Clutterbuck,
nephew of J.W.H.B. Younger. The men involved in the insurance links

of British Linen were Lord Airlie, Lord Clydesmuir, Sir Ernest Wedderburn (partner in Shepherd and Wedderburn), Sir Robert Erskine-Hill
(cousin of Lord Clydesmuir) and Eric J. Ivory.

Linking British Linen and the Bank of Scotland was a cluster of
companies in the paper, ink and rubber industries, the key personnel
in which were W.H. Fraser, A.G. Cowan and Sir Hugh Rose. Connecting
the Bank of Scotland to the central Edinburgh investment interests
were the Ivory and Sime trusts and the North British and Mercantile.
The main figures in Ivory and Sime were A.C. Blair and Basil Ivory,
brother of Eric Ivory. The board of the North British was drawn
extensively from the London financial establishment — particularly
Lord Brand of Lazards and Lloyds Bank, and Cyril Kleinwort — but
Scots representation included Viscount Younger and D.B. Bogle.

The major interests associated with the Bank of Scotland were
undoubtedly Colvilles and Brown, Fleming and Murray. Both Sir John
Craig and Lord Bilsland, governor and deputy governor of the Bank of
Scotland, were on the Colville board along with Craig's son (T.R.
Craig), Andrew McCance and F. Rebbeck, managing director of Harland
and Wolff. The Bilsland family firm was Bilsland Bros bakery of
Glasgow, and both Alex and William Bilsland had kinship relations to
the Colvilles: Alex married John Colville's sister, and William's daughter
had married David Colville, Junior. William's son, Lord Bilsland,
married Ronald Colville's sister. These connections are shown in Figure
3.6. On the board of the Bank of Scotland, Craig and Bilsland were
joined by J.B. Findlay, Lord Polwarth (a partner in Chiene and Tait),
Sir Hugh Rose and H.B. Spens. Bilsland and Spens met again on the
board of Burmah, together with Lord Strathalmond of BP. On the
board of the Scottish National Trust were Bilsland and Sir Robert
Erskine-Hill, the latter being related to the Colvilles. Bilsland, Spens and
Findlay were all to be found on the board of Scottish Amicable,
together with Lord Elgin, whose son (David Bruce) sat on Scottish
Equitable. The Brown, Fleming and Murray trusts and the Moores,
Carson and Watson trusts, as we have already described, were dominated by Hugh Cowan-Douglas, the two Spens brothers, and the two
Murray brothers. Active directors in this group from shipping and
shipbuilding were Lord Maclay and Sir A.M. Stephen. Hugh Spens was
also a director of the textile firm Fleming Reid, though this was under
the control of the Hebblethwaites. The board of New Zealand and
Australian Land was, as in previous years, an important meeting point
for Edinburgh and Glasgow interests, particularly T.P. Spens and
W.H. Fraser (these families being related by marriage).

Figure 3.6: The Colville Family

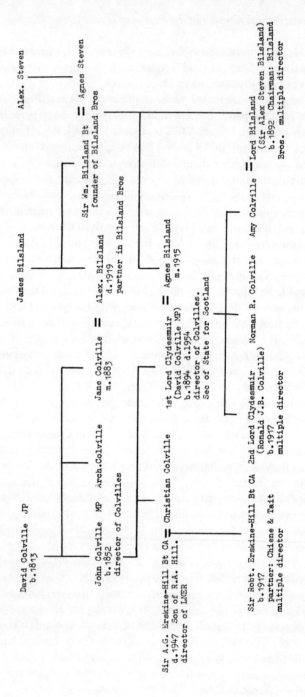

We have already described the close connections between Glenfield and Kennedy, the Baird companies, and North British Loco through the financier Hugh Cowan-Douglas and the family representatives of Lorimer and McCosh. This group was closely entwined with three other family firms. The Saxone board included two Lilleys, and its managing director, J.S. Abbott, linked it to Glenfield. United Turkey Red still included a Christie on its board, though in the 1930s there had been four representatives of the family. Lyle Shipping was interlocked with Glenfield through I.M. Stewart, who had joined the Lyle board as an outside director in 1952. The remaining members of the Lyle board were mainly from the controlling families: the board included two Shearers, two Macfarlanes and one Lyle.

The final sphere of influence was that of the Clydesdale Bank and Coats. Robert Laidlaw, deputy chairman of the Clydesdale Bank was chairman of Coats, though the latter's board included four members of the Coats family and one Clark. Also on the Coats board was Lord McCorquodale, son-in-law of J.O.M. Clark and chairman of McCorquodale & Co. printers. On the Clydesdale board were R.A. Murray and Lord Maclay, A.L. McClure (an Edinburgh solicitor related to Viscount Younger) and Sir Harold Yarrow.

Conclusion

The business network was a mixture of family firms and firms controlled by financial interests. It was the financiers and members of the dominant families who welded these companies together into a densely connected system in which, nevertheless, certain spheres of influence could be identified. There had undoubtedly been a diffusion of share ownership, though many companies remained under family control. Families now controlled their companies through large minority blocks rather than majority ownership, though the latter was not uncommon. Shares sold by families were increasingly taken up by insurance companies and investment trusts which permitted the families to retain control of their firms. A consequence of this diffusion of share ownership was that it was far less easy for mergers to be arranged, since a wider group of interests had to be involved. In particular, the main form of merger was the take-over bid in which offers, often unsolicited, would be made and a struggle for control would ensue. In Scotland the master of this was Hugh Fraser, who also followed the dominant pattern of the 1950s in buying undervalued companies in order to realise their assets.

The companies formed in earlier periods either continued to

consolidate their positions or were incorporated into nationalised concerns. Control over many of the dynamic features of the economy was progressively removed from Scotland to London, and also to the USA. Functional and financial links, even less than in earlier periods, were no longer confined to other Scottish companies, as more and more companies became tied in directly to the English economy.

There was, again, little evidence of a 'managerial revolution'. Some internal managers had been promoted to the boards of their companies, but there was strong evidence that these men were ensuring the recruitment of their sons to the boards. As a result, new family dynasties were created to share control with the older interests, though it is difficult to assess the extent to which this was associated with share ownership. In general, it seems that ownership was becoming more 'depersonalised': blocks of shares were passing into the hands of the financial 'institutions' and families were controlling with smaller and smaller minority stakes. This was the basis for the coming together of family interests and financial interests in the major spheres of influence.

Table 3A: Scotland's Top Companies (1955-6)

Section 'A: Non-Financial Companies

Rank	Company	Industry	Capital (£000)	Multiple Directors
1	Burmah Oil	Oil	45,210	Lord Bilsland, H.B. Spens
2	Distillers	Whisky distillers	44,075	Sir Henry J. Ross (C), L.A. Elgood, J.V. Marshall
3	J. and P. Coats	Textiles	35,000	R. Laidlaw (C), M. McDougall (MD), C.H. Mackenzie, A.M. Watson
4	Stewarts and Lloyds	Steel	20,000	–
5	Colvilles	Steel	14,000	Sir Andrew McCance (C, MD), Sir John Craig (HP), Lord Bilsland
6	Inveresk Paper	Paper man.	6,427	–
7	Scottish Brewers	Brewing	6,342	W.McE. Younger (DC), C.F.J. Younger
8	Metal Industries	Shipbreakers, etc.	5,900	–
9	Linen Thread	Textiles	5,500	W. Miller (S)
10	Bank Line	Shipping	5,451	Lord Teviot
11	United Biscuits	Biscuit man.	4,500	P.G. Macdonald
12	Scottish Cooperative Wholesale	Wholesale distr.	4,372	–
13	Scottish Agricultural Industries	Fertiliser man.	4,220	H.U. Cunningham (MD), E.P. Hudson
14	Saxone, Lilley and Skinner (Holdings)	Shoe man. and retailers	3,843	J.S. Abbott (DC, MD)

Table 3A: Section A—cont.

Rank	Company	Industry	Capital (£000)	Multiple Directors
15	William Baird	Textiles	3,715	A.K. McCosh (C), H.C. Waterston (VC), T.H. Thorneycroft, A.R. McCosh, H.R. Neilson, J.W. Andrew (S)
16	James Finlay	Traders and merch.	3,500	W.H. Marr (C), Sir James Jones (DC), A.M. McGrigor, Sir John Muir, R.J. Clough, C.C.C. Bell
17	Bairds and Scottish Steel	Steel	2,730	A.K. McCosh (C), H.C. Waterston (VC), J.W. Andrew, A.R. McCosh, T.H. Thorneycroft
18	Clan Line Steamers	Shipping	2,710	Lord Rotherwick (C)
19	House of Fraser	Retail distribution	2,699	Hugh Fraser (C, MD)
20	Consolidated Tea and Lands	Tea planters and merchants	2,600	W.H. Marr (C), Sir James Jones (DC), A.M. McGrigor, G. Fellowes, R. Brown, Sir John Muir, A.R.A.G. Cameron, R.J. Clough
21	Glenfield and Kennedy Holdings	Engineers	2,400	H. Cowan-Douglas (C), H.R. Neilson, I.M. Stewart, J.S. Abbott
22	North British Rubber	Rubber products	2,225	Sir Wm Wallace
23	G. and J. Weir	Engineers	2,018	J.K. Weir (C), J.A. Lumsden
24=	Low and Bonar	Jute man.	2,000	–
24=	North British Locomotive	Locomotive eng.	2,000	H. Cowan-Douglas
24=	Singer Manufacturing	Sewing machine man.	2,000	–
24=	Teacher (Distillers)	Whisky distillers	2,000	–
28	Wm Collins & Sons (Holding)	Printers, publishers	1,808	–
29	United Turkey Red	Textile finishers	1,606	H. Cowan-Douglas (C), Sir James I. Campbell, W.H. Marr

Table 3A: Section A –cont.

Rank	Company	Industry	Capital (£000)	Multiple Directors
30	John Dewar and Sons	Whisky distillers	1,600	J.V. Marshall
31	Scottish Motor Traction	Vehicle distrib.	1,509	Earl of Elgin and Kincardine
32	Blackwood, Morton and Sons	Carpet man.	1,500	–
33	Moss Empires	Theatre manage.	1,497	–
34	Fleming, Reid	Textiles	1,488	T.P. Spens (C)
35	Jugra Land and Carey	Rubber planters	1,436	–
36	Amalgamated Tea Estates	Tea planters and merchants	1,377	W.H. Marr (C), Sir James Jones (DC), A.M. McGrigor, G. Fellowes, R. Brown, Sir John Muir, A.R.A.G. Cameron, R.J. Clough
37=	Kanan Devan Hills Produce	Tea planters and merchants	1,300	W.H. Marr (C), Sir James Jones (DC), A.M. McGrigor, G. Fellowes, R. Brown, Sir John Muir, A.R.A.G. Cameron, C.C.C. Bell
37=	James Templeton	Carpet man.	1,300	–
39	Alex Cowan and Sons	Paper man.	1,275	W.H. Fraser (C), A. Harrison (VC), Sir Wm Wallace, Sir Hugh Rose
40	Tharsis Sulphur and Copper	Copper mining	1,250	Lord Glenconner
41	Angus Milling	Flour millers	1,235	–
42	Federated Foundries	Iron and steel founders	1,213	–
43	Anglo-American Direct Tea Trading	Tea planters and merchants	1,162	W.H. Marr (C), Sir James Jones (DC), A.M. McGrigor, G. Fellowes, R. Brown, Sir John Muir, A.R.A.G. Cameron, C.C.C. Bell

Table 3A: Section A—cont.

Rank	Company	Industry	Capital (£000)	Multiple Directors
44	Donaldson Line	Shipping	1,114	I.H.S. Black
45	Alex Pirie and Sons	Paper man.	1,100	–
46	James Howden	Engineers	1,092	–
47	Rivet, Bolt and Nut	Rivet, etc. man.	1,031	J. Gilchrist
48	Sir Wm Arrol	Engineers	1,023	–
49	Lawsons	Retail drapers	1,018	–
50=	Cooper and Cos. Stores	Retail grocers	1,000	–
50=	MacDonald Martin Distilleries	Whisky distillers	1,000	–
50=	United Collieries	Brickworks, etc.	1,000	–
50=	Arthur Bell and Sons	Whisky distillers	1,000	W. Miller
50=	A.B. Fleming	Ink man.	1,000	Sir Hugh Rose
50=	Lyle Shipping	Shipping	1,000	I.M. Stewart

Table 3A—cont.

Section B: Banking Companies

Rank	Company	Deposits (£000)	Multiple Directors
1	Royal Bank of Scotland	319,888	D.F. Landale (C), J.H. Richardson (DC), K. Murray, Earl of Elgin and Kincardine, Sir Wm Y. Darling, L.A. Elgood, T.G. Waterlow, D.H. Cameron of Lochiel, J.M. Prain
2	Bank of Scotland	171,600	Sir John Craig (G), Lord Bilsland (DG), J.S. Abbott, A.C. Blair, J.B. Findlay, Lord Elphinstone, R. McCosh, W.H. Marr, J.T. Dowling, Lord Polwarth, Sir Hugh Rose, J.M. Ross, H.B. Spens, Sir Douglas Thomson, T.H. Thorneycroft, Wm Watson (T)
3	Clydesdale and North of Scotland Bank	170,922	R. Laidlaw (DC), Lord Maclay, A.L. McClure, A. Mitchell, R.A. Murray
4	Commercial Bank of Scotland	125,482	Lord Rotherwick (G), G.T. Chiene, D.M. Wood, I.W. Macdonald, H.U. Cunningham, R.Y. Weir, J. Gilchrist, Sir John M. Erskine
5	National Bank of Scotland	105,278	W.H. Fraser (C), Lord Teviot, J.K. Weir, J.T. Leggatt, I.M. Stewart, P.J. Oliphant, Sir Andrew McCance, Hugh Fraser
6	British Linen Bank	77,401	Earl of Airlie (G), A. Harrison, Lord Clydesmuir, Lord Kinnaird, Sir Wm Wallace, Sir Ernest M. Wedderburn, Wm McE. Younger

Table 3A—cont.

Section C: Insurance Companies

Rank	Company	Life and General Funds (£000)	Multiple Directors
1	Standard Life Assurance	157,527	Sir Jas. C. Campbell (G), A. Harrison (C), Lord Kinnaird, G.P.S. Macpherson, I.R. Pitman, J.H. Richardson, Wm Watson, T.G. Waterlow
2	Scottish Widows Fund and Life Assurance	83,406	A.C. Blair, Sir Ian Bolton, D.H. Cameron of Lochiel, T.J.C. Gifford, K. Murray, H.G. Sharp, D.M. Wood, Wm McE. Younger
3	North British and Mercantile Insurance	80,074	D.B. Bogle
4	Northern Assurance	55,681	Lord Glenconner (C), D.F. Landale
5	Scottish Amicable Life Assurance	43,348	Lord Bilsland (C), J.B. Findlay, Earl of Elgin and Kincardine, H. Cunningham, J.T. Dowling, H.B. Spens
6	General Accident, Fire and Life Assurance	40,088	Sir Stanley Norie-Miller (C, MD), R.G. Simpson (DC), I.H.S. Black
7	Scottish Provident Institution	37,252	A.H. Bowhill, Sir Ernest Wedderburn, R.Y. Weir, Sir Hugh Rose, Lord Clydesmuir, Lord Elphinstone
8	Scottish Union and National Insurance	28,744	C.F.J. Younger (C), J.A. Lumsden (DC), A.W. Blair, H. Cowan-Douglas, Sir Wm Y. Darling, J.L. Mounsey, P.J. Oliphant, H. Watson
9	Scottish Legal Life Assurance	19,682	–
10	Scottish Equitable Life Assurance	18,973	R. McCosh, R.I. Marshall, A.M. Watson, A.C. Murray

Table 3A: Section C—cont.

Rank	Company	Life and General Funds (£000)	Multiple Directors
11	Caledonian Insurance	17,661	P.G. Macdonald (C), Sir John M. Erskine, W.H. Fraser, J.F. Carnegie, Sir Henry J. Ross, W.H. McGregor
12	Scottish Life Assurance	16,316	G.T. Chiene, R.M. Guild, W.L. Milligan, J.M. Prain
13	Scottish Mutual Assurance (formerly Scottish Temperance)	13,827	Sir John Craig (C), I.W. Macdonald, M. MacDougall
14	Life Association of Scotland	10,260	Earl of Airlie (C), Sir R. Erskine-Hill, E.J. Ivory, J.T. Leggat, J.L. Mounsey, G.I. Stewart, Sir D. Thomson

Table 3A—cont.

Section D: Investment and Property Companies

Rank	Company	Capital (£000)	Multiple Directors
1	Scottish American Investment	5,780	A.W. Blair (C), K. Murray, Sir Ian Bolton, P.J. Oliphant
2=	British Assets Trust	4,500	A.C. Blair (C), B.G. Ivory, H.G. Sharp, Lord Polwarth
2=	British Investment Trust	4,500	A.H. Bowhill (C), J.H. Richardson (DC), R.Y. Weir, I.R. Pitman, D.F. Landale
4	Alliance Trust	4,300	A.L. Brown (C, M), T.J.C. Gifford, J.M. Prain, Sir George Cunningham, H.B. Spens, D.F. McCurrach (M), C.N. Thomson
5	Second Scottish Investment	3,150	T.J.C. Gifford (C), R.G. Simpson, E.J. Ivory, Wm McE. Younger, E.P. Hudson
6	Scottish American Mortgage	2,550	R.B. Watson (C), W.H. Fraser, A.L. McClure, D.M. Wood
7	Investors' Mortgage Security	2,541	T.J.C. Gifford (C), J. Chiene, D.J. Bogie, A.L. Brown, A.C. Blair
8	Scottish Mortgage and Trust	2,475	T.J.C. Gifford (C), D.F. McCurrach, R.I. Marshall, H. Watson
9	Northern American Trust	2,300	R.S.L. Macpherson (C), Sir George Williamson, Earl of Airlie
10=	Edinburgh Investment Trust	2,250	A. Harrison (C), Sir Wm Wallace, J. Chiene, W.H. McGregor (M), J.L. Anderson, I.M. Stewart, A.P. Anderson
10=	Great Northern Investment Trust	2,250	G.H. Christie (C), Sir Stanley Norie-Miller, J.G. Stenhouse
10=	New Zealand and Australian Land	2,250	R.I. Marshall (C), T.P. Spens, W.H. Fraser

Table 3A: Section D–cont.

Rank	Company	Capital (£000)	Multiple Directors
13	Scottish United Investors	2,160	H.B. Spens (C), C.H. Mackenzie, R.G. Simpson, H. Cowan-Douglas
14	Realisation and Debenture Corporation of Scotland	1,800	D.M. Wood (C), R.B. Watson, J.M. Ross, T.G. Waterlow
15=	Scottish Investment Trust	1,750	T.J.C. Gifford (C), R.G. Simpson, E.J. Ivory, W. McE. Younger, E.P. Hudson
15=	Second Investors' Mortgage Security	1,750	T.J.C. Gifford (C), J. Chiene, D.J. Bogie, A.L. Brown, A.C. Blair
17	Edinburgh and Dundee Investment	1,663	T.J.C. Gifford (C), A.L. Brown, W.L. Milligan, G.T. Chiene
18=	Scottish Eastern Investment Trust	1,600	G.I. Stewart
18=	Second Alliance Trust	1,600	A.L. Brown (C, M), T.J.C. Gifford, J.M. Prain, Sir George Cunningham, H.B. Spens, D.F. McCurrach (M), C.N. Thomson
20	Aberdeen and Canadian Trust (formerly North of Scotland Canadian)	1,545	J.S.R. Cruickshank (C)
21	Second Scottish Western Investment	1,540	T.P. Spens (C), R.A. Murray (M), Sir Alex M. Stephen, R. Laidlaw
22=	American Trust	1,500	R.B. Watson (C), R.M. Guild, A.L. McClure
22=	Second Edinburgh Investment Trust	1,500	A. Harrison (C), Sir Wm Wallace, J. Chiene, W.H. McGregor (M), J.L. Anderson, I.M. Stewart, A.P. Anderson
24	Clydesdale Investment	1,460	T.P. Spens (C), R.A. Murray (M), Lord Maclay, J.T. Dowling

Table 3A: Section D—cont.

Rank	Company	Capital £000)	Multiple Directors
25	Scottish National Trust	1,400	Lord Bilsland (C), Sir Robert Erskine-Hill, J.F. Carnegie
26=	Clyde and Mersey Investment Trust	1,250	G.H. Christie, J.G. Stenhouse
26=	Scottish Northern Investment Trust	1,250	Sir G. Williamson (C), R.S.L. Macpherson, Sir Ian Forbes-Leith
28=	Scottish Capital Investment	1,200	T.J.C. Gifford (C), R.G. Simpson, D.B. Bogle
28=	Scottish Central Investment Trust	1,200	T.J.C. Gifford (C), D.M. Wood, J.H. Richardson
28=	Scottish Consolidated Trust	1,200	H.B. Spens (C), H. Cowan-Douglas, A.C. Murray, Sir James Jones
31	East of Scotland Trust	1,190	J.S.R. Cruickshank, G.P.S. Macpherson
32	Second British Assets Trust	1,125	A.C. Blair (C), B.J. Ivory, H.G. Sharp, Lord Polwarth
33=	Caledonian Trust	1,100	T.P. Spens (C), J.I. Murray (M), A. Mitchell, W.H. Marr
33=	Scottish Western Investment	1,100	T.P. Spens (C), Sir Alex M. Stephen, R.A. Murray (M), R. Laidlaw

4 THE SEVENTIES: PROSPERITY OR CONTINUED DECLINE?

The late 1960s and early 1970s showed a relative improvement in Scotland's economic prospects as a result of the increased activities of multinational companies in industries such as electronics and chemicals. The coming of North Sea oil was widely seen as consolidating and expanding this improvement. These processes enabled the Scottish economy to withstand some of the problems associated with its unbalanced industrial mix. In many respects 1973-4 was seen as a turning-point for the Scottish economy: oil resources offered the potential that was once offered to indigenous capital by coal and iron in the development of heavy industry. There were even expectations in the business community that Scotland would develop more rapidly than the rest of the United Kingdom. Popular expressions of these expectations were perhaps the growing demands for devolution and the increased support for the Scottish National Party. The potential prosperity of the Scottish economy was seen as a way of overcoming the long-term decline which had led to Scotland being a net recipient of Central Government regional aid: 30 per cent of all regional development aid went to Scotland over the period 1960-72.

Much of the improvement, as we have indicated, was due to the activities of English and foreign firms, and there was considerable concern that Scotland was becoming a 'branch-plant economy'. There continued to be great inequalities within Scotland, and the impact of these new developments was far less in the industrial West of Scotland than in other parts of the country. The general economic slump which made itself felt during 1976 and 1977 saw less investment in Scotland, a cut in regional aid, and a slowdown in the pace of oil development. By 1978 the hopes of the early 1970s had all but disappeared. The oil wealth seemed to have had little impact on employment, investment, or output; the main impact being short-term and concentrated in areas such as the North East. Oil in itself was insufficient to counteract the historical problems of the Scottish economy and its position within the world economy.

In this chapter we shall discuss the Scottish business system in the mid 1970s against the backdrop of the relative prosperity and subsequent slowdown discussed above. In the next chapter we shall

165

discuss the response of Scottish capital to the exploitation of North Sea oil.

Scotland's Top Companies, 1973-4

In 1973-4, as shown in Table 4.A, the 120 top companies comprised 62 non-financial companies, four banking companies, nine insurance companies, and 45 investment and property companies. In Table 4.1 is shown the size distribution of non-financial companies. The capital of these companies was more than double the capital of the top non-financials in 1955-6. The ten largest companies accounted for 80 per cent of total capital, most of this being the capital of the four largest companies. Table 4.A gives the ranking of these companies by their total turnover and indicates their significance in the British economy. The top 100 British companies, as given in *The Times 1,000*, included just five Scottish companies: Burmah (ranked 25th), Distillers (38th), Coats Patons (42nd), House of Fraser (92nd), and Scottish and Newcastle (100th). A total of 36 of the top 62 Scottish non-financial companies were amongst the 1,000 largest British companies, and the top 1,000 included a further ten Scottish companies which were private firms, which had too small a share capital to qualify for inclusion in our list, or which had been floated shortly after its compilation. The major private companies were Christian Salvesen (277th in the top 1,000), General Motors Scotland (650th) and D.C. Thomson (702nd). The newly floated company was Dawson International (484th), and the small companies were J. & W. Henderson (612th), Watson and Philip (616th), Alexanders Holdings (787th), F.J.C. Lilley (793rd), Melville, Dundas and Whitson (836th), and Tullis Russell (913th). A full assessment of the importance of Scottish companies might also include the three companies which were registered in London but had their administrative headquarters in Scotland: Grampian Holdings (380th), Sidlaw Industries (formerly Jute Industries, 458th) and Scott and Robertson (817th). This total of 49 'Scottish' companies in the British top 1,000 shows the extreme under-representation of Scottish interests.

Table 4.2 shows the industrial distribution of the non-financial companies. Certain differences from Table 3.2 are immediately obvious: the loss of the steel firms through nationalisation, and the appearance of house-building and other construction firms. Perhaps the most important feature of the period – the drive towards diversification – is only partly visible from the table. Only three companies appear as diversified concerns: Coltness Group was formed

Table 4.1: Size Distribution of Non-Financial Companies (1973-4)

Companies by Rank	Total share Capital (£)	Cumulative Total (£)
Top 10	551,363,545	551,363,545
11-20	56,354,471	607,718,016
21-30	28,754,296	636,472,312
31-40	21,354,025	657,826,337
41-50	16,646,564	674,472,901
51-62	15,733,638	690,206,539
TOTAL	690,206,539 (N=62)	

Table 4.2: Industrial Distribution of Non-Financial Companies (1973-4)

Industrial Sector	No. of Companies		
	Top 30	Top 50	All
Tea Planters	2	2	4
Food and drink	6	9	9
Oil	1	1	1
Chemicals	1	1	1
Textiles (incl. rubber)	6	8	10
Non-coal mining	1	1	1
Metalworking		2	6
Engineering	4	7	7
Paper and publishing	2	3	3
Timber			1
Construction	1	4	4
Transport		2	2
Distribution	3	5	7
Hotels, entertainments, etc		2	2
Non-trading	1	1	1
Diversified manuf.			1
Mixed Man. and services	2	2	2
TOTAL			62

around the shell of the old Coltness Iron Company and had diversified into many manufacturing industries; Stenhouse Holdings developed out of the former Stenhouse shipbuilding interests and combined a large insurance broking business with interest in engineering and retail distribution; and Scottish and Universal Investments brought together the Fraser holdings ranging from newspapers to whisky distilling. But even a cursory examination of Table 4.A shows that many other companies allocated to specific industrial sectors had diversified away from their primary activities into related and unrelated product areas. It was, in fact, becoming increasingly difficult to use the traditional industrial categories to classify modern combines.

The three operating Scottish banks had total deposits of £2,173m, though if the English deposits of the National and Commercial Group are included this figure would be £3,319m. This latter figure was equivalent to just under 10 per cent of the total deposits of the English clearing banks. As a result of bank mergers the Royal Bank and the Bank of Scotland were similar in size to one another, the Clydesdale being slightly smaller. Total insurance funds were £2,826m, with the lion's share going to Standard Life, General Accident and Scottish Widows. The Scottish life companies had funds of about one-eighth the total of British insurance funds and Standard Life was the fourth largest life company in Britain, after the Prudential, Legal and General, and Commercial Union. Other Scottish companies amongst the top 25 British life companies were Scottish Widows (11th), General Accident (15th), Scottish Amicable (18th), and Scottish Provident (23rd). The top 25 British non-life companies included only one Scottish firm — General Accident — which came third after Commercial Union and Royal Insurance. The 45 investment and property companies had total capital of £408m, and 24 of the trusts were amongst the top 50 British investment trusts. As always, the investment trust sector showed a heavy over-representation of Scottish capital.

Average board size had remained fairly constant at 7.6 since 1955-6. Bank boards diminished slightly in size to 14.3 members, insurance boards increased to an average of 11.7, and investment boards increased slightly to 5.6. The fall in the size of banking boards was matched by a fall in the size of the boards of the top ten companies to 10.7. A total of 719 people (717 men and 2 women) held 912 directorships, with 101 multiple directors holding 32 per cent of all directorships. Whilst 45 per cent of all directorships were in the financial sector, 74 per cent of the directorships held by the multiple directors were financial directorships.

Table 4.3: Multiple Directors on the Board (1973-4)

No. of Multiple Directors on Board	Number of Companies		
	Non-financial	Financial	Total
0	30	5	35
1	17	2	19
2	7	12	19
3	3	6	9
4	1	13	14
5		9	9
6	1	6	7
7		2	2
8	1		1
9	2	3	5
TOTAL	62	58	120

Although the pattern of multiple directors on the boards of non-financial companies shown in Table 4.3 was generally similar to that for 1955-6, financial companies showed a reduction in the average number of multiple directors on their boards. As a result the average number of multiple directors sitting on each interlocked company fell to 3.5. The companies with the most multiple directors were the three operating banks (9 each), Cessnock Holdings (9), Teith Holdings (9), Consolidated Tea (8), Standard Life (7), and Scottish Widows (7). This pattern shows a remarkable continuity with that for 1955-6.

The Financial Sector

(i)   The Banking and Insurance Sector

During the 1960s the movement of concentration in Scottish banking continued, and this process also led to a clarification of the relationship between the Scottish and the English banks. The National Bank and the Commercial Bank had merged in 1959, reducing the number of Scottish commercial banks to five. In 1968 the National Commercial Bank, in which Lloyds Bank held 37 per cent of the shares, acquired the Royal Bank and the resulting National and Commercial Banking Group became a holding company for its Scottish and English banking subsidiaries and its other financial subsidiaries. The major shareholder in the group was Lloyds with 16.37 per cent, the only other important shareholding being 3.79 per cent held by a Bank of England nominee company. In 1969 the Bank of Scotland acquired the British Linen Bank, giving Barclays Bank 35 per cent of the enlarged bank. Thus, by the beginning of the 1970s the number of Scottish commercial banks had been reduced to three, all being subject to English ownership: National and Commercial was minority-controlled by Lloyds, Bank of Scotland was minority-controlled by Barclays, and Clydesdale was wholly-owned by Midland.

The total of deposits and notes for the Scottish commercial banks rose from £943m in 1962 to £2,170m in 1973. In the latter year total advances by the banks to UK residents amounted to £851m, of which 28 per cent was to manufacturing industry, 26 per cent to service industries, and 16 per cent to the financial sector. As compared with British banks as a whole the Scottish banks advanced slightly less to manufacturing and finance and slightly more to the service sector. Some of this expanded lending to the service sector would no doubt represent the involvement of the Scottish banks in the financing of North Sea oil which we discuss more fully in the next chapter.

The ownership of controlling blocks of shares in the Scottish banks by the English commercial banks was complemented by competition from England and abroad. In the early 1970s the Scottish banks faced pressure from National Westminster, the only English bank without a Scottish subsidiary, as well as from various American and other foreign banks. Scottish branches had been opened by 1974 by Bank of America, Credit Lyonnais and the Bank of Nova Scotia, followed later in the 1970s by Continental Illinois National Bank, First National Bank of Chicago, Banque National de Paris, Citibank, Manufacturers Hanover, and others. By 1978 a total of 18 foreign banks had set up operations in Scotland.

A notable feature of the 1960s and 1970s was the growth of merchant banking in Scotland, an area where the Scottish economy had always been weak. During the 1880s James Finlay had been involved in merchant banking in relation to the tea trade and in connection with its shipping and insurance interests, but the only really significant Scottish merchant banks had been set up in the inter-war period: British Bank of Commerce was formed in 1935 and Glasgow Industrial Finance in 1946. The British Bank of Commerce was registered in London, though it had a Glasgow head office, and the company was restructured in the 1960s

by Samuel Montagu the London merchant bankers. The bank was run
by a Glasgow solicitor Alex Stone who, together with his fellow
directors, held over a half of the shares, a minority stake of 11 per cent
being held by Guardian Royal Exchange Assurance. In the secondary
banking crash of 1973 and 1974 the company lost almost three quarters
of its deposits and was taken over by National and Grindlays Bank late
in 1974, becoming first the Scottish arm of its William Brandt subsidiary
and then Grindlays Bank (Scotland) Ltd. Glasgow Industrial Finance
had been backed by the Brown, Fleming and Murray trusts and other
Scottish interests. In the 1950s its chairman had been H.B. Spens and
its manager had been R.A. Murray, whose brother J.I. Murray was also
a director. The bank subsequently became a part of the Finance For
Industry group in which the Scottish commercial banks held 9.5 per
cent of the shares, the remainder being held by the London commercial
banks and the Bank of England.

During the 1960s and 1970s a number of new Scottish merchant
banks were formed. Edward Bates, an English company, was acquired
by Atlantic Assets in 1963 and became an integral part of the Ivory and
Sime group. Noble Grossart was formed in 1969 with the backing of a
number of Scottish financial interests and soon became a major figure
on the Scottish financial scene. In the early 1970s there were also some
subsidiaries or joint ventures of English companies registered as
merchant banks in Scotland: National Commercial and Schroders,
Scottish Financial Trust (set up by First National Finance Corporation
and suffered in the secondary banking crash together with its parent),
and Dalton Barton (Scotland) Ltd. To these could be added the
merchant banking subsidiaries of the three Scottish commercial banks,
which were also involved in agricultural finance through their joint
ownership of Scottish Agricultural Securities, and the Scottish offices
of a number of English merchant banks including Singer and
Friedlander, Henry Ansbacher, Slater Walker, Morgan Grenfell, and Hill
Samuel. Finally, the middle and late 1970s saw the reconstruction of
Dalton Barton (Scotland) as Dalscot, the establishment of James Finlay
Corporation (which marked the return of the Finlay group to merchant
banking), the resurrection of the British Linen Bank as the merchant
banking arm of the Bank of Scotland (replacing the Bank of Scotland
Finance Corporation), and the establishment of Edinburgh Financial
and General Holdings by Peter de Vink (formerly of Ivory and Sime).

We have already mentioned the consequences of the secondary
banking crash for British Bank of Commerce and Scottish Financial
Trust. However, the repercussions of the crash went further than this

and hit at the heart of the Scottish financial system. Ivory and Sime had made the shares of Edward Bates publicly available and had sold 24.8 per cent to London Merchant Securities, though Atlantic Assets retained a controlling stake of 31.6 per cent. During the course of 1974 Bates acquired a number of American oil and gas interests and built up its merchant banking and insurance activities, but this was to bring about serious liquidity problems. Bates's insurance subsidiary had to be sold at a loss, though Bates Oil Corporation was sold to Atlantic Assets at a considerable profit and so increased Bates's liquidity. After heavy losses in 1975 the company was reorganised and the London Merchant Securities stake was acquired by the First Arabian Corporation of Saudi Arabia (a nominee for a consortium headed by Prince Abdullah Rahman). The losses continued and, in early 1976, the Bank of England was forced to mount a rescue operation. However, in 1977 Bates was forced into liquidation.

The rising star of Scottish finance during the 1970s was undoubtedly Noble Grossart, which was formed in 1969 by Iain Noble and Angus Grossart together with Sir Hugh Fraser. In the first allocation of shares Noble and Grossart acquired 16.6 per cent each, four investment trusts held 59.7 per cent (Scottish American Investment, American Trust and Scottish Northern with 17.7 per cent each, and Ailsa Investment with 6.6 per cent), and Stenhouse Holdings held 2.8 per cent, the remaining shareholdings all being of less than 250 shares. The initial board included Noble, Grossart and Fraser, together with a representative of Stenhouse. In a new allocation of shares in 1970 a large holding was acquired by Sir Hugh Fraser and as a result the two largest holders became Fraser and Stenhouse with 10.0 per cent each, the four trusts holding 24.0 per cent, and Noble and Grossart holding 6.9 per cent each. The two main directors and the Fraser-Stenhouse interests together held 33.8 per cent and so shared minority control of the company.

Noble Grossart advised House of Fraser on the take-over of the Army and Navy Stores and advised Stenhouse on its merger with the Canadian firm Reed, Shaw, Osler. In 1970 it formed a property company, International Caledonian Assets, in partnership with the two Fraser companies. One of ICA's major deals occurred in 1974 when it was involved in a sale and lease-back arrangement with John Menzies. Wylie Hill's department store had been acquired by Menzies and the site was immediately sold to Prudential Assurance. The Prudential granted a long lease to ICA which, in turn, granted a long lease to John Menzies. In this way Menzies was able to recoup the cost of purchasing Wylie Hill.

During 1974 Iain Noble resigned from the bank board and Angus Grossart became the dominant figure. Table 4.4 shows that the three major interests held exactly half of the shares in 1974. Over the following years the company's general merchant banking business and its oil activities grew, the main shareholders remaining the same. By the later 1970s Sir Hugh Fraser, who faced numerous business problems of his own, was neither a director nor a large shareholder, and the controlling stake of the major interests had fallen to 44.5 per cent.

Table 4.4: Major Shareholdings in Noble Grossart (1974 and 1978)

	Percentage Holding	
Shareholder	1974	1978
A. Grossart	17.3	19.3*
Sir H. Fraser	16.3	
Stenhouse Holdings	16.4	20.0
Scottish American Investment	11.6	11.5
American Trust	11.7	12.5
Scottish Northern Investment	11.7	12.5
Ailsa Investment	4.4	4.5
Scottish Investment		4.7
Scottish United Investors		3.1
Noble Grossart Investments		5.2
TOTALS	89.4	93.3

*Figure for 1978 comprises Grossart's holding together with those of other directors and executives. In 1974 other directors and executives held 8.9 per cent in addition to Grossart's holding.

As a result of a merger between Dalton Barton and Keyser Ullman in 1973, Dalton Barton's Scottish banking subsidiary was taken over by a group of Scottish financial institutions. The company was renamed Dalscot, its head office was transferred from Glasgow to Edinburgh, and the whole company was restructured. The largest shareholders in the new bank were four Scottish companies: Scottish Life Assurance (23.3 per cent), Scottish American Investment (20.0 per cent), Scottish Northern Investment (17.1 per cent), and Scottish Homes Investment (11.4 per cent). The dominant directors, R. McNeill and J. Pearson, together with the other directors and executives, held 8.2 per cent and the remaining 20 per cent was held by various Scottish financial institutions. In the mid-1970s the main non-executive director was D.M. Young, the chairman of Scottish Homes, and he was replaced in the late 1970s by W. Berry of Scottish American Investment. By 1977 the restructuring of the company was more or less complete: Dalscot itself functioned as an investment company, its merchant banking activities having been transferred to its subsidiary McNeill Pearson. Dalscot was clearly following in Noble Grossart's footsteps, with similar financial backing, and it had built up a substantial business amongst private Scottish companies.

The development of merchant banking in Scotland shows the close involvement of the investment trusts at each stage. Indeed, the investment management companies such as Ivory and Sime, Baillie Gifford, and Brown, Fleming and Murray (now Murray Johnstone) operated in a very similar way to merchant banks themselves. In view of their similarity to 'true' merchant bankers such as Robert Fleming, it is hardly surprising to find them strengthening their corporate finance activities through banking subsidiaries or through participation in banks. It is particularly significant that Ivory and Sime have always treated Atlantic Assets as something of a holding company with interests in Bates, other trusts, the Save and Prosper Group, Haw Par of Singapore (bought from Slater Walker), and so on.

The development of Scottish insurance during the 1960s and 1970s was less dramatic than events in the banking sector. Since the late 1950s, five companies disappeared from the list through merger, either losing their separate quotation or being completely absorbed. Commercial Union acquired Northern Assurance and North British, Guardian Royal Exchange acquired Caledonian Insurance, and Norwich Union acquired Scottish Union. The Dutch company Nationale Nederlanden acquired Life Association after a take-over battle in which the latter was advised by Slater Walker Securities. Life Association had originally planned to mutualise and Scottish Life had converted from a proprietary company to a mutual company in 1968, leaving General Accident as the only non-mutual Scottish insurance company.

The shares of General Accident were held very widely by a constellation of financial interests; the 20 largest shareholders in 1975 possessed 15.60 per cent of the shares. These 20 holders comprised nine bank nominee and trust companies (representing unit trusts and pension funds as well as private individuals), three insurance companies, four pension funds, two unit trusts, one investment trust, and the Church Commissioners. The largest single holder was a Royal Bank

nominee company with 1.96 per cent of the shares, a holding matched
in size by other large holdings — a Lloyds Bank nominee with 1.20 per
cent, a Williams and Glyn's account with 1.03 per cent, a Bank of
Scotland nominee with 0.97 per cent, and a unit trust (held *via* National
Westminster Bank) with 0.82 per cent. Together these five largest
interests held 5.98 per cent of General Accident's shares, yet they do
not seem to have comprised a unified controlling group. It is perhaps
most accurate to see the General Accident board as having a certain
amount of autonomy from any particular ownership interest though
being constrained by the controlling constellation as a whole. Of the
17 directors 11, including the chairman and deputy chairman, seem to
have had most of their directorships within the General Accident group.
The remaining directors comprised two Scottish industrialists
(G.M. Menzies and D.W. Nickson), a stockbroker (G.R. Simpson), a
director of Schroders merchant bank (Earl of Airlie), a director of the
National Westminster Bank (Sir John Partridge), and a director of the
Pennsylvania Banking and Trust Co. (E.T. Moynahan). Only one of
these interests was represented amongst the top 20 shareholders —
National Westminster had three nominee holdings — though Schroders
nominees were the 24th largest holder. It seems likely that those who
participated in the controlling constellation ensured that the board
included some representation of their interests, but they did not
attempt to act together to dominate the composition of the board.
Thus, the traditional controlling interests in the company, represented
by I.H.S. Black, continued to run its affairs.

The links between banking and insurance companies are depicted in
Figure 4.1. It can be seen that the total number of links was fewer than
in previous periods. Of the nine interlocks, three were plural lines and
five involved office holders. The strongest links were those between the
National and Commercial Group and Scottish Widows, Bank of Scotland
and Standard Life, and Bank of Scotland and Scottish Provident. The
Clydesdale Bank not only acquired insurance links which it lacked in
previous years, it had 'captured' the link with Scottish Amicable
formerly held by the Bank of Scotland.

(ii)   The Investment and Property Sector

The investment and property sector comprised 42 investment trusts
and three property companies. The three property companies were very
different from the property and mortgage companies of the late-
nineteenth and early-twentieth centuries in so far as their investments
were in urban property rather than agriculture or mining. Argyle

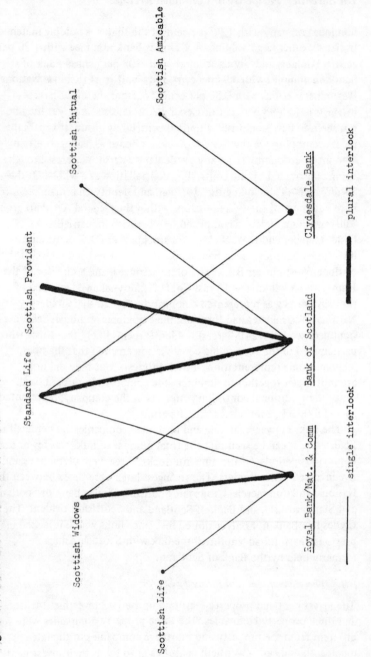

Figure 4.1: Bank and Insurance Interlocks (1973-4)

Scottish Amicable

Scottish Mutual

Clydesdale Bank

Scottish Provident

Standard Life

Bank of Scotland

Royal Bank/Nat. & Comm

Scottish Widows

Scottish Life

single interlock

plural interlock

Securities had been set up in 1958, passed into the control of Slater
Walker Securities in the 1960s, and had the Hamilton shopping precinct
as one of its major properties. In the early 1970s the Slater Walker 40
per cent holding was sold to Jimmy Goldsmith's Anglo-Continental
Investment, a further 14 per cent being held by G.M. Rivkin and his
fellow directors. Over the course of the 1970s the Goldsmith holding
was increased as part of a general restructuring of the whole Goldsmith
group. By 1975 Anglo-Continental held 47 per cent and in 1976 it
held 97 per cent, the balance being held by the directors. Both
Amalgamated Securities and Scottish Metropolitan were based on older
property companies – Northern Loan and St Mungo Property
respectively. The dominant influence in Scottish Metropolitan was Issy
Walton and his family who held 29.6 per cent of the shares. However,
two major insurance companies which made mortgage loans on Scottish
Metropolitan's properties also held large stakes: Guardian Royal

**Table 4.5: Owners of Commercial Property in Glasgow City Centre
(1971-2)**

Company	Aggregate Rateable Value (£000)
Prudential Assurance	550
Great Universal Stores	320
Legal and General Assurance	310
Scottish Metropolitan Property	300
Stock Conversion & Investment Trust	300
Scottish & Universal Investments	300
John Lewis Partnership	300
Guardian Royal Exchange	150
Artagen Properties	150
Scottish Amicable Life Assurance	150
Ronex Properties	150
Cooperative Insurance	150
Capital & Counties Securities	125

Note: Large property owners not included in Cable's table were British Rail,
Strathclyde University and Glasgow Corporation. Artagen Properties was an
associate of Sun Life Assurance, Ronex Properties was a subsidiary of Heron
Corporation, and Capital and Counties Securities was an indirect associate
(through Charter Consolidated) of two South African companies.
Source: Adapted from V. Cable, 'Glasgow: Area of Need', in G. Brown (ed), *The
Red Paper on Scotland* (Edinburgh University Student Publications Board, 1975),
p. 246.

Table 4.6: Scottish Investment Trust Assets (1976)

Group	No. of Trusts	Group Assets (£m)	Trusts Included in Present Analysis	Assets (£m)
Baillie Gifford	4	224.8	Scottish Mortgage	93.4
			Edinburgh & Dundee	72.5
Murray Johnstone	7	196.2	Scottish Western	58.1
			Clydesdale	52.1
			Caledonian	34.3
			Second Great Northern	18.6
			Glendevon	14.0
			Glenmurray	4.8
Martin Currie	6	173.6	Scottish Eastern	78.5
			Securities Trust	48.3
			Scottish Ontario	19.7
			St Andrew*	15.9
Alliance	2	164.7	Alliance	124.1
			Second Alliance	40.6
Ivory and Sime	4	131.9	British Assets	68.2
			Atlantic Assets	34.3
			Edinburgh American Assets**	21.2
–	–	–	British Investment	106.8
Scottish Investment	2	93.9	Second Scottish Investment	60.4
			Scottish Investment	33.5
Scottish United Invs. Man.	–	–	Scottish United	81.7
Edinburgh Fund Mans	4	80.4	American Trust	51.0
			Crescent Japan	14.4
			General Scottish*	8.3
			Wemyss Investment*	6.7
East of Scotland Inv. Man.*	4	78.7	Aberdeen Trust	37.2
			Pentland	22.5
			Aberdeen, Edinburgh and London	9.5
			Dominion & General	9.5
Belsize House	2	75.1	Northern American	40.6
			First Scottish	34.5
Gartmore Investment (Scotland)	3	73.1	Scottish National	57.2
			Glasgow Stockholders	14.7
–	–	–	Edinburgh Investment	69.4

Table 4.6 continued

Group	No. of Trusts	Group Assets (£m)	Trusts Included in Present Analysis	Assets (£m)
Stewart Fund Managers	2	63.0	Scottish American	48.6
			Scottish European	14.4
–	–	–	Investors Capital Trust**	59.8
–	–	–	Great Northern	55.9
Paull & Williamsons	–	–	Scottish Northern	41.6
–	–	–	Dundee & London	13.1
Thomson McLintock	2	10.8	Ailsa Investment	9.0
Rea Bros. (London)	–	–	Scottish Cities	4.8

*Management changes 1973-6: St Andrew Trust was formerly independent; General Scottish and Wemyss were formerly managed by Robertson and Maxtone Graham; investment interests of Brander & Cruickshank and Chiene & Tait merged into East of Scotland Investment Management.
**Name changes 1973-6: Edinburgh American Assets was formerly Second British Assets; Investors Capital was formerly Investors Mortgage Security.
Note: see note to Table 3.5.
Source: Calculated from A.A. Arnaud, *Investment Trusts Explained*, (Woodhead-Faulkner, Cambridge, 1977), Appendix B, p. 135 ff.

Exchange held 17.7 per cent and Royal Insurance held 15.3 per cent. As shown in Table 4.5, Scottish Metropolitan was one of the largest property owners in the City of Glasgow.

Table 4.6 shows the asset values of the investment trusts for 1976. Although some alterations in management groups occurred between 1973 and 1976, the general pattern remained the same. The largest group was Baillie Gifford with total assets of £224.8m, followed by Murray Johnstone with £196.2m and Martin Currie with £173.6m. The largest single trust was the Alliance with assets of £124.1m, followed by British Investment with £106.8m, and Scottish Mortgage (part of the Baillie Gifford group) with £93.4m.

A number of the trusts and trust groups had undergone reorganisation during the 1960s and 1970s. Baillie Gifford reorganisation began in 1960 when two of the London trusts, the Abbotts and the Friars, were merged into Monks Investment Trust. In 1969 Scottish Central Investment became the basis of a new Edinburgh and Dundee Investment Trust which absorbed both the old Edinburgh and Dundee and

Second Edinburgh and Dundee. In the same year Scottish Mortgage and Trust absorbed both its 'second' trust and Scottish Capital Investment. The chairman of the two Scottish Baillie Gifford trusts was George Chiene and there were no other interlocks between the two trusts. Linkages to jute interests and to the Alliance trust continued to be an important feature of Baillie Gifford interlocks.

Murray Johnstone was set up as a management company for the trusts formerly managed by Brown, Fleming and Murray, and this group underwent a complex restructuring between 1959 and 1972. In 1959 Scottish Western absorbed the Caledonian Trust, and a year later the Second Clydesdale and Second Scottish Western merged to become the new Caledonian Trust. In 1961 Clydesdale Investment absorbed Second Caledonian, Third Caledonian and Third Scottish Western. In a period of three years eight trusts had been reduced to three and the names of these trusts bore little relation to the trusts of the same names in earlier years. The final steps in the reconstruction of the group involved the founding of three new trusts: Glenmurray in 1966, Scottish and Continental in 1971, and Glendevon in 1972. The Murray Johnstone group was a tightly integrated group. James Lumsden, senior partner in Maclay, Murray and Spens, was chairman of all the trusts in the group, and a number of other directors had two or three directorships within the group: J.R. Johnstone sat on Scottish Western, Caledonian, and Glenmurray, A.I. Mackenzie sat on Scottish Western, Second Great Northern, and Glendevon, James I. Murray sat on Caledonian and Second Great Northern (his son, J. Iain Murray, sat on Glenmurray), W.D. Coats of Coats Patons sat on Caledonian and Glendevon, and R.D. Fairbairn of the Clydesdale Bank sat on Scottish Western and Second Great Northern. Shipping interests were particularly prominent on the boards of Caledonian and Clydesdale Investment: the latter's board included A.M.M. Stephen and W.F. Robertson (of Gem Line and on whose board J.A. Lumsden sat), and Caledonian's board included J.F. Denholm (whose brother, R.F. Denholm, was a director of Scottish Amicable and Scottish National Trust).

The Martin Currie group, like Baillie Gifford, had a looser form of group structure than Murray Johnstone, though it too was restructured during the 1960s. In 1961 Securities Trust absorbed Oregon Mortgage, Melville Trust and Second Securities Trust, and in 1966 Scottish Eastern absorbed Second Scottish Eastern and Scottish American Mortgage. In 1968 St Andrew Trust absorbed United States Investment and later became a member of the Martin Currie group. The group had only one internal interlock in 1973-4 — Hamish Falconer, senior partner, was chairman of Scottish Ontario and a director of Scottish Eastern — though A.L. McClure was chairman of both Scottish Eastern and St Andrew Trust, the latter being independently managed at the time.

Within the Ivory and Sime group the main change was the growing importance of Atlantic Assets over the period, though Second British Assets was renamed Edinburgh American Assets in 1975 to mark a change in investment policy (the original name of the trust had been Edinburgh American Land Mortgage). British Assets and Second British Assets had identical boards and both were chaired by Sir Alistair Blair. Atlantic Assets was chaired by J.V. Sheffield, founder of Norcros, and was linked to the other group trusts through E.J. Ivory and J.C.R. Inglis. Edinburgh-based Chiene and Tait and Aberdeen-based Brander and Cruickshank had long had a close relationship. In the early 1970s East of Scotland Trust was absorbed by Aberdeen Trust, and the investment management activities of the two firms were merged into East of Scotland Investment Management. The internal interlocks of the group were maintained primarily through Sir Robert Erskine-Hill of Chiene and Tait, who sat on all four boards, and J.S.R. Cruickshank of Brander and Cruickshank, who sat on the two Aberdeen boards.

Eleven investment trusts from the 1955-6 list had disappeared through merger by 1973-4, and five of them have been discussed above. Of the others, Investors' Mortgage and Edinburgh Investment both acquired their 'second' trusts, Realisation and Debenture was acquired by British Investment in 1960, Clyde and Mersey was acquired by Home and Foreign in 1964 (the latter was itself acquired by Great Northern in 1969), Scottish Consolidated was acquired by Scottish United in 1961, and New Zealand and Australian by Dalgety. A total of 23 trusts were common to both the 1955-6 list and the 1973-4 list, the majority of the 22 newcomers being flotations of older companies or companies which had not previously qualified for inclusion. Perhaps the most interesting newcomer was Wemyss Investment, which had appeared in the 1904-5 list as Wemyss Collieries. As a result of coal nationalisation the Wemyss family had used the compensation funds to convert the company into an investment trust in 1956. By the early 1970s the family's master company, Wemyss Development, had two subsidiaries (Wemyss Hotels and Wemyss Brick) and held a third of the shares of Wemyss Investment. This profitable company attracted considerable outside interest and by 1977 the Wemyss Development stake of 31.1 per cent in Wemyss Investment was supplemented by a 9.8 per cent stake held by Prudential Assurance and a 5.1 per cent stake held by the Kuwait Investment Office.

What were the ownership characteristics of the investment trusts? Only a very few of the trusts, as might be expected, were substantially controlled by particular interests. Apart from Wemyss Investment there was only Aberdeen, Edinburgh and London Trust, which had been the subject of a struggle for control between the Slater Walker group and Cable Trust and which eventually became a wholly-owned subsidiary of Cable Trust. The more usual situation was for control to lie with a diverse constellation of interests, though share concentration was significantly higher than the previously discussed case of General Accident. A very good example of such a control situation was Scottish United Investors, presented in Table 4.7. The ten largest shareholders comprised six insurance companies, two unit trusts and two bank nominees and they together held 28.62 per cent. Within this constellation of interests the smallest group capable of outvoting the remainder was the first three holders, who held 15.20 per cent but were unlikely to form an exclusive coalitition. As in the case of General Accident, it is likely that the board was constrained not by *particular* interests but by the constellation as a whole.

Table 4.7: Ownership of Scottish United Investors (1975)

Rank	Shareholder	Size of Holding (%)
1	Prudential Assurance	6.28
2	Scottish Widows Fund	4.56
3	Unknown unit trust (held *via* Midland Bank)	4.36
4	Pearl Assurance	2.84
5	Royal Insurance	2.45
6	Save and Prosper Group	1.97
7	Standard Life	1.64
8	Royal Bank nominee company	1.60
9	Williams and Glyns bank account	1.50
10	Equity and Law Life Assurance	1.42
	TOTAL	28.62

The distinction between groups with a loose organisation and those with a tight structure is apparent for shareholders as well as for director-ships, as can be seen by comparing the Ivory and Sime group with the

Baillie Gifford group. In 1973 British Assets held 10.99 per cent of Atlantic Assets' shares, Second British Assets held 6.24 per cent (which it had acquired from British Assets earlier that year), and the directors of Atlantic Assets themselves held 5.64 per cent. Thus the total 'in-house' holding in Atlantic Assets was 22.87 per cent. Over the next few years this total was reduced: Second British Assets sold its stake in 1974, the British Assets holding was reduced to 5.66 per cent in the same year, and the directors' holding remained at about ten per cent. Atlantic Assets can therefore be regarded as minority-controlled by Ivory and Sime, the largest rival shareholder being Save and Prosper with 3.92 per cent – and Atlantic Assets was a quarter-owner of Save and Prosper. By contrast, the two Baillie Gifford trusts had no mutual shareholdings. The five largest shareholders in Edinburgh and Dundee Investment held 15.77 per cent with the largest holder, D.C. Thomson, having 5.28 per cent, though this was insufficient to outvote the next two shareholders. In 1977, Edinburgh and Dundee was acquired in a controversial move by the British Rail pension fund which formerly was the seventh largest shareholder with 1.27 per cent. Take-overs of investment trusts are likely when the share price is low in relation to the underlying assets and this situation prompted many members of the financial community to propose conversion into unit trusts, where the price of a unit is automatically linked to its asset value. This option has not, so far, proved popular in Scotland even though British Investment Trust shared the fate of Edinburgh and Dundee and was acquired in 1978 by the National Coal Board pension fund.

Groups with a similar structure to Baillie Gifford were Martin Currie and the East of Scotland Investment group. The two Aberdeen trusts in the East of Scotland group, formerly managed by Brander and Cruikshank, had close links with the Electra Group of investment trusts in London. We have already described the takeover of Aberdeen, Edinburgh and London by Cable Trust. In 1977 the latter was merged with Globe Investment Trust, the holding company for the Electra Group. Although the largest holder in Aberdeen Trust was the Prudential, with 6.96 per cent, its second largest holder was Globe Investment with 5.27 per cent. Together with the 5.07 per cent holding by London and Manchester Assurance, the three largest shareholders in Aberdeen Trust held 17.3 per cent. Control in both these companies was shared by the East of Scotland group (J.S.R. Cruickshank and Sir Robert Erskine-Hill sitting on both boards) and the Electra Group (A.F. Roger sitting on Aberdeen, Edinburgh and London, A.W. Anderson sitting on Aberdeen Trust). The two largest shareholders of the two

Edinburgh trusts formerly managed by Chiene and Tait were identical: Kuwait Investment Office held 7.7 per cent of Dominion and 7.9 per cent of Pentland, London and Manchester Assurance held 9.6 per cent of Dominion and 5.0 per cent of Pentland. Neither of these interests were directly represented on the board though most of the directors were drawn from the Edinburgh and London financial establishments: Dominion's board included W.M. Cunningham from the Cayzer group and J.R. Johnstone of Murray Johnstone; Pentland's board included P.J. Oliphant of Stewart Fund Managers, Hamish Falconer of Martin Currie and G.P.S. Macpherson of Kleinwort Benson. The Martin Currie group itself comprised three trusts from our list, though St Andrew Trust subsequently joined the group. Each of these four trusts showed a different dominant stockholder. The directors of Scottish Ontario themselves held 8.52 per cent of the shares, most being held by Falconer, and were rivalled only by the Kuwait Investment Office holding of 7.00 per cent. Scottish Ontario's board overlapped with that of Pentland Investment, including Falconer, Erskine-Hill and G.M. Menzies. The dominant shareholder in Securities Trust was Equity and Law Life Assurance with 5.99 per cent, and the board included no partners from Martin Currie. The main character of the board was the representation of a number of major Scottish interests: Scottish Provident, Standard Life, Sidlaw Industries and Scottish and Newcastle Breweries. The board of Scottish Eastern, in which Prudential held 6.02 per cent, also included representatives of Standard Life and Scottish and Newcastle. Both Scottish Eastern and St Andrew Trust (in which Scottish Widows held 5.08 per cent and the directors held 1.26 per cent) seem to have been closely linked to the Edinburgh legal firm Brodies: R.K. Watson was a director of Scottish Eastern, A.L. McClure was chairman of both trusts, and the St Andrew board included members of the Watson and Cuthbertson families associated with Brodies. The pattern of control in the Martin Currie group was very complex. There was no integration of the group through cross-shareholdings or interlocking directorships, nor were major outside ownership interests represented on the board. Various overlapping coalitions of interests were able to control the companies subject only to the general constraints of their particular ownership constellations.

By contrast, the Murray Johnstone group had a tightly integrated structure. Table 4.8 shows that share ownership was highly concentrated for most of the group trusts. In the case of the four largest trusts between 42 and 54 per cent of the shares were held by the major holders, but there was considerable concentration within this top group. The

Table 4.8: Share Distribution in the Murray Johnstone Group (1973-4)

Company	No. of Holdings Over 10,000 Shares	% Held by Major Holders
Caledonian	44	42.6
Clydesdale	47	53.9
Glendevon	7	17.4
Glenmurray	3	76.1
Scottish Western	47	44.0
Second Great Northern	16	49.9

Note: The data for Glenmurray refer not to all holders over 10,000 but simply to the three largest shareholders.
The other trust in the group, Scottish and Continental, had 15 large holders with 42.3 per cent of the shares.
Source: Adapted from J. Scott and M. Hughes, 'Ownership and Control in a Satellite Economy', *Sociology* 10, 1, 1976, p.31.

five largest holders in Clydesdale Investment held 19.49 per cent, Scottish Western's top five holders held 19.50 per cent, and in Second Great Northern the three largest holders held 20.7 per cent. While the largest shareholders in each of the bigger trusts varied, Prudential and Standard Life appeared prominently in all of them and the trusts were closely linked through shared directors. Glendevon was formed in 1972, and by 1973 the four largest holders held 13.1 per cent of its shares. It is likely that the other Murray Johnstone trusts held the controlling stake, which they were gradually reducing as the shares were sold to a wider group. This seems to have been the case for Glenmurray, which was floated in 1966: holdings in Glenmurray by Caledonian, Clydesdale Investment and Scottish Western were reduced from 76.11 per cent in 1973 to 63.49 per cent in 1977.

The only Aberdeen trust not discussed so far is Scottish Northern, which was controlled by two partners in Paull and Williamsons together with other Aberdeen interests. By far the largest shareholder was the Save and Prosper Group with 6.38 per cent, though this company had no board representation. The main outside link was with Clydesdale Bank — Iain Tennant was a director and together with Roger Fleming sat on the Clydesdale Northern Area board. Most of the Dundee trusts also seem to have been characterised by local control, and they showed a high degree of interconnection. The Alliance trusts both had D.C. Thomson (publishers of *Beano*, *Dandy*, etc.) as their major

shareholder — Thomson held 6.43 per cent of Alliance and 9.99 per
cent of Second Alliance. This link was reinforced by the presence of
Brian Thomson on the two boards. Apart from G.T. Chiene, all the
outside directors had Dundee interests: J.M. Prain and Sir William
Walker were from the jute industry and G.W. Dunn was a director of
the supermarket group William Low. Dundee and London Investment
was managed by Tay and Thames Investment Trust Services, an
associate company of Robert Fleming run from the Belsize House
offices of the Northern American Trust group and chaired by Ivor
Guild. The latter was a partner in Shepherd and Wedderburn (formerly
Guild and Shepherd) and was a descendant of John Guild who joined
with Robert Fleming to establish many of the early investment trusts.
John's son was A.M. Guild a Dundee stockbroker and his grandson was
R.M. Guild, a partner in Shepherd and Wedderburn. (see Figure 1.8.)
Both A.M. Guild and R.M. Guild had been directors of Dundee and
London Investment and Scottish Cities Investment during the 1950s.
The major shareholder in Dundee and London was a Lloyds Bank
nominee company, though the second largest holder was John Leng
and Company of Dundee with 5.32 per cent. Dundee and London was
interlocked only with Low and Bonar, and Sir John Leng (who died in
1906) had married a daughter of William Low. The two Belsize House
trusts had a stake of 2.80 per cent in Dundee and London and were
themselves tightly controlled. The boards of the two companies
included Ivor Guild, Sir Herbert Bonar of Low and Bonar, and two
directors of Robert Fleming — Hugh S. Spens (son of H.B. Spens) and
Richard E. Fleming. The latter was a director of the Save & Prosper
Group which was partly owned by Fleming and which was the largest
shareholder in Northern American Trust with 7.94 per cent. Save and
Prosper was the third largest holder in First Scottish American with
2.83 per cent, the largest holders being Standard Life with 5.87 per
cent and John Leng and Co. with 4.17 per cent.

The Edinburgh trusts most closely linked to the Dundee trusts were
the Baillie Gifford group, Edinburgh Investment and Investors' Mortgage
(subsequently re-named Investors' Capital Trust), though the latter was
less closely linked to Dundee than in previous years. Edinburgh investment was chaired by Ivor Guild and its board included John Chiene,
who chaired Investors' Mortgage and was the brother of George Chiene.
With 7.13 per cent Save and Prosper was the largest shareholder in
Edinburgh Investment. The 24 holdings of over 100,000 shares together
held 25 per cent of the voting capital and were all financial companies.
Though individuals (11,500 of them) owned over half of the shares,

just 16 individuals held more than 25,000 shares (accounting for 2.1 per cent) and one of the largest individuals holdings was that of Ivor Guild. During 1973 Edinburgh Investment moved into the general area of investment advice and investment management, a strategy which some other trusts had already adopted. Edinburgh Fund Managers was set up by American Trust and managed its investments together with those of Crescent Japan Investment and the Crescent group of unit trusts. In the mid-1970s two trusts formerly managed by Robertson and Maxtone Graham, General Scottish Trust and Wemyss Investment, also joined the EFM group. The directorate of the four companies was drawn overwhelmingly from law and accountancy firms associated with the trusts or from EFM executives – nine directors, including A.L. McClure. The main 'outside' directors were Angus Grossart (American Trust being a major shareholder in Noble Grossart) and G.P.S. Macpherson of Kleinwort Benson. The family nature of control in Wemyss Investment was unique and has already been discussed. None of the other three trusts seems to have had direct board representation of major ownership interests, though there was considerable share concentration: the two largest holders in American Trust (Post Office pensions fund, Save and Prosper) held 11.70 per cent; the three largest holders in Crescent Japan held 27.27 per cent, with Commercial Union alone holding 15.29 per cent; and the four largest holders in General Scottish held 25.84 per cent, with Scottish Widows holding 9.05 per cent.

Stewart Fund Managers, in which the Stewart family were prominent, managed Scottish American Investment and Scottish European and were heavily involved in oil development and in the ownership of other financial companies. Scottish American, for example, had 22 per cent of all its investments located in the financial sector in 1977, including a 20 per cent stake in Dalscot and an 11 per cent stake in Noble Grossart. Scottish American was also the major shareholder, with 7.67 per cent, in Scottish European. In 1975 the top five holders of Scottish European shares held 24.25 per cent, over a half of this being accounted for by Scottish American's holding and a 6.67 per cent block held by Norwich Union. By 1977 the Electricity Supply pension fund had become a major holder with 5.70 per cent. Control in the group seems to have rested with various legal interests associated with Stewart Fund Managers and to have been buttressed by the Norwich Union holding: P.W. Turcan and P.J. Oliphant sat on both boards, and Oliphant was also a director of Norwich Union. Scottish Investment and Second Scottish Investment have always had identical boards, though an accident of timing shows Angus Grossart as sitting only on the second board. The chairman of the two companies was Sir William McEwan Younger, who retired in 1975 and was replaced by Grossart. The following year the two companies were merged together to form a larger trust. The only remaining Edinburgh trust on our list is Scottish Cities Investment which had no Scottish interlocks and was managed by Rea Brothers of London. The trust seems to have been closely controlled by its management group since all of its directors were associated with Rea Brothers or its associated companies, and Scottish Cities was a major shareholder in Rea Brothers itself.

Apart from Murray Johnstone, the major Glasgow investment interests comprised the Great Northern, Ailsa and Gartmore. The largest shareholder in Great Northern was Prudential with 12.42 per cent, more than half of the total for the top five holdings. However, the Prudential was not represented on the board, which drew its membership from Glasgow industry and commerce: J.P. Agnew of Lyle Shipping, J.G. Stenhouse of Stenhouse Holdings, and W.K.J. Weir of Weir Group. Ailsa Investment was managed, like its smaller sister Alva, by Glasgow accountants Thomson McLintock. In 1977, Ailsa's two largest shareholders were Cornhill Insurance (part of the Tilling Group) with 9.55 per cent and American Trust with 9.00 per cent. Ailsa owned 13.90 per cent of Alva, of which Cornhill also held 9.94 per cent. The Tilling group was not represented on the board, the major outside link being to Scottish Mutual Assurance. Gartmore Investment (Scotland) was set up to take over the investment management activities of Grahams Rintoul. The management company was a subsidiary of Gartmore Investment of London, itself a subsidiary of the Cayzer group company British and Commonwealth Shipping. The largest shareholders in Scottish National were Scottish Widows (6.28 per cent) and Equity and Law Life (5.48 per cent), and the largest holder in Glasgow Stockholders was Save and Prosper with 6.16 per cent, though Kuwait Investment Office had acquired 6.94 per cent by 1977. None of these interests was represented on the trust boards, which were recruited mainly from Glasgow accountants and businessmen. W.C. Allen, who sat on Glasgow Stockholders, was the only representative of the Cayzer group to sit on either board.

It is clear that control over investment and property companies varied from city to city and according to the character of the management company. In some companies control was dispersed amongst a constellation of interests which permitted lawyers, accountants and local businessmen to run the company. In other cases, control was vested in a particular corporate or familial interest. This mixture of control types was also apparent in the industrial sector.

The Industrial Sector

Of the 55 large non-financial companies of 1955-6, 28 were still to be found amonst the top 62 of 1973-4. Of the 27 companies lost over the period three were lost due to nationalisation (Colvilles, Stewarts and Lloyds, Bairds and Scottish), three were liquidated (North British Loco, Donaldson Line, United Collieries), Singer was no longer quoted, two were too small to appear in the list (Anglo-American Direct Tea, Angus Milling), five were fully incorporated into their parent groups (Clan Line, Dewar, Jugra Land, Pirie, Scottish Motor Traction), and the remaining 13 were acquired by other companies. The 13 acquired are listed in Figure 4.2. It can be seen that all the acquired companies were taken over by English-based concerns, though Patons and Baldwins merged with Coats in 1961. Of the 34 companies new to the list in 1973-4, 18 had been small public companies in 1955-6 and 16 were new flotations. Some of the new flotations were in fact, very old companies. Carron Company, for example, was first quoted in 1966 but had been founded in 1759 by Samuel Garbett, John Roebuck and William Cadel – though by the end of the nineteenth century control rested with the inter-married Dawson, Stainton and Maclaren families. One of the newest flotations was Reo Stakis, which had been formed on the basis of a small shell company Frederick J. Malcolm. A number of the companies changed their names between 1956 and 1973: Aberdeen Construction Group (formerly Wm Tawse), Nairn Floors (formerly Jas. Williamson and Nairn-Williamson), Tayforth (Dundee Ice and Cold Storage), Scottish Automobile (Rossleigh), North British Steel (Atlas Steel Foundry), Ayrshire Metal (Ayrshire Dockyard), and certain other minor name changes. Culter Guard Bridge Holdings was formed to consolidate Culter Paper Mills and Guard Bridge Paper, both of which had been small in 1955-6.

A number of name changes mask the continuity of companies over the period. Certain companies, such as Coats Patons and Scottish and Newcastle Breweries, clearly show the links with their predecessor companies, but others are not so straightforward. The American parent company of North British Rubber was reorganised during the 1960s and the Scottish company was renamed Uniroyal. In 1979 Uniroyal was sold to the West German tyre-maker Continental Gummiwerke in a deal which surprised even the British management. Conti-Gummi was partly-owned by the massive Bayer Corporation. The Linen Thread Company

Figure 4.2: Acquisitions of Scottish Companies (1955-74)

Company	Acquired by
Sir Wm Arrol	Clarke Chapman
Bank Line	Andrew Weir
Cooper	Associated British Foods
Alex Cowan	Reed International
A.B. Fleming	Croda International
Fleming, Reid	Patons and Baldwins
Federated Foundries	Glynwed
Lawsons	UDS Group
Rivet, Bolt and Nut	Guest Keen and Nettlefolds
Saxone, Lilley & Skinner	Sears Holdings
Scottish Cooperative Wholesale	Cooperative Wholesale Society
James Templeton	Guthrie Corporation
United Turkey Red	Tootal

Note: Patons and Baldwins merged with J. & P. Coats in 1961. A.B. Fleming is now called Croda Polymers.

was renamed Lindustries in order to underline its diversification into engineering and polymers. Finally, a number of the Finlay tea companies were renamed as part of a reconstruction of the group, and we discuss this more fully below.

A total of 32 of the non-financial companies were interlocked, only 14 having interlocks with other industrial companies. Figure 4.3 shows the industrial network, which had been further reduced in density since 1955-6. The network comprised five components: the Finlay group of four plurally connected companies, three pairs, and a component of five companies. As in 1955-6, functional links were few and far between. The interlock between Culter Guard and Richards was a regional link generated through Roger Fleming. However, Fleming's own firm was a timber dealer and there may have been a functional link with Culter Guard. The only other case of a functional link was that between Lindustries and Wm Baird, both of which had textile interests. The remaining connections seem to have been financial or control links: Sir Hugh Fraser linked House of Fraser and Scottish and Universal (SUITS), John Chiene linked Brownlee and Scotcros, and the large component was primarily due to the directorships held

Figure 4.3: Industrial Interlocks (1973-4)

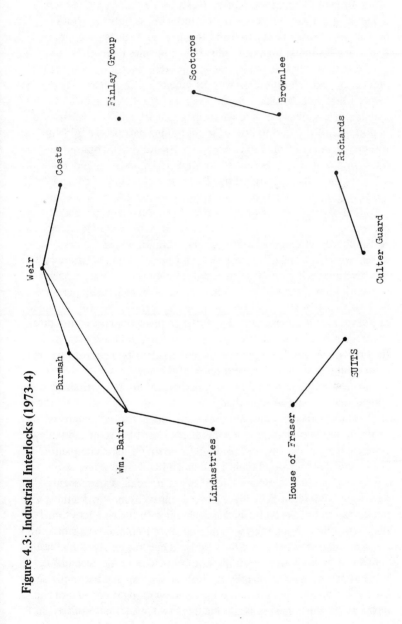

by James Lumsden. It is perhaps significant that the largest component of 1955-6 (see Figure 3.3) was, in large part, a product of the interlocks of the Brown, Fleming and Murray trusts, while that of 1973-4 was induced by Murray Johnstone trust interlocks. As in the previous period links between industrial and financial companies were more important than links amongst industrial companies themselves.

It was argued in Chapter 3 that an important factor in reducing the number of Scottish interlocks was the growth of English and American ownership, a trend which involved the complete disappearance of companies as well as partial ownership. As an attempt to quantify the importance of this and to assess the continuing part played by family ownership and control, Tables 4.9 and 4.10 give the distribution of ownership characteristics for the non-financial companies and Table 4.C gives the full company listing. Three general modes of control are distinguished — majority, minority, and control through a con- stellation of interests — and each of the former two are subdivided according to whether control is exclusive, shared , or limited. (See Appendix for a fuller discussion of these definitions.) In the case of minority control and control through a constellation of interests it is particularly important to investigate board representation so as to see whether those with controlling shareholdings actually participate in the exercise of strategic control. It can be seen that majority control decreased in frequency as the size of the company increased, and that the frequency of control through a constellation of interests varied in the opposite direction. It proved possible to identify a controlling ownership interest for all except seven of the non-financial companies, and in each of the latter a dominant participant in the controlling constellations could be identified.

A total of 20 companies were subject to some form of majority control, only two of these involving shared control (two of the Finlay companies which we discuss more fully below). Of these companies, eight were controlled by families and individuals and the rest were controlled by other companies. Most of the personal owners seem to have been Scottish or Scottish resident families. In most cases the families seem to have had a long association with the company which they controlled, though the tycoon-controlled Reo Stakis Organisation was a prominent exception. Stoddard Holdings, for example, had been controlled by the Renshaw family until shortly after the Second World War but had been controlled by Sir Robert Maclean and his family since then. Maclean had spent much of his career working for Stoddard and in the 1970s the company board included two Macleans. Similarly, in

Table 4.9: Mode of Control in Non-Financial Companies (1973-4)

Mode of Control		Number of Companies
Majority		20
Wholly owned	7	
Exclusive majority	11	
Shared majority	2	
Minority		35
Exclusive minority	19	
Shared minority	12	
Limited minority (exclusive or shared)	4	
Control through a constellation of interests		7
TOTAL		62

Note: Due to additional information being available, some companies have been classified differently to the findings reported in an earlier paper.

Table 4.10: Mode of Control and Size of Non-Financial Companies (1973-4)

Rank	Wholly -owned	Exc. maj.	Shared maj.	Exc. min.	Shared min.	Limited min.	Constellation
Top 10	1	1		3	1		4
11-20	1	1		4	3		1
21-30	2	1		2	2	2	1
31-40	2	2		3		2	1
41-50	1	3		3	3		
51-62		3	2	4	3		
TOTALS	7	11	2	19	12	4	7

Carron Company control was vested in a Dawson family trust and the board included a member of the founding Cadell family and was chaired by Charles H. Burder, a member of the Stainton family. Of the newer companies, James Scott Engineering was controlled by its board of directors with large holdings by the chairman, I. Sclar, S.S. Cohen, and a smaller holding by James I. Scott. During 1976, however, the company was taken over by William Press of London, which had gradually built up a large holding. No family had a majority stake in more than one company – the Menzies families controlling John Menzies and North British Steel were not related to one another.

Thirty-five companies were characterised by control through owner-ship of a substantial minority holding. In the case of both exclusive and shared minority control the most typical holding was between 20 and 30 per cent. The strongest cases of minority control were the Wilson family holding in Ayrshire Metal, the Duncanson family and directors' holdings in Arthur Bell, the Fraser stake in SUITS, the Morton family and directors' holdings in Blackwood Morton, and the Thomas Duff and Co. stake in Titaghur Jute. Slightly weaker cases were those with exclusive minority control based on holdings of between 20 and 30 per cent. Six of these nine companies were family-controlled, the exceptions being House of Fraser (though this was indirectly under family control), Inveresk and Culter Guard. The weakest cases of exclusive minority control, those involving blocks of between 10 and 20 per cent, involved four cases of personal control and one of control by a corporate interest. The companies in which minority control was shared between two or more shareholders show a rather more complex pattern. Families or individuals shared control in nine of the 12 companies, mainly sharing control with industrial or financial companies. In most cases the companies and institutions were supports to continuing family control and did not have direct board representation. For example, the Coltness Group was controlled by the Gibbons and Walker families who were represented on the board with A.L. Telfer, a descendant of a former top manager. However, in two cases shared control did actually involve shared representation. Tharsis Sulphur had just under half of its board drawn from the Spanish interests, though the top positions were occupied by the Tennant (Lord Glenconner) and Rutherford families (the board included two descendants of W. Rutherford who had run the company for a long period). Similarly, the board of Scotcros included John Chiene of Edinburgh Investment as well as Walter Alexander. The four cases of limited minority control involve three cases of an established family remaining in control with between five and ten per cent of the shares: Goldberg's board included three Goldbergs, Aberdeen Construction's board included two Andersons, and the Brown and Tawse board included two members of the Rae family. In the fourth case, United Wire, the Green family had a rather small stake buttressed by the holding of the Scottish Amicable, the latter having no board representation.

The nature of minority control can best be illustrated through a comparison of United Biscuits with Wm Baird. United Biscuits was classified as being under exclusive minority control by its directors, predominantly Sir Hector Laing and his family. The total of shares held by the directors and their families, according to the annual report, was 22.8 per cent. However, examination of the share register showed a complex pattern of holdings. The 20 largest holdings on the register held a total of 29.17 per cent, with the largest holding — by the Prudential — being 6.25 per cent. However, the list of the 20 largest holdings included no less than eight Laing family trust holdings. The controlling block was split into a number of separate small blocks. In the case of Baird the share concentration appeared, from the register, to be greater; the 20 largest holders held 45.05 per cent, with the ten largest holding 33.44 per cent. Duplication of entries, though not on the scale of the Laing holdings, reduced the number of separate holders amongst the top 20. There were, in fact four M and G Group holdings and four Save and Prosper holdings. The three largest holdings apart from these unit trusts were Prudential (4.68 per cent), Norwich Union (1.87 per cent) and Britannic Assurance (1.78 per cent). Collectively these insurance companies held only a third of the shares held by the unit trusts. However, neither of the unit trust groups were represented on the Baird board: executives and former controlling families (such as McCosh) continued to run the company. But they could only do this for as long as the dominant ownership interests wanted them to. There seems to be an important distinction between minority control which arises through the dilution of a family holding (as in United Biscuits) and minority control which develops, unintentionally, out of the growth of 'institutional' shareholdings (as in Baird).

The companies classified as controlled through a constellation of interests show an extension of the type of control found in Baird. Each of the seven companies had a wide distribution of shares, though the 20 largest holders always held sufficient for minority control (see Table 4.11). Within the general constraints set by the controlling constellations the boards could achieve a certain autonomy, though intervention by the dominant ownership interests was an ever present possibility. Thus a number of variations were found within this category. Scottish and Newcastle Breweries shows very clear continuity of family control. The descendants of H.J. Younger were the largest shareholders with just under four per cent, and four members of the Younger families were represented on the board and held key executive

Table 4.11: Share Distribution in Controlling Constellations (1973-4)

Cumulative % held by:	Distillers	Burmah	Coats	S & N	Lindustries	Howden	Highland Distilleries	Average % held
Largest holder	2.86	1.67	6.22	3.91	6.38	8.64	6.42	5.16
Top 2 holders	4.35	2.93	8.37	6.06	11.95	14.83	11.44	8.56
Top 3 holders	5.43	4.18	10.01	8.04	16.78	19.84	15.70	11.43
Top 4 holders	6.49	5.40	11.31	9.86	21.19	24.61	18.91	13.97
Top 5 holders	7.51	6.52	12.52	11.23	24.58	30.24	21.70	16.33
Top 10 holders	11.81	10.79	17.31	16.88	35.88	39.93	31.62	23.46
Top 20 holders	18.21	17.43	23.98	25.96	46.90	49.36*	44.14	32.28
Average held by a large holder	0.91	0.87	1.20	1.30	2.35	2.74*	2.21	1.61

Note: Some of the information on the four largest companies was provided by M. Thwaite.
*Data for Howden relates to 18 largest holders only.

positions. The remaining members of the board were mainly internal
managers — though the Earl of Airlie was also a director of General
Accident, which was S & N's second largest shareholder with 2.15 per
cent. In Coats Patons, Distillers and Lindustries family influence
persisted in a weaker form. Lord Forteviot was a member of the
Distillers board and had a family shareholding of only 0.23 per cent,
being the 47th largest shareholder. (It is of course possible that there
were further nominee holdings for this family.) The majority of the
members of the Distillers board were internal managers and there was
no direct representation of major shareholders, though institutional
pressure led to a solution of the Thalidomide case in which Distillers
was involved. Similarly the Coats Patons board consisted almost
exclusively of internal managers, with W.D. Coats representing the
Coats family which no longer had (or appeared to have) a large holding.
The only obvious personal holding was that of the Heathcote Amory
family (0.82 per cent) whose family firm John Heathcote had been
taken over by Patons and Baldwins. It seems clear that family members
and executives could continue to run Coats and Distillers with little or
no ownership stake, because the dominant ownership interests were
willing to let them remain *in situ*. The Lindustries board included two
Lukes and one Knox from the old controlling families, though there
were no large family shareholdings. Although the two largest shareholders (Barclays Nominees and Midland Bank Trust Co.) owned more
than 10 per cent of the shares, neither was represented on the board.
Once again, family rule continued under sufferance from the dominant
ownership interests. A very similar situation held in Highland Distilleries
where the board consisted of five people having their main business
interests within the firm itself.

It can be concluded that family control was far from dead in the
1970s. A total of 37 of the 62 non-financial companies can realistically
be regarded as having been subject to control by particular families or
individuals, whether on a secure or limited basis. At least a further five
companies had strong family or individual influence, often with
extremely small shareholdings. The remaining 20 companies were
controlled by other companies. The seven wholly-owned companies
were all controlled by other companies, of which two were American
and the rest were English. These corporate controllers were all non-
financial companies and most were independent loci of strategic
control (the National Freight Corporation was a nationalised concern
and Nairn Williamson, an English company with Scottish origins, was
subsequently acquired by Unilever). The subsidiary boards consisted

mainly of internal managers with the parent company having board representation in virtually every case, the exceptions being Tayforth, and Glenfield and Kennedy. The three companies with corporate controllers in positions of exclusive majority control showed a similar pattern. All three showed board representation by their parent companies and one showed apparent representation of minority interests: the Scottish Agricultural Industries board included A.H. Carnwath of Barings and Save and Prosper. In Scottish Automobile, however, the Alexander family minority of interest of 5.38 per cent was not represented on the board.

Only one of the four companies subject to exclusive minority control by other companies was controlled by a non-financial company. Titaghur Jute was controlled by Thomas Duff of India, a director of which sat on the Titaghur board together with Sir John Brown of McLeod Russell. In none of the three companies controlled by financial companies did there seem to be board representation. Inveresk Group was controlled by London and County Securities, a company backed by Eagle Star, Keyser Ullman and National Westminster and which had built up a holding in Inveresk as a prelude to a take-over bid. The offer was withdrawn after considerable opposition from the board and in 1974 London and County ran into secondary banking problems and went into liquidation. Culter Guard was controlled by clients of Arbuthnot Latham, but the main outside interest represented on the board was National and Commercial Banking. The identity of the controllers of Culter Guard is not known, but it is known that Credit Suisse of Geneva held 6.7 per cent in 1977. Of the companies subject to shared minority control by other companies, one was a Finlay company and the other, Brunton's, was controlled by two financial interests neither of which was represented on the board.

The two remaining companies, Howden and Burmah, were controlled through a constellation of interests and showed interestingly different characteristics. The top 18 shareholders in Howden Group comprised four insurance companies, two unit trusts, two pension funds, one investment trust, one person, one public body, and seven bank nominees. Although they collectively held almost half of the shares, there were no obvious coalitions amongst them. The leading interest in the constellation was a nominee of the merchant banking subsidiary of Midland Bank, but this company was not represented on the board. In fact, the board included men such as Sir Norman Elliott and J.D.H. Hume who had been associated with the firm for some time. The chairman of Burmah, J.A. Lumsden, represented the Murray

Johnstone holding and continued a long association between Burmah and the trusts. Similarly, Richard Fleming continued the association between Burmah and Fleming's Bank. None of the other large holders was represented on the board and it is clear that this traditional pattern of control could only continue for as long as the major interests remained in the background − and, as we shall show in a later discussion of Burmah, this form of control is inherently unstable.

The companies subject to family control had a predominantly Scottish character, but Scottish participation was far less marked in those companies controlled by corporate interests. The major example of Scottish control was to be found in the Finlay group, though this was shared with English interests. Just one bank subsidiary and three investment trusts represented Scottish participation in strategic control, though many Scottish participants were to be found amongst the controlling constellations. In a later section we shall examine the extent to which these features of ownership were associated with changes in the personnel of the top directorate. The important issue to investigate here is the significance of the Scottish companies in the Scottish economy. Unfortunately statistics of turnover, assets, capital, etc., are not available for the Scottish company sector, the most comprehensive and accessible data being on manufacturing employment. Nevertheless, some assessment can be made.

During the 1970s just under a third of the Scottish workforce was employed in manufacturing industry and just over a half in the service

Table 4.12: Employment in Top Scottish Companies (1973-4)

Company	No. of Employees
Coats Patons	32,965
House of Fraser	29,713
Scottish and Newcastle	27,544
United Biscuits	26,000
Burmah Oil	19,329
Distillers	18,600
Weir Group	12,856
Wm Baird	10,127
Lindustries	8,912
John Menzies	6,422

Source: Extracted from *Business Scotland*, July, 1974.

sector. The largest categories of manufacturing employment were engineering (particularly mechanical engineering), textiles, and food, drink and tobacco. Table 4.12 shows the ten largest Scottish employers, though it is important to recognise that not all of the employees of these companies would have been Scottish residents. The list includes three companies operating in the food and drink industry, two textile firms, one engineering firm, one company operating in both textiles and engineering (Lindustires), one oil firm, and two retail distributors. Just as many of the employees of these companies would have been English or foreign, so many Scottish residents were employed by branches of English or foreign companies. As is well known, foreign and English firms tended to operate in the most strategic sectors: English companies in oil, metal manufacture and chemicals, and American firms in electrical and instrument engineering, vehicles and mechanical engineering. Employment in American manufacturing companies rose from about 8 per cent in the mid 1960s to about 15 per cent in the mid 1970s. Much of this expansion was due to growth in the dynamic industries where American ownership was concentrated, together with stagnation in the heavy traditional industries. A study carried out for 1973 suggested that employment in Scottish-owned manufacturing firms amounted to just over 40 per cent of the manufacturing workforce, whilst employment in English-owned firms amounted to just under 40 per cent. In addition, it was argued that Scottish firms were predominantly small-scale as compared with the larger English and American firms. It is figures such as these which have led to much debate about Scotland as a 'branch plant' economy.

The 114 large manufacturing plants with more than 1,000 employees in 1974 accounted for 40 per cent of Scotland's total manufacturing employment. These plants were owned by 96 firms, of which 20 were included in our list of top Scottish companies. These 20 companies included two English-owned firms (Nairn Floors and Scottish Agricultural Industries) and two US-owned firms (Uniroyal and Glenfield Kennedy). In total, 48 English-owned firms, 21 North American-owned firms, and one Dutch firm operated large manufacturing plants. The Scottish firms which were not on our list were mainly private companies. Six of the Scottish companies owned more than one of the 114 large plants, and will also have owned smaller plants: Distillers owned four large plants, and Aberdeen Construction, Carron, Coats, United Biscuits and Weir owned two each. We have previously shown all of these companies to be subject to family control or family influence. In fact, all except two of the 16 Scottish companies with large plants were family-controlled firms. English companies with more than one large plant were BP, Guthrie Corporation, Unilever, GEC and ICI, and the foreign companies with more than one plant were Burroughs of the USA and Hiram Walker of Canada. It is clear that the Scottish registered and controlled companies remained an important element in the Scottish economy, though not so important as in earlier periods. It must be noted, however, that a number of major Scottish companies had severed many of their links with Scotland and had transferred their head offices to England — Burmah, Lindustries and United Biscuits had all moved south. Nevertheless, this movement was counterbalanced by the presence of London registered firms with Scottish headquarters: Grampian Holdings, Sidlaw Industries and Scott and Robertson being the most prominent. Any attempt to quantify the significance of the Scottish firms is hampered by a general lack of data and by problems of method, though it can be concluded that the Scottish element in the Scottish economy is far from having disappeared.

At the beginning of this section we discussed some of the restructuring which the industrial companies had experienced since the 1950s, and our analysis of ownership and control has taken this a step further. In order to fill out the details of the various processes which we have described we propose to investigate in greater depth some of the most important aspects of the restructuring of Scottish industrial capital during the 1970s. We look first at the interlinked steel, shipbuilding and shipping industries in order to see how nationalisation, long-term decline and economic crises have transformed companies operating in these sectors. An analysis of Burmah Oil shows how the problems of the shipping industry, in this case oil tankers, led to the virtual collapse and restructuring of an important Scottish company. By contrast, an analysis of the Finlay group shows the resilience of an old Scottish firm and the way in which it has been restructured. Finally, we discuss the two Fraser companies to show the successes and failures of a more recent generation of Scottish businessmen.

The steel and shipbuilding companies had traditionally had a close relationship to one another, particularly since the 1930s. In the mid 1960s, however, this relationship was transformed from connections between private companies to connections between state-controlled concerns. In 1967 the British steel industry was again nationalised, though the nationalisation plan extended only to the 14 largest crude steel companies. The assets of the firms were vested in the British Steel

Corporation which abolished the old company structure and adopted a geographical and functional structure. Within this structure Colvilles became the basis of the General Steel division and Stewarts and Lloyds, which had merged into British Steel and Tube in the early 1960s, became the basis of the Tubes division. The 1960s continued to be bad years for the shipbuilding industry, and in 1965 Fairfield, the Lithgow shipbuilding company, had gone bankrupt and had been rescued by a government-private consortium headed by Sir Iain Stewart. This intervention failed to solve the continuing problems of the shipbuilding industry and in 1967-8 the findings of the Geddes Report were implemented. The lower Clyde yards of Scott and Lithgow were amalgamated into Scott-Lithgow, whilst the upper Clyde yards of Fairfield, Yarrow, John Brown, Alexander Stephen and Charles Connell were amalgamated into Upper Clyde Shipbuilders (UCS). In 1970 the shareholders of UCS, which operated as a holding company for the independent yards, were the government with 48.44 per cent, the five shipbuilding companies with 42.59 per cent, various trades unions with 2.37 per cent and various other interests (including Thomson Scottish Associates, Stenhouse, and the Salvesen family) with the balance. Amongst the private shipbuilders the largest holdings were those of John Brown (20.71 per cent) and Yarrow (12.50 per cent). In 1970 Yarrow bought their yard out of the consortium but retained their participation in the holding company. Meanwhile UCS itself moved towards bankruptcy as a result of the pressure of its creditors, chief amongst which was the British Steel Corporation. As a result of the pressure of a 'work-in' another government rescue of the upper Clyde yards occured in 1972. The Clydebank yard of John Brown was acquired by a US company, Marathon, backed by public funds and was converted to the construction of oil production platforms. The other three yards were formed into Govan Shipbuilders, which was fully-owned by the government. With the return of a Labour government in 1974 the whole shipbuilding industry was nationalised in 1978 and ownership of Govan Shipbuilders, Yarrow and Scott-Lithgow passed to British Shipbuilders. The form of nationalisation, however, was a holding company which was particularly easy to dismantle, and the Conservative election victory of 1979 meant that the future of the Scottish yards of British Shipbuilders remained uncertain.

The only shipping company which remained in the list of top companies in 1973-4 was Lyle Shipping, though Salvesen and Hogarth were important private companies. All the companies proved themselves able to survive the chronic over-capacity problems of shipping in the 1970s. Lyle had been set up by Abram Lyle, who later expanded into sugar refining. In the 1870s two of Lyle's grandsons ran the shipping firm while another two grandsons ran the sugar firm. The shipping interests became increasingly separate from the sugar firm and in the early years of this century Sir Archibald Lyle went into partnership with Peter Macfarlane and James Shearer, most of their ships being built by Russells (later Lithgow). These three families continued to run the firm after its public flotation in 1952, though Iain Stewart joined the board in that year and the Lyle and Macfarlane families have not been represented on the board since the late 1960s. In 1968 the problems of the shipping industry led Lyle to join with Hogarth in forming Scottish Ship Management which had day-to-day control of the two fleets. The board of SSM comprised Herbert Walkinshaw and Tom Shearer from Lyle with John Walkinshaw (Herbert's brother) and Walter Scott from Hogarth. During 1975-6 foreign interests purchased Lyle shares which were later transferred to Hogarth and the Kuwait Investment Office. As a result, Hogarth held 30 per cent of the Lyle shares. The company developed into insurance broking and engineering and has been heavily involved in oil development. Its major foray into oil was the establishment of Seaforth Maritime in 1972. The company was formed by Noble Grossart (Iain Noble joining the Lyle board) with Lyle and Hogarth taking 30 per cent each and companies such as Sidlaw Industries taking the balance of the shares. The relative buoyancy of the Scottish oil industry, however, did not prevent Burmah Oil from experiencing serious difficulties.

The over-capacity problems of the shipping industry had serious repercussions outside the shipping industry itself; the tanker problems of Burmah Oil led to a total restructuring of the company. Burmah had traditionally operated very much like an investment trust owing to its 21.5 per cent holding in BP and its two per cent holding in Shell. During the 1960s and early 1970s, however, the company used these holdings as collateral to finance its development into a diversified and integrated oil company. Having fought off a joint take-over from BP and Shell in 1962 and having had its Burmese assets nationalised the following year, Burmah expanded into chemicals, industrial products and engineering. Successful bids for Castrol in 1966 and Rawlplug in 1968 were followed by an abortive bid for Laporte Industries, also in 1968, and the successful take-over of Halfords in 1970. In 1972, Burmah acquired Quinton Hazell, a major vehicle component firm, and the company reached its peak in 1973 with its take-over of the US company Signal Oil and Gas, having failed to pull off a merger with

Continental Oil in 1971. During 1972 and 1973 the board suggested
that the BP and Shell holdings might be sold off in order to finance
further acquisitions, but this was opposed by a group of shareholders
led by Dennis Blake who had become the third largest individual shareholder in Burmah following the acquisition of Hazell. However, the
acquisition of Signal brought this dispute to a close since the holdings
had once more been used as collateral for a loan. But all was not going
well for Burmah. Serious financial over-stretching combined with
disastrous losses in the oil tanker subsidiary led to financial collapse
at the end of 1974. The government, through the Bank of England,
guaranteed Burmah's dollar borrowings and took the BP and Shell
holdings as security. Peat, Marwick and Mitchell the accountants were
called in to oversee Burmah's affairs, the group managing director and
the chief of Burmah Oil Tankers resigned, and James Lumsden the
non-executive chairman became acting managing director. Burmah's
problem was that the security of the loans it had raised in the past
depended upon the BP and Shell holdings maintaining their value, and
this could not happen when stock market prices were falling. Burmah
was, further, supposed to earn sufficient profit to cover its interest
payments by up to one and a half times and profits were not sufficient
for this. Gradually some of Burmah's assets were sold off to try to
rationalise its position and the purchase of the BP holding by the
government at a 'knock-down' price led to the establishment of the
Burmah Institutional Shareholders Committee, representing a third of
the votes and concerned with maintaining the value of the institutional
holdings. Dissatisfaction with the terms of the sale led also to the
creation of a more radical group of individual shareholders, the Burmah
Shareholders Action Group. Early in 1975 Alistair Down, formerly a
managing director of BP, was appointed chief executive of Burmah,
James Lumsden remaining as deputy chairman until 1976. The final
humiliation for Burmah's aspirations was perhaps the sale, in mid 1975,
of the former Signal oil and gas interests to Reynolds Industries of the
USA. Following Down's appointment a number of the non-executive
directors resigned, including R.E. Fleming, the Earl of Inchcape, and
L.M.H. Gow. By 1977 the restructuring of Burmah was more or less
complete with the newly appointed non-executive directors (two of
whom were directors of Tarmac and one a director from the Inchcape
Group) formed into an audit committee.

We have already discussed the return of James Finlay to merchant
banking and in the following chapter we shall discuss its participation
in the oil industry. The years between 1973 and 1977 saw important

transformations in the whole structure of the group in relation to outside interests. This restructuring has affected both the parent company and its subsidiaries. In the early 1970s the Slater Walker group acquired a holding of 22.65 per cent of Finlay, with Sir John Muir and his fellow directors holding an additional 4.28 per cent. However, the problems faced by Slater Walker during the secondary banking crisis led to its holding being sold to John Swire and Company. By 1977 the Swire holding had been increased to 29.9 per cent and British and Commonwealth Shipping (based around Clan Line with which Finlay had once been associated) had acquired 10.6 per cent. Running parallel with these changes in the ownership of Finlay were other changes in the ownership of its subsidiary and associate companies. Ownership of these companies had for some time been shared with McLeod Russell (36 per cent owned by Assam Trading) though the boards were filled exclusively with men from the Finlay group. In the early 1970s Finlay owned 36 per cent of Amalgamated Tea Estates and 30 per cent of Consolidated Tea; McLeod Russell held 14 per cent of Amalgamated and 13 per cent of Consolidated. The other two companies were owned in a more complex way. Anglo-American Direct Tea was owned as to 29 per cent by Consolidated, 29 per cent by Amalgamated and 21 per cent by Kanan Devan Hills Produce. The latter was owned 18 per cent by Finlay, 32 per cent by Amalgamated and 31 per cent by Consolidated. Over the course of the 1970s Finlay attempted to buy out the McLeod Russell holdings and to this end three of the old companies became subsidiaries of new holding companies, though the old pattern of ownership remained: in 1970 West Nile Holdings was set up as a holding company for Anglo-American, and in 1973 Teith Holdings was set up to hold Amalgamated, and Cessnock Holdings to hold Kanan Devan. Eventually it was agreed to reorganise the boards of Teith and Consolidated to represent the two parent groups equally, but it was not until 1977 that agreement was reached between Finlay and McLeod Russell that each would acquire two of the group companies as wholly-owned subsidiaries. McLeod Russell purchased Teith and West Nile, Finlay acquired Cessnock and Consolidated. In this way the Finlay group ended the 1970s as a slimmed-down and more streamlined group with interests in banking, insurance and oil to counterbalance the traditionally-strong tea interests.

The final companies that we wish to discuss here are the two Fraser companies House of Fraser and SUITS. In 1948 Hugh Fraser formed SUITS as a holding company for his various interests, but it was not until 1960 that the company was floated, with its main attraction as a

15 per cent holding in House of Fraser. A major acquisition was made in 1964 when Fraser (who had been made a baronet in 1961 and a baron in 1964 for his political services) bought George Outram, the proprietors of the Glasgow Herald. Outram had originally invited Fraser onto the board to help prevent a possible take over by the Thomson Organisation. Fraser himself owned ten per cent of the Outram shares and was the largest holder. When the Thomson bid was made Fraser resigned his directorship, made a counter bid, and won control of the company. Lord Fraser died in 1966 and control of the two companies passed to his son, who renounced the peerage and became Sir Hugh Fraser. In the early 1970s Fraser interests owned 47.74 per cent of SUITS, which in its turn held 25.03 per cent of House of Fraser. During 1974 much of the SUITS holding in House of Fraser was sold to the US department store Carter Hawley Hale. Fraser's personal stake in the company at this time stood at 8.53 per cent. By 1976 CHH held 20.54 per cent and Sir Hugh Fraser held 10.82 per cent. However, the CHH holding was sold to Lonrho during 1977 and the other major holdings were SUITS with 10.29 per cent and the Fraser family trust with 9.81 per cent. In that same year Sir Hugh Fraser sold a two per cent stake in SUITS to Lonrho which managed to build its total holding up to 29 per cent, at which time Fraser resigned as chairman in favour of Tiny Rowland the head of Lonrho. Subsequently Lonrho made an offer for the whole of the SUITS capital which was supported by Sir Hugh Fraser and opposed by the non-executive directors, prominent amongst whom was Henry Cowan of Maclay, Murray and Spens who had replaced Angus Grossart on the company board. In late 1978 Fraser changed his mind about the offer and joined the rest of his board in opposition, whilst Lonrho had made an offer for House of Fraser and again faced board opposition. In April 1979 Sir Hugh Fraser and his assistant managing director once again supported the Lonrho bid for SUITS, though the opposition from the non-executive directors was supported by the company's merchant bankers Charterhouse Japhet. The dispute became increasingly acrimonious when it was announced that the Fraser trust holdings of nine per cent had been pledged to Lonrho and that Charterhouse Japhet had mobilised eight of the institutional shareholders to oppose the bid. At this time the institutions as a whole held 26 per cent of SUITS shares and Lonrho's 29 per cent holding had been supplemented by the Fraser trust holdings and a further eight per cent 'in friendly hands'. By early May 1979 the battle was over and Lonrho had obtained more than 50 per cent of the SUITS shares.

The Structure of the Business Network

Eighty-five of the 120 companies were interlocked with one another, only two of the isolated companies having interlocks with smaller Scottish companies (Carron, Scottish Metropolitan Property). A total of 280 lines between companies were generated by the 101 multiple directors listed in Table 4.B. It can be seen from Table 4.13 that the number of lines had fallen from its level for 1955-6, as had the number of plural lines. Although a slightly higher proportion of the lines had a value of three or more, the proportion with five or more fell. The density of the network fell to 3.99 per cent and the connectivity fell to 50.85 per cent, both facts reflecting the fall in the proportion of companies which were interlocked. The network comprised just one component of 85 companies, which indicated the continued decrease in the amount of clustering in the network.

Table 4.13: Plural and Single Company Linkages (1973-4)

Value of Line	No. of Lines
1	235
2	32
3	3
4	4
5	1
6	2
7	
8	2
9	1
TOTAL	280

Table 4.14 shows that companies had fewer connections than during the 1950s. The modal number of connections for each interlocked company was four, though a substantial number had just two. The number of companies with extremely high centrality scores had fallen considerably and Table 4.15 shows the three banks way ahead of the other central companies. In 1955-6 the 14 most central companies included no industrials, whereas the 15 most central companies in 1973-4 included two industrials. Also apparent from Table 4.15 is the

Table 4.14: Distribution of Company Connections (1973-4)

No. of Companies Connected to	No. of Companies	No. of Connections
0	35	0
1	9	9
2	10	20
3	5	15
4	14	56
5	4	20
6	8	48
7	8	56
8	5	40
9	4	36
10	1	10
11	2	22
12	3	36
13	3	39
14	3	42
15	3	45
22	3	66
TOTALS	120	560

predominance of the Murray Johnstone group of investment trusts which derived their high centrality scores from their links to one another and to two of the banks. In fact, the two industrials seem to owe their high centrality scores to their links with the Murray Johnstone group. As in the 1950s the links of industrial companies to the business network were mainly through direct connections to financial companies, and within the core of central financial companies the three operating banks had emerged into a clear leading position.

In the following section we shall give a full analysis of the primary business interests of the multiple directors but we shall preview some of that information here in order to clarify the role of the banks and other companies in the business system. Directors with their primary interests in one of the four banking companies tended to represent their banks on the boards of other financial companies. Only National and Commercial was represented on industrial boards: the holding company was represented on United Biscuits and Culter Guard, and its Royal Bank

Table 4.15: Most Central Companies (1973-4)

Company	No. of Connections
Bank of Scotland	22
Clydesdale Bank	22
Royal Bank	22
Burmah	15
Scottish Provident	15
Scottish Western	15
Caledonian Trust	14
Pentland Investment	14
Second Great Northern	14
Glendevon	13
Scottish Widows Fund	13
Weir Group	13
Clydesdale Investment	12
Glenmurray	12
Scottish Eastern	12

subsidiary was also represented on Culter Guard. The banks were represented on five insurance companies and seven investment trusts. Similarly, people with their primary interests in an insurance company represented their companies on the boards of three investment trusts. A great many of the links between the financial and industrial sectors were due to the representation of investment trusts on industrial boards. However, also of importance was the representation of industrial interests on financial boards. The outside directors in the National and Commercial group with two or more Scottish directorships were evenly divided between industrial and financial interests: Distillers, Salvesen and Hall-Thermotank were represented on the two boards as were three legal firms involved in investment management. Two industrial interests were represented on the Bank of Scotland board (Scottish and Newcastle, Robertson Ship Management) together with four investment managers, two of whom were partners in Maclay, Murray and Spens. The Clydesdale board showed three industrial representations (Coats, Yarrow and Sidlaw) amongst the multiple directors on its board, though the board also included a retired industrialist and the family interests of Alexander and Tennant. The industrial company which was represented on the largest number of other boards was undoubtedly

Scottish and Newcastle Breweries which was represented on the boards of the Bank of Scotland, Scottish Widows and seven investment trusts. The typical pattern was for industrials to be represented on the investment trust boards, with less representation on bank and insurance boards.

We can describe the main pattern of linkages as follows. Industrial and investment boards exchanged members in roughly equal numbers, as did investment and insurance boards. Insurance boards showed minority representation from industrials and banks in addition to their core of investment trust directors. Bank boards were recruited, apart from representatives of the London holding companies, from investment trusts and industrial boards. There were, of course, exceptions to this pattern but the description fits the majority of cases. The structure of relations between industrial and financial companies cannot be described simply in terms of the presence of bankers on industrial boards, or of industrialists on bank boards. Equally, if not more important, was the presence of investment trust directors on both bank and industrial boards as 'brokers' between the two.

Table 4.16: Distribution of Plural Linkages (1973-4)

No. of Plural Lines per Company	No. of Companies
0	36
1	26
2	11
3	9
4	1
5	1
6	1
TOTAL	85

Table 4.16 shows that 36 of the interlocked companies were involved in the network of plural lines and, compared with 1955-6, companies were far more likely to have just one plural connection. The plural network was far more fragmented than earlier years, comprising one component of 12 companies, one of seven, one of five, one of four, one of three and nine pairs. Only two industrials were members of the network: Scotcros had a double interlock with Investors' Mortgage, and

Weir Group had double interlocks with two of the Murray Johnstone trusts. These data suggest that the clustering of the business network was far less than previously. Only four relatively tight 'cliques' could be identified: the Finlay group, the Ivory and Sime trusts, the Murray Johnstone trusts together with Weir, and the Alliance, Second Alliance and Scottish Mortgage grouping. The banks were important members of the plural network with the National and Commercial Group being allied to the Alliance-Baillie Gifford cluster, and the Bank of Scotland allied to Murray Johnstone and Scottish Provident.

Figure 4.4 depicts the overall structure of the business network and shows that certain features of a regional pattern persisted. Within the network two of the major insurance companies functioned as bridges between the various sectors of the network. Standard Life connected with all three banking groups and with British Investment Trust; Scottish Widows connected with two of the banks, the Murray Johnstone trusts, Scottish and Newcastle Breweries and Edinburgh Investment. The Clydesdale Bank was closely linked with some Glasgow interests as well as having numerous links with North of Scotland industrial interests, and it had connections with some Edinburgh financial interests which had northern or eastern industrial links. The National and Commercial Group retained its Edinburgh character as well as its particular links with Dundee firms but also had important links to the Glasgow-based Finlay group and the companies associated with General Accident and Scottish United Investors. As in previous years the Bank of Scotland had both Edinburgh and Glasgow linkages. Its major Edinburgh links were through the Ivory and Sime trusts and the insurance companies, whilst the Glasgow links were through the Murray Johnstone group and its allied industrial and shipping companies. A notable feature of the network is that the non-banking spheres of influence were less distinct and integrated than earlier. The Murray Johnstone sphere, the Balfour-Falconer sphere and the Fraser-Grossart sphere did not match the scale and power of the Tennant empire or even the Lithgow-Colville group.

The major uninterlocked companies were tied directly to the American and English networks, but external interests were also allied to the main business network itself. The main points of entry for English interests were the Scottish banks, each of which had substantial ownership and director links with English clearing banks.

The area around the National and Commercial Bank was the point of entry not only for Lloyds Bank but also for Norwich Union and Schroders which linked with Scottish and Newcastle, General Accident,

Figure 4.4: The Structure of the Business Network (1973-4)

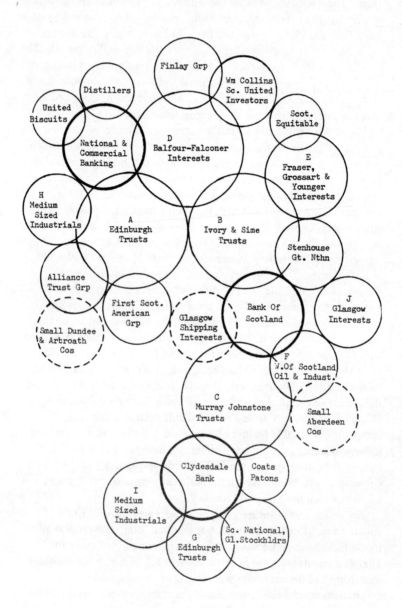

Key to Figure 4.4

A: Edinburgh Trusts

British Investment
Sc. Mortgage & Trust
Edinburgh Investment
Investors' Mortgage
Stewart Fund Managers

B: Ivory & Sime Trusts

Br. Assets
Atlantic Assets
Sec. British Assets
Nth Sea Assets
Viking Resources

C: Murray Johnstone Trusts

Sc. Western Inv.
Clydesdale Investment
Sec. Great Northern
Sc. Amicable Life

D: Balfour-Falconer Interests

Sc. & Newcastle Breweries
Sc. Eastern Investment
General Accident
Sc. Life Assurance
Securities Trust

E: Fraser, Grossart & Younger Interests

Sc. & Universal Investments
House of Fraser
Noble Grossart
Scottish Investment

Note: This figure includes some smaller and unquoted Scottish companies. The Scottish Widows and Standard Life 'bridges' are not shown.

F: West of Scotland Oil & Industrials

Weir Group
Burmah Oil
Wm Baird
Hugh Baird
Lindustries

G: Edinburgh Trusts

American Trust
Crescent Japan
East of Scotland Group

H: Industrials

Anderson Mavor
Fife Forge
Titaghur Jute
Waverley Cameron
Bertrams
Brownlee
Scotcros

I: Industrials

Sc. Automobile
Nairn Floors
Culter Guard Bridge
W. Alexander Group
Richards
J. Smart
Glenlivet
Ellis & McHardy
Sc. Television
Grampian Television
Sc. Northern Investment

J: Glasgow Interests

Sc. Mutual Assurance
Melville, Dundas & Whitson
Ailsa Investment
Alva Investment

Scottish Life and a number of Edinburgh trusts. In the English network itself Lloyds was linked with the Commercial Union and Guardian Royal Exchange. The latter linked Lloyds with Midland Bank, as did Hill Samuel, Rothschilds and Eagle Star. Hill Samuel and Morgan Grenfell had links with companies in the National and Commercial sphere of influence. The Midland Bank had a major link to the Clydesdale Bank, its Scottish subsidiary, which was also connected with Eagle Star. Phoenix Assurance, which linked Barclays, National Westminster and Lloyds, had links to the Clydesdale, Scottish Provident and the Glasgow industrials. Companies around the Bank of Scotland were predominantly linked to Barclays and to Robert Fleming, with Fleming linking Barclays and National Westminster. Royal Insurance was linked with these same two banks and had Scottish links to United Biscuits and the Finlay group. Some of these English links undoubtedly involved the direct or indirect representation of external interests and a certain number derived from Scottish directors sitting on English boards. However, the main pattern of linkages must be seen as a consequence of the position of the Scottish business system within an overall British network. Without a full analysis of British companies it is impossible to describe these relations fully, but it seems clear that the diffuse nature of interlocking in both England and Scotland ensures that there were no simple links between English and Scottish groupings. The various spheres of influence overlapped and intersected with one another to produce the structure depicted in Figure 4.4.

The People of Business

Table 4.17 shows that 101 multiple directors held a total of 294 directorships: 14 per cent of the directors held 32 per cent of the directorships. Of those who had been multiple directors in 1955-6, 29 were to be found on the list for 1973-4 (Table 4.B). There was in addition, direct father to son continuity for the Airlie, Craig, Fraser, Spens and Stephen directorships. Although the multiple directors were exclusively male, the Scottish directorate as a whole included two women: Helen Bett sat on Bett Brothers and Miss E.G. Robertson sat on Highland Distilleries. Women had certainly been directors of top companies before, though none had ever appeared in our lists.

Table 4.18 shows that 19 of the multiple directors (19 per cent) had titles. The gradual disappearance of the higher titles continued with only one man having a title higher than that of baron. This decline was accompanied by a fall in the number of barons to two. By contrast, the resilient baronetcy increased its representation to become the single

Table 4.17: Distribution of Directorships (1973-4)

No. of Directorships per Person	No. of People	No. of Directorships
1	618	618
2	49	98
3	28	84
4	16	64
5	5	25
6	2	12
11	1	11
TOTALS	719	912

Table 4.18: Multiple Directors and Their Titles (1973-4)

No. of Directorships per Person	No. of People				
	Knights	Baronets	Barons	Earls	Totals
2	2	6		1	9
3	3		2		5
4	1	2			3
5		1			1
6		1			1
TOTALS	6	10	2	1	19

largest category. The number of knights fell markedly to six, though all the titled directors with four or more directorships were either knights or baronets. The majority of the titles were hereditary and many were of long pedigree. Indeed, even the life peerage had yet to appear amongst the Scottish directorate.

The primary business interests of the multiple directors show an interesting pattern (Table 4.19). The second largest category comprised the lawyers and accountants involved in fund management, and if the men who were fully involved in investment management are added to the total the group of fund managers exceeded in size the total number of Scottish industrialists. It is clear that the majority of the multiple directors had their primary interest in Scotland: only ten had primary

Table 4.19: Primary Business Interests (1973-4)

Primary Interest		No. of Directors
Bankers		15
Scottish banks	10	
English merchant banks	5	
Industrialists		38
Scottish industrials	36	
English industrials	2	
Professionals		26
Lawyers	16	
Accountants	10	
Insurance (Scottish)		4
Investment (Scottish)		12
Other		6
TOTALS		101

Note: The category of 'professionals' includes both current and retired partners and all 26 were Scottish. The 'other' category includes three retired English industrialists, one Scottish stockbroker, and two Scottish directors of family investment interests. Sidlaw Industries is counted as a Scottish industrial company in this table.

interests in England and most of these men were Scotsmen or were directors of companies with strong Scottish linkages. Eight men had five or more directorships in the top Scottish companies: James Lumsden (11), George Chiene (6), Sir Robert Erskine-Hill (6), and five men with five directorships each (W.D. Coats, J.C.R. Inglis, J.R. Johnstone, Sir John Muir and A.L. McClure). These eight men comprised two Scottish industrialists and six fund managers. Table 4.20 gives the most central directors — those who met the most other directors. There were 11 men who met 15 or more multiple directors and nearly all owed their positions to their bank directorships. Three men were directors of the Bank of Scotland, two of the Clydesdale, and three of the Royal Bank. Those who sat on the two Edinburgh banks sat also on one or other of the major insurance companies. The only central director not to have a bank directorship, E.H.M. Clutterbuck, sat on Scottish and Newcastle and Scottish Widows.

We have already shown that kinship was an important feature of company control and we wish here to show its continuing importance for inter-corporate linkages, both in the 1970s and over time.

Table 4.20: Central Directors in the Network (1973-4)

Director	Number of Directors Met
J.A. Lumsden	21
G.T. Chiene	20
Sir A.C. Blair	18
L.M.H. Gow	18
J.C.R. Inglis	17
Sir T.G. Waterlow	17
R.D. Fairbairn	16
E.H.M. Clutterbuck	15
J.G.S. Gammell	15
A.L. McClure	15
P.J. Oliphant	15

Figure 4.5 shows the family tree of the Fleming family which includes directors from top Scottish companies in all the periods studied. Robert Fleming, who founded many of the investment trusts and was a director of the British Investment Trust until his death, had two grandsons among the Scottish directorate: M.V. Fleming was a director of many Brown, Fleming and Murray trusts in the 1930s and R.E. Fleming was a director of Burmah Oil and the Northern American trusts in the 1970s. During the 1970s the Scottish directorate also included Roger Fleming who was a grandson of Robert Fleming's brother and sat on various North of Scotland boards. The remarkable continuity of the Fleming interests is also exhibited in the continuing presence of Fleming bank directors such as W.K. Whigham and H.A. Jamieson (directors of British Investment in the 1930s), D.J. Robarts (British Investment in the 1950s), and most recently Joe Burnett-Stuart (British Investment 1973-4), H.S. Spens (Northern American trusts 1973-4), and G.L.A. Jamieson (Scottish Mortgage and Trust 1973-4).

Another family with a long business history is the Ivory family. Eric Ivory was a director of the Ivory and Sime trusts in 1973-4 and his nephew, James Gammell, was the chairman of Ivory and Sime. Gammell and Eric Ivory had managed the trusts during the 1950s when Basil Ivory, Eric's brother, had been a director. James Ivory, father of Basil and Eric, had been a director of the group trusts and Standard Life in the 1930s and had been a trust manager and a director of Standard Life and various trusts since at least 1904-5. James's father, Holmes Ivory, had married a

Figure 4.5: The Fleming Family

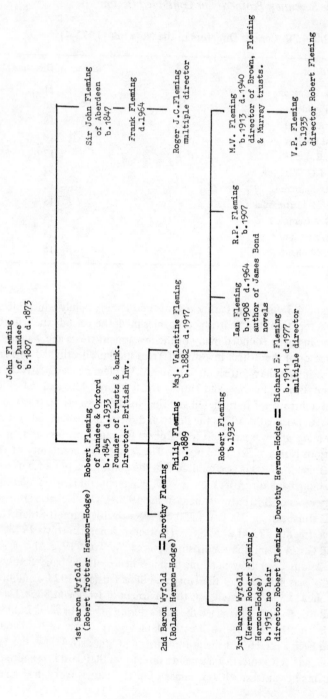

Figure 4.6: The Family of H.J. Younger

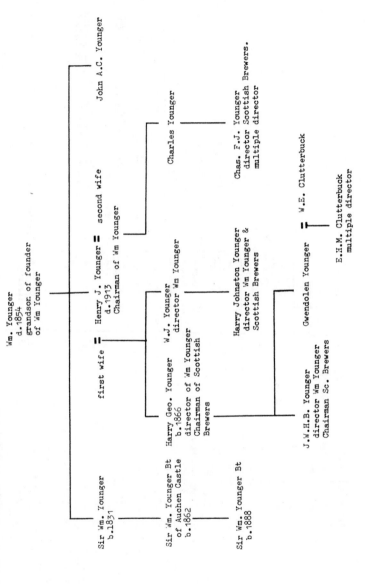

Figure 4.7: Intermarriage in Scottish Industry and Finance — Section A: The Younger and Balfour Families

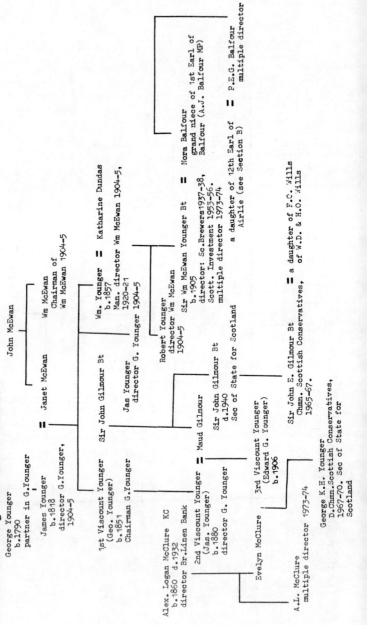

**Figure 4.7: Intermarriage in Scottish Industry and Finance —
Section B: The Tennant and Ogilvy Families**

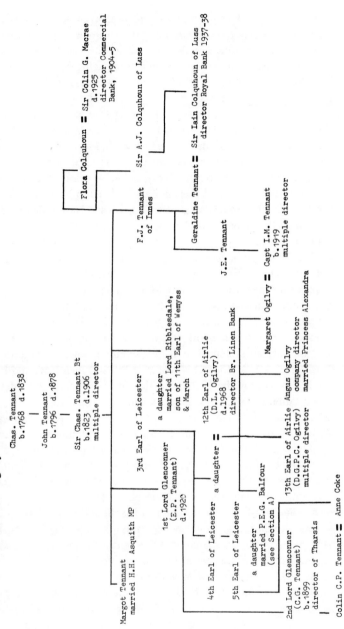

daughter of J. Dick Peddie (a founding director of Scottish American Investment) and had set up a number of investment trusts during the 1880s. From the same founding generation we have already mentioned the continued representation of families such as Inglis, Guild and Pitman. The descendants of many of the nineteenth-century businessmen were still to be found in the Scottish directorate of the 1970s.

Descendants of industrial entrepreneurs were also directors of top Scottish companies in 1973-4. In particular, the Younger families were prominent members of the business network. Figure 4.7 shows the family of H.J. Younger who ran the brewing firm of Wm Younger which became the core part of Scottish and Newcastle Breweries. In 1973-4 three members of this family, C.F.J. Younger, D.A.H. Younger and E.H.M. Clutterbuck, sat on the Scottish and Newcastle board. Because of the merger with Wm McEwan in 1931 the other Younger family acquired an interest in the merged company, Sir William McEwan Younger being managing director of the company for some time and Peter Balfour being chairman in 1973-4. Sir William had been a prominent member of the Scottish Conservative Party along with many of his kinsmen: both Sir John Gilmour and George Younger held the post of Secretary of State for Scotland. The Youngers were part of an extensive kinship network which bridged a number of sectors of the Scottish business system. The third Viscount Younger had married a daughter of A.L. McClure, a director of British Linen Bank and Edinburgh Assurance in the 1920s, and McClure's son – also A.L. McClure – was a director of Clydesdale Bank and American Trust in 1973-4. Peter Balfour married a daughter of the 12th Earl of Airlie and was thereby related to the Tennant family which stretched back to the 'empire' of Sir Charles Tennant in 1904-5 and was represented in 1973-4 by Lord Glenconner's directorship of Tharsis and Iain Tennant's directorship of the Clydesdale Bank and a number of North of Scotland companies. Iain Tennant had become chairman of Glenlivet and Glen Grant Distilleries (later Glenlivet Distilleries) in 1964 as successor to Sir Henry Houldsworth whose family firm, Coltness Iron, had formerly been associated with the Tennant empire. This kinship network came full circle with the directorship of the 13th Earl of Airlie on Scottish and Newcastle Breweries.

Family dynasties were still an important feature of the business network in the 1970s, and the links of kinship – only a few of which have been discussed here – were one of the bonds linking Scottish companies together into an extensive system. Numerous other examples of kinship links could be cited: for example, A.M.M. Stephen was brother-in-law to John F. Denholm, P.J. Oliphant was a grandson of Abram Lyle, Sir Alistair Blair was the son of Sir William Blair, Sir William Walker was a grandson of Sir Michael Nairn, and many other cases have been given throughout this chapter. The Scottish business system must be seen as the outcome of overlapping shareholdings, interlocking directorships, and the bonds of kinship.

Conclusion

In this chapter we have tried to show the structure of Scottish capital in the context of the continued 'anglicisation' and 'commercialisation' of the Scottish economy. The position of Scotland within the world economy set certain constraints on Scottish development and the prospects of oil wealth seemed, for a time, to offer an escape route. Scottish companies, however, did experience considerable growth and diversification during the 1960s and early 1970s, and the financial sector proved particularly dynamic. The whole of the post-war period was marked by the growth of 'institutional' shareholdings, yet many Scottish companies grew under the control of their traditional controlling interests. Family control remained a potent element in Scottish capital. The economy itself became more bank-centred and more integrated with the English economy, but the controlling directorate of the major companies was drawn from a long line of prominent business families.

Table 4A: Scotland's Top Companies (1973-4)

Section A: Non-Financial Companies

Rank	Company	Industry	Capital (£000)	Rank in Times 1000 British	Scottish	Multiple Directors
1	Distillers	Whisky distillers	181,585	38	(2)	Sir A. McDonald (C)
2	Burmah Oil	Oil production	161,685	25	(1)	J.A. Lumsden (C), R.E. Fleming, L.M.H. Gow
3	Coats Patons (formerly J. & P. Coats)	Thread & textile	67,796	42	(3)	W.D. Coats
4	Scottish & Newcastle Breweries (formerly Scottish Brewers)	Brewers	54,458	100	(5)	P.E.G. Balfour (C, JMD), E.H.M. Clutterbuck (JMD), Earl of Airlie, Sir H. Hamilton-Dalrymple, T.S. Lewis, C.F.J. Younger
5	House of Fraser	Retail stores	28,018	92	(4)	Sir H. Fraser
6	United Biscuits (Holdings)	Biscuits & cakes	18,807	126	(6)	I.W. Macdonald
7	Wm Baird	Textiles & engineering	11,251	302	(10)	J.A. Lumsden, J.P. Van den Bergh
8	Metal Industries	Electrical engineering	10,277	–	–	–
9	Inveresk Group	Paper & packaging	9,037	542	(21)	–
10	Scottish Agricultural Industries	Fertilisers, etc.	8,450	–	–	–
11	Stenhouse Holdings	Insurance broking, engineering	7,684	145	(7)	J.G. Stenhouse (VC)
12	Uniroyal (formerly North British Rubber)	Tyres & rubber goods	7,554	415	(18)	–
13	Scottish & Universal Investments	Holding company	6,942	543	(22)	Sir H. Fraser (C, MD), A.M.M. Grossart

Table 4A: Section A—cont.

Rank	Company	Industry	Capital (£000)	Rank in Times 1000 British	Scottish	Multiple Directors
14	Lindustries (formerly Linen Thread)	Engineering, polymers and textiles	6,747	310	(11)	J.P. Van den Bergh (VC)
15	Anderson Mavor	Electrical & mining engineering	5,927	625	(25)	B.D. Misselbrook (C)
16	Arthur Bell & Sons	Whisky distillers	5,650	343	(13)	—
17	Weir Group (fomerly G. & J. Weir)	Engineering	4,504	227	(8)	W.K.J. Weir (C), W.D. Coats, J.A. Lumsden
18	Low & Bonar Group	Textiles, packaging, etc.	4,410	338	(12)	Sir H.V. Bonar (C), I.C. Low (DC)
19	Jas Finlay	Traders & merchant bankers	3,500	767	(31)	Sir J. Muir (C), Sir C. Campbell (DC), R.J. Clough, N.S. Coldwell
20	Wm Collins & Sons (Holdings)	Publishers	3,436	604	(23)	D.W. Nickson (MD)
21	A. Goldberg & Sons	Retail stores	3,139	796	(32)	—
22	Tharsis Sulpher & Copper	Copper mining	3,000	—	—	—
23	John Menzies (Holdings)	Retail stores	2,968	229	(9)	J.M. Menzies (C)
24	Alexandra Building Services	Non-trading	2,945	—	—	—
25	Robertson Foods	Jams & preserves	2,933	438	(19)	—
26	Teacher (Distillers)	Whisky distillers	2,890	385	(17)	—

Table 4A: Section A—cont.

Rank	Company	Industry	Capital (£000)	Rank in Times 1000 British	Scottish	Multiple Directors
27	Howden Group (formerly Jas Howden)	Air & gas handling plant	2,859	349	(15)	T.N. Risk
28	Aberdeen Construction Group	Construction	2,758	370	(16)	—
29	Nairn Floors	Floorcoverings	2,662	—	—	—
30	Consolidated Tea & Lands	Tea merchants	2,600	—	—	Sir J. Muir (C), Sir C. Campbell (DC), C.C.C. Bell, R.J. Clough, N.S. Coldwell, H. Ferguson, W.W. Mayne, G.R. Muir
31	Highland Distilleries	Whisky distillers	2,559	—	—	—
32	Glenfield & Kennedy Holdings	Engineering	2,401	—	—	—
33	Brown & Tawse	Steel stockholders	2,320	739	(29)	—
34	United Wire Group	Steel wire man.	2,097	—	—	—
35	Tayforth	Freight carriers	2,053	—	—	—
36	Reo Stakis Organisation	Restaurants & hotels	2,026	871	(35)	—
37	Lyle Shipping	Shipping	2,006	—	—	J.P. Agnew (C), Sir I.M. Stewart
38=	Blackwood, Morton & Sons	Carpet yarn spinners	2,000	634	(26)	—
38=	Scottish Automobile	Motor distributors	2,000	346	(14)	—
39	Titaghur Jute Factory	Jute spinners	1,893	701	(27)	W.L. Milligan
41	Culter Guard Bridge Holdings	Paper makers	1,867	—	—	Sir D.H. Cameron (C), J.O. Blair-Cunynghame, R.J.C. Fleming

Table 4A: Section A—cont.

Rank	Company	Industry	Capital (£000)	Rank in Times 1000 British	Rank in Times 1000 Scottish	Multiple Directors
42	Scotcros	Food distributors, packaging	1,863	837	(33)	W.R. Alexander (C), J. Chiene
43	Glenlivet Distillers	Whisky distillers	1,845	–	–	I.M. Tennant (C)
44 =	MacDonald Martin	Whisky distillers	1,750	–	–	J. Burnett-Stuart
44 =	Scottish Homes Investment	Construction	1,750	–	–	J.A.R. Falconer (DC)
46	Jas Scott Engineering Group	Electrical engineering	1,613	469	(20)	–
47	Giddings & Lewis-Fraser	Industrial plant man.	1,517	–	–	–
48	Bett Brothers	Construction	1,500	868	(34)	W.F. Robertson
49	M.E. Theatres (formerly Moss Empire)	Theatre management	1,495	–	–	–
50	Hewden-Stuart Plant	Construction plant hirers	1,446	613	(24)	–
51	Carron Co. (Holdings)	Metal products	1,400	751	(30)	–
52	Wm Low	Retail stores	1,388	730	(28)	G.W. Dunn
53	Bremner	Warehousemen	1,380	–	–	–
54	Teith Holdings (holding company for Amalgamated Tea Estates)	Tea merchants	1,377	–	–	Sir J. Muir (C), Sir C. Campbell (DC), C.C.C. Bell, A.R.A.G. Cameron, R.J. Clough, N.S. Coldwell, H. Ferguson, W.W. Mayne, G.R. Muir

Table 4A: Section A—cont.

Rank	Company	Industry	Capital (£000)	Rank in Times 1000 British	Scottish	Multiple Directors
55=	Cessnock Holdings (holding company for Kanan Devan Hills)	Tea merchants	1,300	–	–	Sir J. Muir (C), Sir C. Campbell (DC), C.C.C. Bell, A.R.A.G. Cameron, R.J. Clough, N.S. Coldwell, H. Ferguson, W.W. Mayne, G.R. Muir
55=	Stoddard Holdings (formerly A.F. Stoddard)	Carpet man.	1,300	883	(36)	–
57	Richards	Synthetic yarn	1,286	–	–	R.J.C. Fleming
58	Brownlee	Sawmills	1,281	–	–	J.F. Carnegie, J. Chiene
59	North British Steel Group	Metal founders	1,273	–	–	G.M. Menzies, Sir G.C. Harvie-Watt
60=	Ayrshire Metal Products	Metal products	1,250	–	–	–
60=	Bruntons (Musselburgh)	Steel wire & ropes	1,250	–	–	–
60=	Coltness Group (formerly Coltness Iron)	Holding company	1,250	–	–	–

Table 4A—cont.

Section B: Banking Companies

Rank	Company	Deposits (£000)	Multiple Directors
–	National & Commercial Banking Group	*	J.O. Blair-Cunynghame (C), I.W. Macdonald (DC), Sir A.F. McDonald, Sir T.G. Waterlow
1	Royal Bank of Scotland	889,392	J.O. Blair-Cunynghame (C), Sir T.G. Waterlow (DC), D.H. Cameron (VC), G.T. Chiene (VC), Sir I.M. Stewart, L.M.H. Gow, J.C.R. Inglis, I.W. Macdonald, P.J. Oliphant
2	Bank of Scotland	767,201	Lord Clydesmuir (G), T.R. Craig (DG), Lord Balfour of Burleigh, Sir A. Blair, J.G.S. Gammell, J.A. Lumsden, T.N. Risk, W.F. Robertson, C.F. Younger
3	Clydesdale Bank	516,143	A.L. McClure (DC), R.D. Fairbairn (VC), W.R. Alexander, W.D. Coats, J.S.R. Cruikshank, Sir G. Harvie-Watt, I.M. Tennant, Sir W.G.N. Walker, Sir E. Yarrow

* The total deposits of the National & Commercial Banking Group were £2,035,156,000, comprising the deposits of the Royal Bank together with those of the English based Williams & Glyns Bank.

Table 4A—cont.

Section C: Insurance Companies

Rank	Company	Funds (£000)	Multiple Directors
1	Standard Life Assurance	1,056,626	T.N. Risk (C), J.G.S. Gammell, G.P.S. Macpherson, B.D. Misselbrook, I.R. Pitman, Sir T.G. Waterlow, Sir E. Yarrow
2	General Accident, Fire & Life Assurance	508,662	I.H.S. Black (C), Earl of Airlie, G.M. Menzies, D.W. Nickson, G.R. Simpson
3	Scottish Widows Fund & Life Assurance	506,142	L.M.H. Gow (C), J.L. Anderson, Sir A.C. Blair, Sir D.H. Cameron, E.H.M. Clutterbuck, A.I. Mackenzie, A.M.M. Stephen
4	Scottish Amicable Life Assurance	307,691	J.R. Johnstone, R.F. Denholm, W.C.C. Morrison, R.D. Fairbairn
5	Scottish Provident Institution	192,639	J.C.R. Inglis (C), Sir H. Rose, Lord Clydesmuir, J.A. Lumsden
6	Scottish Equitable Life Assurance	136,206	R.K. Will (DC), C.F. Sleigh
7	Scottish Life Assurance	119,717	P.W. Turcan (C), R.K. Watson (DC), W. Berry, G.T. Chiene, W.L. Milligan, J.G. Wallace (GM)
8	Scottish Mutual Assurance	100,786	W.R. Ballantyne (C), T.R. Craig, H.A. Whitson
9	Scottish Legal Life Assurance	33,431	–

Table 4A—cont.

Section D: Investment and Property Companies

Rank	Company	Capital (£000)	Rank in Times 100 British	Rank in Times 100 Scottish	Multiple Directors
1	Scottish American Investment	30,651	18	(9)	P.J. Oliphant (C), W. Berry, Sir H. Hamilton-Dalrymple, P.W. Turcan
2	Edinburgh Investment Trust	29,420	28	(16)	I.R. Guild (C), J.L. Anderson, L.M.H. Gow, W.H. McGregor, J. Chiene
3	British Assets Trust	25,250	5	(2)	Sir A.C. Blair (C), P.E.G. Balfour, C.A. Fraser, J.C.R. Inglis, E.J. Ivory
4	Scottish Mortgage & Trust	19,911	9	(4)	G.T. Chiene (C), J.O. Blair-Cunynghame, D.F. McCurrach, T.R. Macgregor
5	Investors' Mortgage Security	17,301	26	(15)	J. Chiene (C), D.J. Bogie, C.F. Sleigh, W.R. Alexander
6	Second Scottish Investment Trust	16,650	15	(8)	Sir W.McE. Younger (C), R.K. Will, T.R. Macgregor (M), Lord Balfour of Burleigh, A.M.M. Grossart
7	Clydesdale Investment	16,498	19	(10)	J.A. Lumsden (C), W.F. Robertson, A.M.M. Stephen
8	Scottish Eastern Investment Trust	15,820	13	(6)	A.L. McClure (C), W.L. Milligan (VC), E.H.M. Clutterbuck, J.A.R. Falconer, R.K. Watson
9	British Investment Trust	15,600	7	(3)	I.R. Pitman (C), G.R. Simpson (DC), J. Burnett-Stuart, Sir T.G. Waterlow
10	Alliance Trust	14,800	3	(1)	D.F. McCurrach (C, MD), G.T. Chiene, G.W. Dunn, B.H. Thomson, C.N. Thomson, Sir W.G.N. Walker
11	Scottish Western Investment	14,368	25	(14)	J.A. Lumsden (C), Lord Clydesmuir, R.D. Fairbairn, J.R. Johnstone, A.I. Mackenzie

Table 4A: Section D–cont.

Rank	Company	Capital (£000)	Rank in Times 100 British	Scottish	Multiple Directors
12	Great Northern Investment Trust	13,767	24	(13)	J.P. Agnew (C), W.R. Alexander, J.G. Stenhouse, W.K.J. Weir
13	Scottish United Investors	13,744	14	(7)	I.H.S. Black, Sir J. Muir, D.W. Nickson
14	Edinburgh & Dundee Investment (formerly Scottish Central Investment)	12,837	12	(5)	G.T. Chiene (C), W.L. Milligan, J.M. Weir
15	Caledonian Trust (formerly Second Scottish Western)	10,112	42	(21)	J.A. Lumsden (C), W.D. Coats, J.R. Johnstone, J.I. Murray
16	Scottish Northern Investment Trust	9,945	29	(17)	R.J.C. Fleming (C), I.M. Tennant
17	Scottish National Trust	9,404	21	(11)	A. Rintoul (C), Sir R. Erskine-Hill, J.F. Carnegie, W.D. Young, R.F. Denholm
18	North American Trust	9,048	32	(18)	I.R. Guild (C), A.K. Aitkenhead, W.D. Marr, Sir H.V. Bonar, R.E. Fleming, H.S. Spens
19=	Scottish Cities Investment Trust	8,750	–	–	–
19=	Scottish Investment Trust	8,750	43	(22)	Sir W.McE. Younger (C), R.K. Will, T.R. Macgregor (M), Lord Balfour of Burleigh
21	First Scottish American Trust	8,091	49	(24)	I.R. Guild (C), Sir H.V. Bonar, R.E. Fleming, H.S. Spens, W.D. Marr, A.K. Aitkenhead
22	Securities Trust of Scotland (formerly Reversionary Association)	7,848	42	(23)	Sir H. Rose (C), W.H. McGregor, J.M. Weir, J.G. Wallace, T.S. Lewis, W.C.C. Morrison

Table 4A: Section D–cont.

Rank	Company	Capital (£000)	Rank in Times 100 British	Scottish	Multiple Directors
23	Atlantic Assets Trust	7,561	–	–	J.C.R. Inglis, E.J. Ivory, J.G.S. Gammell, J.M. Menzies
24	Aberdeen Trust (formerly Aberdeen & Canadian Investment)	6,607	40	(20)	J.S.R. Cruickshank (C), Sir R. Erskine-Hill (DC)
25	Second Alliance Trust	5,600	33	(19)	D.F. McCurrach (C, MD), G.T. Chiene, G.W. Dunn, B.H. Thomson, C.N. Thomson, Sir W.G.N. Walker
26	Pentland Investment Trust	5,389	–	–	P.J. Oliphant (C), Sir R. Erskine-Hill, J.A.R. Falconer, G.P.S. Macpherson, G.M. Menzies
27	Second Great Northern Investment Trust	5,085	–	–	J.A. Lumsden (C), R.D. Fairbairn, J.I. Murray, A.I. Mackenzie
28	Dundee and London Investment Trust	4,625	–	–	I.C. Low (C)
29	Scottish Metropolitan Property	4,353	–	–	–
30	Scottish Ontario Investment	3,959	–	–	J.A.R. Falconer (C), Sir R. Erskine-Hill, G.M. Menzies
31	Scottish European Investment	3,750	–	–	P.W. Turcan (C), P.J. Oliphant
32	Argyle Securities	3,062	–	–	–
33	American Trust	2,965	23	(12)	A.L. McClure (C), A.M.M. Grossart, G.P.S. Macpherson, J.W. Turnbull
34	Second British Assets Trust	2,775	–	–	Sir A.C. Blair (C), P.E.G. Balfour, C.A. Fraser, J.C.R. Inglis, E.J. Ivory

Table 4A: Section D–cont.

Rank	Company	Capital (£000)	Rank in Times 100	Multiple Directors
35	General Scottish Trust	2,538	–	P.W. Turcan (C), A. Cassels (MD)
36	Glendevon Investment Trust	2,521	–	J.A. Lumsden (C), W.D. Coats, A.I. Mackenzie
37	Crescent Japan Investment Trust	2,500	–	A.L. McClure (C), J.W. Turnbull
38	Aberdeen, Edinburgh & London Trust	2,271	–	J.S.R. Cruickshank (DC), Sir R. Erskine-Hill
39	Glasgow Stockholders Trust	2,268	–	A. Rintoul (C), W.D. Young
40	Wemyss Investment (formerly Wemyss Collieries Trust)	2,250	–	D.J. Bogie (C), A. Cassels
41	Ailsa Investment Trust	2,224	–	W.R. Ballantyne (C), H.A. Whitson
42	Amalgamated Securities	2,169	–	–
43	St Andrew Trust	2,092	–	A.L. McClure
44	Glenmurray Investment Trust	1,513	–	J.A. Lumsden (C), J.R. Johnstone
45	Dominion & General Trust	1,400	–	Sir R. Erskine-Hill, J.R. Johnstone

Table 4B: Scotland's Multiple Directors (1973-4)

Director	Primary Business Interest	Directorships
James Percival Agnew, O St J, DL, LLD, CA	Chairman of Lyle Shipping	Lyle Shipping (C); Great Northern Investment (C)
Rt Hon The 13th Earl of Airlie, DL	Director of Schroders, London	General Accident; Scottish and Newcastle
Alexander Kidd Aitkenhead, CA, JP	Director of Northern American Trust	Northern American Trust; First Scottish American
Walter Ronald Alexander, MA	Cleveleye Investment (family trust)	Scotcros (C); Clydesdale Bank; Great Northern Investment; Investors' Mortgage
John Leslie Anderson, FIA, FFA, MA	Scottish Widows Fund (retired general manager)	Scottish Widows Fund; Edinburgh Investment
Rt Hon The 12th Baron Balfour of Burleigh, C Eng, FIEE	Director of Bank of Scotland	Bank of Scotland; Scottish Investment; Second Scottish Investment
Peter Edward Gerald Balfour	Joint Managing Director of Scottish & Newcastle	Scottish & Newcastle (C, JMD); British Assets; Second British Assets
Walter Robert Ballantyne, JP, LLB	Retired General Manager of Royal Bank	Ailsa Investment (C); Scottish Mutual Assurance (C)
Cecil Charles Campbell Bell	Director in Finlay Group	Consolidated Tea and Lands; Cessnock Holdings; Teith Holdings
William Berry, WS	Partner in Murray, Beith & Murray WS	Scottish American Investment; Scottish Life Assurance
Ian Hervey Stuart Black	Chairman of General Accident	General Accident (C); Scottish United Investors
Sir Alastair Campbell Blair, KCVO, TD, WS, JP	Partner in Dundas & Wilson, Davidson & Syme WS	Bank of Scotland; Scottish Widows Fund; British Assets (C); Second British Assets (C)

Table 4B—cont.

Director	Primary Business Interest	Directorships
James Ogilvy Blair-Cunynghame, OBE, LLD, DSc	Chairman of National & Commercial	National & Commercial (C); Royal Bank (C); Culter Guard; Scottish Mortgage
David James Bogie, TD, B Comm, PhD, CA	Retired partner in Graham, Smart & Annan	Investors' Mortgage; Wemyss Investment (C)
Sir Herbert Vernon Bonar, CBE, LLD, JP	Chairman of Low & Bonar Group	Low & Bonar (C); Northern American Trust; First Scottish American
Joseph Burnett-Stuart	Assistant managing director of Robert Fleming	British Investment; MacDonald Martin Distilleries
Angus Ronald Alistair Graham Cameron, MBE	Director in Finlay Group	Cessnock Holdings; Teith Holdings
Colonel Sir Donald Hamish Cameron of Lochiel	Vice chairman of Royal Bank	Royal Bank (VC); Scottish Widows Fund; Culter Guard (C)
Sir Colin Moffat Campbell Bt, MC	Deputy chairman of James Finlay	James Finlay (DC); Consolidated Tea (DC); Cessnock Holdings (DC); Teith Holdings (DC)
James Forrest Carnegie	Director of Brownlee	Brownlee; Scottish National Trust
Alexander Cassels, CA	Partner in Robertson & Maxtone Graham	General Scottish Trust (MD); Wemyss Investment
George Turcan Chiene, DSO, MC, TD, WS	Retired partner in Baillie Gifford	Royal Bank (VC); Scottish Life Assurance; Edinburgh & Dundee Investment (C); Scottish Mortgage (C); Alliance Trust; Second Alliance Trust
John Chiene, OBE, TD, CA	Director of Edinburgh Investment Trust	Edinburgh Investment; Investors' Mortgage; Brownlee; Scotcros

Table 4B—cont.

Director	Primary Business Interest	Directorships
Richard Julian Clough	Director of James Finlay	James Finlay; Consolidated Tea; Cessnock Holdings; Teith Holdings
Edmund Harry Michael Clutterbuck, OBE, BA	Joint managing director of Scottish & Newcastle	Scottish & Newcastle (JMD); Scottish Widows Fund; Scottish Eastern Investment
Rt Hon 2nd Baron Clydesmuir of Braidwood, KT, CB, MBE, TD, LLD, DSc	Governor of Bank of Scotland	Bank of Scotland (G); Scottish Provident; Scottish Western Investment
William David Coats	Director of Coats Paton	Coats Patons; Clydesdale Bank; Weir Group; Caledonian Trust; Glendevon Investment
Newcomb Spence Coldwell, OBE, MC	Director of James Finlay	James Finlay; Consolidated Tea; Cessnock Holdings; Teith Holdings
Thomas Rae Craig, CBE, TD, LLD	Deputy Governor of Bank of Scotland	Bank of Scotland (DG); Scottish Mutual Assurance
James Stanley Rowland Cruickshank, BA, LLB, WS	Partner in Brander & Cruickshank	Aberdeen Trust (C); Aberdeen, Edinburgh & London (DC); Clydesdale Bank
Robert Ferguson Denholm	Director of Denholm Ship Management	Scottish Amicable Life; Scottish National Trust
George Willoughby Dunn, CBE, DSO, MC, TD, DL	Partner in Clark, Oliver, Dewar & Webster	Alliance Trust; Second Alliance Trust; Wm Low
Sir Robert Erskine-Hill Bt, CA	Partner in Chiene & Tait	Aberdeen Trust (DC); Aberdeen, Edinburgh & London; Dominion & General; Pentland Investment; Scottish Ontario; Scottish National Trust
Robert Duncan Fairbairn, JP	Vice chairman of Clydesdale Bank	Clydesdale Bank (VC); Scottish Amicable; Second Great Northern; Scottish Western Investment

Table 4B—cont.

Director	Primary Business Interest	Directorships
James Alexander Reid Falconer, BA, CA	Senior partner in Martin Currie	Scottish Ontario Investment (C); Scottish Homes Investment (DC); Scottish Eastern Investment; Pentland Investment
Hugh Ferguson, BSc, FRSE	Director in Finlay Group	Consolidated Tea & Lands; Cessnock Holdings; Teith Holdings
Richard Evelyn Fleming, MC, TD	Director of Robert Fleming	Burmah Oil; Northern American Trust; First Scottish American
Roger John Cary Fleming, OBE, TD, DL	Managing director of John Fleming	Scottish Northern Investment (C); Culter Guard; Richards
Charles Annand Fraser, MVO, WS, MA, LLB	Partner in W. & J. Burness WS	British Assets; Second British Assets
Sir Hugh Fraser Bt	Chairman of Scottish and Universal Investments	House of Fraser (C); Scottish & Universal Investments (C, MD)
James Gilbert Sydney Gammell, MBE, CA	Chairman of Ivory & Sime	Atlantic Assets; Bank of Scotland; Standard Life Assurance
Leonard Maxwell Harper Gow, MBE	Chairman of Christian Salvesen	Burmah Oil; Royal Bank; Scottish Widows Fund (C); Edinburgh Investment
Angus Macfarlane McLeod Grossart, MA, LLB, CA	Managing director of Noble Grossart	Scottish & Universal Investments; American Trust; Second Scottish Investment
Ivor Reginald Guild, WS	Partner in Shepherd & Wedderburn WS	Northern American Trust (C); First Scottish American (C); Edinburgh Investment (C)
Sir Huw Fleetwood Hamilton-Dalrymple Bt	Assistant managing director of Scottish & Newcastle	Scottish & Newcastle (AMD); Scottish American Investment
Brigadier Sir George Steven Harvie-Watt Bt, TD, DL, QC	Retired chief executive of Consolidated Goldfields	Clydesdale Bank; North British Steel

Table 4B—cont.

Director	Primary Business Interest	Directorships
James Crawford Roger Inglis, BA, LLB, WS	Partner in Shepherd & Wedderburn WS	Atlantic Assets; British Assets; Second British Assets; Royal Bank; Scottish Provident
Eric James Ivory	Retired partner in Ivory & Sime	Atlantic Assets; British Assets; Second British Assets
John Raymond Johnstone, BA, CA	Senior managing director of Murray Johnstone	Caledonian Trust; Scottish Western Investment; Glenmurray Investment; Dominion & General; Scottish Amicable
Timothy Stuart Lewis	Director of Scottish & Newcastle	Scottish & Newcastle; Securities Trust
Ian Campbell Low, BSc, CA	Deputy Chairman of Low & Bonar	Low & Bonar (DC); Dundee & London Investment (C)
James Alexander Lumsden, MBE, TD, DL, MA, LLB	Partner in Maclay, Murray & Spens	Caledonian Trust (C); Clydesdale Investment (C); Glendevon Investment (C); Glenmurray Investment (C); Scottish Western Investment (C); Second Great Northern (C); Bank of Scotland; Scottish Provident; Wm Baird; Burmah Oil (C); Weir
William Donald Marr, CA	Director in Northern American Trust Group	Northern American Trust; First Scottish American
Walter Wilson Mayne, OBE, BSc, MIBiol	Director in Finlay Group	Consolidated Tea & Lands; Cessnock Holdings; Teith Holdings
George Macbeth Menzies	Chairman of North British Steel	North British Steel (C); General Accident; Pentland Investment; Scottish Ontario Investment
John Maxwell Menzies	Chairman of John Menzies	John Menzies (C); Atlantic Assets

Table 4B–cont.

Director	Primary Business Interest	Directorships
William Laidlaw Milligan, JP, BA, CA	Partner in Chiene & Tait	Scottish Eastern Investment (VC); Edinburgh & Dundee; Scottish Life Assurance; Titaghur Jute
Betram Desmond Misselbrook, CBE	Former manager of British American Tobacco	Anderson Mavor; Standard Life Assurance
William Charles Carregie Morrison, CA	Partner in Thomson McLintock	Scottish Amicable; Securities Trust
Lt Comdr Gerald Robin Muir, OBE. RN (retd)	Director in Finlay Group	Consolidated Tea; Cessnock Holdings; Teith Holdings
Sir John Harling Muir Bt, TD, DL	Chairman of James Finlay	James Finlay (C); Consolidated Tea (C); Cessnock Holdings (C); Teith Holdings (C); Scottish United Investors
James Ian Murray, CA	Director of Murray Johnstone Trusts	Caledonian Trust; Second Great Northern
Alexander Logan McClure, WS	Partner in Mackenzie & Black WS	American Trust (C); Crescent Japan Investment (C); Scottish Eastern Investment (C); St Andrew Trust (C); Clydesdale Bank (DC)
David Fleming McCurrach, OBE, BL	Managing director of Alliance Trust	Alliance Trust (C, MD); Second Alliance Trust (C, MD); Scottish Mortgage
Sir Alexander Forbes McDonald, DL, BL, CA	Chairman of Distillers	Distillers (C); National & Commercial
Ian Wilson Macdonald, MA, D.Litt, CA	Deputy chairman of National & Commercial	National & Commercial (DC); Royal Bank; United Biscuits
Thomas Robert Macgregor	Manager of Scottish Investment	Scottish Investment (M); Second Scottish Investment (M); Scottish Mortgage

Table 4B–cont.

Director	Primary Business Interest	Directorships
William Haldane McGregor, FCIS	Retired manager of Edinburgh Investment	Edinburgh Investment; Securities Trust
Alexander Irvine Mackenzie, BA, CA	Partner in Whinney, Murray	Scottish Western Investment; Second Great Northern; Glendevon Investment; Scottish Widows Fund
Brigadier George Philip Stewart Macpherson, OBE, D.Litt, CA, TD	Director of Kleinwort, Benson, London	American Trust; Pentland Investment; Standard Life Assurance
David Wigley Nickson	Managing director of Collins	Wm Collins (MD); General Accident; Scottish United Investors
Patrick James Oliphant, TD, DKS	Partner in Pearson, Robertson & Maconochie WS	Scottish American Investment (C); Scottish European Investment; Pentland Investment (C); Royal Bank
Ian Robert Pitman, WS	Retired partner in J. & F. Anderson WS	British Investment; Standard Life Assurance
Andrew Rintoul, CBE, BA, CA	Chairman of Gartmore Investment (Scotland)	Glasgow Stockholders (C); Scottish National Trust
Thomas Neilson Risk, BL	Partner in Maclay, Murray & Spens	Bank of Scotland; Standard Life (C); Howden
William Francis Robertson, LLD	Chairman of Wm Robertson Shipowners	Bank of Scotland; Clydesdale Investment; Bett
Sir Hugh Rose Bt, TD, DL	Director of Scottish Provident	Scottish Provident; Securities Trust (C)
Gordon Russell Simpson, DSO, TD	Partner in Bell, Lawrie & Robertson & Co (Stockbrokers)	British Investment (DC); General Accident
Charles Frederick Sleigh, CA, TD	Partner in Thornton Baker (Martin Currie)	Investors' Mortgage; Scottish Equitable Life

Table 4B–cont.

Director	Primary Business Interest	Directorships
Hugh Stuart Spens, MBE, MC, TD	Director of Robert Fleming	Northern American Trust; First Scottish American
John Godwyn Stenhouse, TD, FCIB	Vice chairman of Stenhouse	Stenhouse (VC); Great Northern Investment
Alexander Moncrieff Mitchell Stephen, BA	Director of Alex Stephen & Sons	Clydesdale Investment; Scottish Widows Fund
Sir Iain Maxwell Stewart, BSc, FI Mech E, FINA, FI Mar E	Director of Hall Thermotank	Royal Bank; Lyle Shipping
Captain Iain Mark Tennant, FRSA, JP	Innes Trading (family trust)	Glenlivet Distillers (C); Scottish Northern Investment; Clydesdale Bank
Brian Harold Thomson	Director of D.C. Thomson	Alliance Trust; Second Alliance Trust
Colonel Charles Newbigging Thomson, CBE, DSO, TD, DL, CA	Retired partner in R.C. Thomson & Murdoch	Alliance Trust; Second Alliance Trust
Patrick Watson Turcan, WS	Partner in Dundas & Wilson CS	Scottish European Investment (C); Scottish American Investment; General Scottish Trust (C); Scottish Life Assurance (C)
James Wilson Turnbull, CA	Partner in Wallace Guthrie	American Trust; Crescent Japan Investment
James Philip Van den Bergh, CBE	Retired director of Unilever	Lindustries (VC); Wm Baird
Sir William Giles Newsom Walker, TD, DL	Honorary president of Sidlaw Industries	Alliance Trust; Second Alliance Trust; Clydesdale Bank
John Galloway Wallace, MA, FFA, ASA	General manager of Scottish Life	Scottish Life Assurance (GM); Securities Trust
Sir Thomas Gordon Waterlow Bt, CBE, D. Litt	Deputy chairman of Royal Bank	Royal Bank (DC); National & Commercial; Standard Life Assurance; British Investment

Table 4B—cont.

Director	Primary Business Interest	Directorships
Ronald Kenneth Watson, WS	Partner in Brodie, Cuthbertson & Watson WS	Scottish Life Assurance (DC); Scottish Eastern Investment
John McNair Weir, TD	Director of Sidlaw Industries	Edinburgh & Dundee Investment; Securities Trust
Hon. William Kenneth James Weir, BA	Chairman of Weir Group	Weir Group (C); Great Northern Investment
Harold Alexander Whitson, CBE, BA	Chairman of Melville, Dundas & Whitson	Ailsa Investment; Scottish Mutual Insurance
Ronald Kerr Will	Partner in Dundas & Wilson CS, Davidson & Syme WS	Scottish Equitable Life (DC); Scottish Investment; Second Scottish Investment
Sir Eric Grant Yarrow Bt, MBE, DL	Chairman of Yarrow & Co	Clydesdale Bank; Standard Life Assurance
William David Young, CA	Director of Gartmore Investments (Scotland)	Glasgow Stockholders; Scottish National Trust
Charles Frank Johnston Younger, DSO, TD	Director of Scottish & Newcastle	Scottish & Newcastle; Bank of Scotland
Sir William McEwan Younger Bt, DSO, DL	Retired managing director of Scottish & Newcastle	Scottish Investment (C); Second Scottish Investment (C)

Table 4C: Shareholdings in Top Scottish Non-Financial Companies (1973-4)

Note: The information in this table relates to the share registers for the years 1974 and 1975, together with the annual reports of the companies. In some cases data relates to 1976 or 1977 and these companies are indicated with †. Where a major change in ownership has occurred during the period 1973-7, the companies are marked with * and are discussed in the text or below. These are the main changes in the companies not discussed in the text:

Inveresk — Following the collapse of London and County Securities in 1974 the holding was sold. The 1977 annual report records no shareholders with five per cent or more of the shares.

Teacher — The company was acquired by Allied Breweries in 1976.

Weir — The 1977 annual report records no substantial holding by Pearson.

Brownlee — By 1978 McLeod Russell had acquired 11.97 per cent.

Company	Ownership	Dominant Ownership Interest
Distillers	Constellation	Prudential Ass, 2.86%
Burmah	Constellation	Murray Johnstone trusts, 1.67%
Coats Patons	Constellation	Prudential Ass, 6.22%; Securities Management Trust, 2.15%
Scottish & Newcastle	Constellation	Younger family, 3.91%; General Accident, 2.15%
House of Fraser*	Exclusive minority	Scottish & Universal Investments, 25.03%
United Biscuits	Exclusive minority	Laing family and directors, 22.88%
Wm Baird	Shared minority	M. & G. Group, 16.51%; Save and Prosper, 9.45%
Metal Industries	Wholly-owned	Thorn Electrical Industries, 100%

Table 4C—cont.

Company	Ownership	Dominant Ownership Interest
Inveresk*	Exclusive minority	London & County Securities, 29.62%
Scottish Agricultural Industries	Exclusive majority	ICI, 62.4%
Stenhouse	Exclusive majority	Stenhouse family and directors, 72.02%
Uniroyal	Wholly-owned	Uniroyal Inc., USA, 100%
Scottish & Universal	Exclusive minority	Sir Hugh Fraser, 47.74%
Lindustries	Constellation	Barclays nominees, 6.38%; Midland Bank (Unit Trust Dept), 5.57%; Guardian Royal Exchange Ass., 4.83%; M. & G. Group, 4.41%
Anderson Mavor	Shared minority	Anderson family and directors, 7.73% +; Save & Prosper, 9.12%; M. & G. Group, 7.9%
Arthur Bell	Exclusive minority	Duncanson and other directors, 48.34%
Weir Group*	Shared minority	Weir family and directors, 10.86%; S. Pearson & Son, 5.31%
Low & Bonar	Exclusive minority	Low and Bonar families and directors, 27.39%
James Finlay*	Shared minority	Muir family and directors, 4.28%; Slater Walker Securities, 22.65%
Wm Collins	Exclusive minority	Collins family and directors, 23.92%
Goldberg	Limited minority	Goldberg family and directors, 8.69%
Tharsis	Shared minority	Directors, 2.88%; Bank of Santander, Spain, 16.67%
John Menzies	Exclusive majority	John Menzies and directors, 54.45%
Alexandra Building	Wholly-owned	Thomas Tilling Limited, 100%
Robertson Foods	Exclusive minority	Robertson family and directors, 10% approx
Teacher*	Exclusive minority	Bergius, Dunlop, Anderson and other directors, 25.16%
Howden	Constellation	Midland Bank nominee, 8.64%; Prudential Assur., 6.19%; Save & Prosper, 5.63%; Securities Management Trust, 5.01%

Table 4C—cont.

Company	Ownership	Dominant Ownership Interest
Aberdeen Construction	Limited minority	Anderson family and directors, 5.15%
Nairn Floors*	Wholly-owned	Nairn Williamson, 100%
Consolidated Tea	Shared minority	James Finlay Group, 33.9% +; McLeod Russell, 13.04%
Highland Distilleries	Constellation	Prudential Ass., 6.42%; Brittanic Ass., 5.02%; Bank of Scotland nominees, 4.26%
Glenfield & Kennedy	Wholly-owned	Crane Corporation, USA, 100%
Brown & Tawse	Limited minority	Rae family and directors, 7.41%
United Wire†	Limited minority	Green family and directors, 3.91%; Scottish Amicable, 5.00%
Tayforth	Wholly-owned	National Freight Corporation, 100%
Reo Stakis	Exclusive majority	R. Stakis and directors, 70.12%
Lyle Shipping	Exclusive minority	Directors, 14.36%
Blackwood Morton	Exclusive minority	Morton family and directors, 41.75%
Scottish Automobile	Exclusive majority	Heron Corporation, 68.62%
Titaghur Jute	Exclusive minority	Thomas Duff & Co, India, 33.79%
Culter Guard Bridge	Exclusive minority	Arbuthnot Latham nominee, 20.00%
Scotcros†	Shared minority	W.R. Alexander family trust, 10.20%; Edinburgh Investment Trust, 9.53%; Scottish Northern Investment, 9.53%
Glenlivet	Shared minority	Mitcalf, Grant, and other directors, 10.01%; Imperial Group, 27.26%
MacDonald Martin	Shared minority	Walker, Rattray, and other directors, 29.83%; Securities Trust of Scotland, 18.44%
Scottish Homes	Exclusive minority	P. Oppenheim and other directors, 26.07%
James Scott*	Exclusive majority	Directors, approx 54%

Table 4C—cont.

Company	Ownership	Dominant Ownership Interest
Giddings & Lewis Fraser	Exclusive majority	Gidding & Lewis Inc., USA, 92.00%
Bett	Exclusive majority	Bett family and directors, 58.71%
M.E. Theatres	Wholly-owned	Associated Television, 100%
Hewden-Stuart	Exclusive minority	Directors, 21.24% (mainly Goodwin, Jamieson and Stuart)
Carron	Exclusive majority	Directors and Dawson family trust, 60% +
Wm Low	Exclusive minority	Directors, 11.51%
Bremner	Shared minority	Bremner family and directors, 17.93%; Keyser Ullman nominee, 10.91%
Teith*	Shared minority	James Finlay Group, 36.30%; McLeod Russell, 14.40%
Cessnock*	Shared majority	James Finlay, 18.30%; Teith Holdings, 32.00%; Consolidated Tea, 31.30%
Stoddard	Exclusive majority	Maclean family and directors, 64.32%
Richards	Exclusive minority	National & Commercial Banking nominee, 14.8%
Brownlee*	Exclusive minority	Paisley, Forrest and other directors, and Brownlee Pension Fund, 12.69%
North British Steel	Exclusive majority	Menzies family and directors, 92.89%
Ayrshire Metal	Exclusive minority	W.S. Wilson and directors, 49.93%
Bruntons†	Shared minority	Keyser Ullman nominee, 5.67%; ITC Pension Trust, 5.00%
Coltness	Shared minority	Gibbons, Walker and other directors, 24.55%; Bank of Scotland Finance Company, 9.00%

5 THE RESPONSE TO OIL

We do not intend here to give a comprehensive analysis of recent oil developments in Scotland. Such surveys are available in a number of other places (see Bibliography). Our aim is to give an overview of some of the main features of North Sea oil development, focusing mainly on the participation of Scottish capital in this development. Scottish involvement in a home-based oil industry is not new. The total production of shale oil in Scotland in 1894 was 1.5m tons and the many shale oil producers were eventually amalgamated into Scottish Oils, which became a part of BP. Nevertheless, the scale and importance of the recent developments are such that they have called forth a fundamentally new response. Much of the buoyancy of the financial sector which we discussed in the previous chapter was directly consequent upon the possibilities opened up by North Sea oil.

Drilling concessions were awarded in the Netherlands, Denmark and Germany following the discovery of a massive natural gas field off Groningen in 1959. Explorations began in British waters in 1964, in 1965 gas was discovered by BP and Continental Oil (Conoco), and the following year a Shell-Esso consortium also struck gas. It was not until 1969 that the first big oil strike was made, in Norwegian waters, by a consortium headed by Phillips Petroleum of the USA and including ENI (Italy), Petronord (French-Norwegian) and Petrofina (Belgium). This oil strike was the first sign of the Ekofisk field. Late in 1969 another Phillips consortium, which included British representation through Oil Exploration (Holdings), discovered oil in the British Josephine field off Aberdeen. The pace of discovery soon quickened: in 1970 consortia headed by BP, Shell-Esso and Hamilton Brothers (which included participation by Burmah Oil) all discovered oil in the area of the Forties field, and in 1971 another Hamilton consortium discovered the Argyll field.

Exploration was organised through the allocation of drilling licences whereby each consortium was granted the right to drill in particular 'blocks' of the North Sea. The first three licensing rounds — in 1964, 1965 and 1970 — all involved the allocation of licences through administrative discretion, since this was seen as the most effective way to ensure rapid development. Much of the exploration depended on foreign capital, though the government policy did ensure that British participation increased with each round. The fourth round, in 1971, introduced an innovation of allocating a small number of blocks by competitive tender and this principle was also followed in the 1976 round.

The search for oil in the North Sea has involved two main aspects: exploration and production, and supply and service. Once exploration has led to the discovery of suitable oil resources production can begin, but throughout this process there is a further need for offshore supplies and services to keep the whole operation working. The exploration phase requires massive investment in the building and siting of the exploration rigs and the production phase requires similar investment in production platforms. The supply and service activities involve a greater mixture of operations from costly pipe-laying barges to relatively inexpensive catering facilities. By the end of 1977, £1,700m had been spent on exploring 600 wells in the UK sector, British companies being responsible for 37 per cent of the total. More than three-quarters of the British expenditure was accounted for by British Gas, British National Oil Corporation (BNOC), BP and Shell. The rest of the British expenditure was accounted for by 45 companies. By the same period £5,600m had been spent on 18 developments. Most of the funds for exploration and development were raised from the companies' internal resources with smaller companies such as London and Scottish Marine Oil (LSMO) and Tricentrol raising most of the external funds. External funds came mainly in the form of bank loans, though investment trusts subscribed for a considerable amount of share capital and loan stock. By the end of 1978 a total of £1,816m was outstanding as loans for North Sea oil developments by banks based in the UK. The bulk of this, 37 per cent, came from American banks and a further 25 per cent from other foreign banks. The Scottish clearing banks had loans outstanding of £69m, representing 10 per cent of the British bank total. It has been estimated that just over one-tenth of all Scottish bank advances in the late 1970s related to North Sea oil. The Bank of Scotland was the first Scottish bank to set up a separate oil division and as well as backing companies such as North Sea Assets it became a member of the International Energy Bank which has participated in a number of syndicated loan agreements (see Table 5.1). The Royal Bank has also participated in consortium finance and helped to finance the offshore drilling contractors BEN-ODECO, though its specialist area was leasing. The Clydesdale Bank has been more heavily involved in oil finance than its proportionate share in general banking business would suggest, largely because of its strong links with the North East of

Scotland. Its main areas of finance have been in supply and service operations though it has also financed construction at yards such as Nigg.

Table 5.1: Ownership of the International Energy Bank (1973)

Company	Nationality	% held
Bank of Scotland	Scotland	15
Barclays Bank	England	15
Soc. Financière Européenne	Luxembourg	20
Banque Worms	France	10
Canadian Imperial Bank of Commerce	Canada	20
Republic National Bank of Dallas	USA	20

Note: Barclays owns 35 per cent of Bank of Scotland, which owns 7.5 per cent of Banque Worms.

The main involvement of Scottish capital has been at one remove from the active operations themselves. Whilst a number of companies have certainly moved into active development work, the bulk of the capital has been channelled through the investment trusts into specialist oil investment companies, many based in London. In the rest of this chapter we shall examine the extent of Scottish participation in the two main areas identified earlier.

Exploration and Production

Each exploration consortium is led by one or two companies which actually operate in the block, the other participants support the operating companies and have mainly a financial interest. The companies involved as participants in consortia include established oil companies such as BP and Shell, non-oil companies such as P & O, Rio Tinto Zinc and British Electric Traction, oil subsidiaries of companies engaged in other industries (for example, Blackfriars Oil was a subsidiary of Associated Newspapers, Whitehall Petroleum was a subsidiary of S. Pearson, and Rank Exploration was a subsidiary of the Rank Organisation), and various specialist investment and exploration companies such as LSMO, Viking Oil and Caber Oil. In 1972 there were

23 consortia in the UK which had Scottish participants, but only two Scottish companies acted as operators. Burmah was involved in four consortia as joint operator (three with ICI and one with Total) and Premier Consolidated Oilfields was an exclusive operator. Both companies were old-established firms whose main interests had been in Burma and Trinidad respectively. We have already discussed the difficulties faced by Burmah in the mid-1970s. The main arm of its North Sea activities, which were concentrated in the Thistle field, had been Burmah Oil Developments but this was sold off in 1976 as part of Burmah's 'slimming down'. The company was renamed BODL Ltd, following its acquisition by BNOC, which also acquired a majority interest in Burmah's remaining North Sea interests. Premier Consolidated Oilfields had been set up in 1934 to unite a number of Trinidad oil interests and the company only really developed when it entered the North Sea in 1972 following its technical link-up with the Ball and Collins group. In 1975 the major shareholders in Premier were Sir George Bolton's family firm (London United Investments) with

Table 5.2: The Largest North Sea Oilfields (1974)

Field	Estimated reserves (million barrels)	Licensee
Ninian	2,100	(a) BP-Ranger Group
		(b) Burmah Group
Brent	2,000	(a) Shell-Esso
		(b) Texaco
Piper	800	Occidental Petroleum Group
Thistle	750	Burmah Group
Magnus	750	BP
Claymore	600	Occidental Petroleum Group
Dunlin	600	(a) Shell-Esso
		(b) Conoco-Gulf-NCB
Beryl	500	Mobil
Maureen	450	Phillips Group
Andrew	400	BP
Cormorant	400	Shell-Esso
TOTAL	9,350	

Source: Adapted from G. MacKay and D.I. Mackay, *The Political Economy of North Sea Oil* (Martin Robertson, London, 1975), p. 61, Table 3.3.

22.9 per cent, though Ball and Collins held a small stake of 4.6 per cent. The relationship between Premier and Ball and Collins became closer until the two companies merged in 1977 to form an enlarged Premier, which took over all the Ball and Collins participations.

The total estimated reserves of oil in the UK sector of the North Sea in 1974 amounted to 13,800m barrels and it can be seen from Table 5.2 that the 11 largest fields accounted for two-thirds of this total. British and American firms were represented almost equally amongst the operators and it has been estimated that British companies were operating in blocks having 44 per cent of the total reserves. An area in which foreign capital was very heavily represented was the building (or 'fabricating') of rigs and production platforms. Although BP purchased one of its early rigs from Harland and Wolff and both Phillips and Atlantic-Richfield had bought from John Brown at Clydebank, only five rigs had been built in the UK before 1973. In the mid-1970s only two British yards were building rigs – Marathon (based on John Brown) and Scott-Lithgow. Perhaps the most important occurrence in this area was the establishment of BEN-ODECO as a joint venture to provide rigs on a contract basis. ODECO (Ocean Drilling and Exploration Co.) was formed in the USA in 1953 by Murphy Oil to build rigs for use in the Gulf of Mexico and it soon became established as the largest rig constructor in the USA. Ben Line Contractors (BLOC) was set up by Ben Line Steamers which was supported by minority holdings from the Royal Bank with eight per cent and North Sea Assets with 39 per cent. The joint venture between American and Scottish capital BEN-ODECO highlights the importance of the specialist investment companies such as North Sea Assets. The building of production platforms had rather more British participation, though direct Scottish involvement was little. Four of the major builders were joint ventures between British and foreign companies: RDL North Sea brought together Redpath Dorman Long (a subsidiary of British Steel) and various Italian companies; Laing Offshore was an Anglo-French venture involving John Laing Construction; McAlpine Sea Tank was an Anglo-French venture involving Sir Robert McAlpine; and Highland Fabricators brought together George Wimpey and the American firm Brown and Root, a subsidiary of Halliburton Co., of Dallas. The establishment of the deepwater construction yards required for production platforms led to considerable public disquiet and a number of enquiries about developments such as Ardyne Point (McAlpine Sea Tank), Nigg Bay (Highland Fabricators), and Loch Kishorn (Howard-Doris).

The main areas of Scottish involvement were exploration and

Table 5.3: Major Scottish Holdings in Oil Exploration Companies (1972)

Shareholder	LSMO	SCOT	Caledonian Offshore	Viking Oil	Caber Oil	Pict Petroleum
Scottish American Inv.	7.06	8.87	7.6			5.1
General Accident	5.88	8.87	4.8	4.8		
Great Northern Inv.	2.94	4.44				4.0
Standard Life			19.0	9.5		4.0
Edinburgh Inv.	5.88					4.9
Bank of Scotland				4.8		4.0
Finlay Group	6.47	8.87				
Scottish United Inv.	2.94	8.87				
Ivory & Sime			28.9	15.6		
Scottish Provident			4.8	4.8		
Wemyss Inv.	2.94					
General Scottish Tr.	2.94					
Scottish National Tr.		7.10				
Murray Johnstone Group		5.32				
Glasgow Stockholders		3.55				
Scottish Equitable		2.78				
Scottish Life					10.0	
Aberdeen Construction					8.6	
Hewden-Stuart					14.3	
American Trust						9.8
British Investment						5.3
Second Scottish Inv.						6.2
Securities Trust						9.8
Lyle Shipping						4.0
Stenhouse Holdings						4.0
Christian Salvesen						4.0
Scottish Northern Inv.						4.0
TOTALS	37.05	58.67	65.1	37.6	32.9	69.1

Note: Pict Petroleum held 31.4 per cent of Caber Oil. The Ivory and Sime holdings include those of Edward Bates. Scottish American Investment also held 17.5 per cent of Enjay Holdings and 12.5 per cent of Sea Search. Scottish Northern held 23.5 per cent of Triton Petroleum. Pict, Securities Trust and Edinburgh Investment together held 20.8 per cent of Oil and Gas Enterprises.

production themselves rather than the construction of rigs and platforms. Table 5.3 shows the major Scottish participations in oil and production companies in 1972. Pict Petroleum and Caber Oil were both formed by Noble Grossart in 1971 and were intended to spread their own invest-ments over a number of exploration groups. Pict took a 31.4 per cent stake in Caber and most of the rest of the shares of the two companies were taken by Scottish interests. Pict was predominantly owned by investment trusts, though Stenhouse, Lyle and Salvesen had minority holdings. Minority holdings in Caber were taken by Aberdeen Construction and Hewden-Stuart. By 1972 the companies were participating in six licensed consortia and Pict saw itself as evolving into a fully integrated oil company. Under the management of Noble Grossart Pict's shares were spread to a larger group of investors, with each of the major holders taking a smaller percentage share and groups such as Ivory and Sime acquiring larger holdings. Caledonian Offshore and Viking Oil were both set up by Edward Bates and both companies had substantial backing from Ivory and Sime and had similar aims to Pict and Caber. The directors of the two companies were drawn from those who sat on the Ivory and Sime trust boards and the boards of other financial backers: Peter Balfour, Lord Balfour, James Gammell, Sir William McEwen Younger and Lord Clydesmuir. Like the two Noble Grossart companies Caledonian and Viking Oil spread their ownership to a wider group, though in 1975 Ivory and Sime still held 9.6 per cent of Caledonian and 10.8 per cent of Viking Oil. This group of oil companies was typical of the participation of Scottish capital in oil developments. The growth of these companies and the restructuring of Scottish merchant banking were processes which went hand-in-hand. Despite the failure of Edward Bates, the companies and their backers prospered.

Many of these same Scottish interests were involved in the develop-ment of London-based exploration companies. London and Scottish Marine Oil (LSMO) and Scottish Canadian Oil and Transportation (SCOT) were set up in London in 1970 by the stockbrokers Cazenove and the Canadian firm Ranger Oil. The backing for these companies came particularly from Glasgow, in contrast to the Edinburgh backing for the Grossart and Bates companies. Their main participation was in the BP-Ranger operated block in the Ninian field, where LSMO held 15 per cent and SCOT held seven per cent. By 1975 the companies still attracted considerable institutional backing and had bought out the participations of Cawoods Holdings and National Carbonising in the BP-Ranger consortium. The companies underwent a major reorganisation when LSMO acquired SCOT and Morgan Grenfell arranged a stock exchange flotation. By 1970 the percentage holdings of the investment trusts had declined somewhat and the major shareholders were Cawoods Holdings with 12.5 per cent and National Carbonising with 6.8 per cent. LSMO had not had the management backing of the Scottish merchant banks and had become a London-based company with Scottish minority holdings, albeit a highly successful company. A more equal representation of English and Scottish interests seems to have occurred in another London-based company, Oil Exploration (Holdings), which was set up by the Ionian Bank in 1964 to take part in a Phillips consortium. The company was floated in 1971 and by 1977 the largest shareholders were Ivory and Sime with 37.3 per cent and Premier Consolidated with 8.9 per cent. Finally we might mention a more recent company, Clyde Petroleum, which was set up in Glasgow in 1973 by merchant bankers Singer and Friedlander (part of the Bowring group). Like Pict and Caledonian Offshore, Clyde Petroleum invested in a number of exploration groups and aimed to become a fully-integrated oil company. It was originally set up as a way of channelling Glasgow investment funds into a consortium in which Sun Oil was the operator. As part of its move towards becoming a more broadly-based oil company it acquired Phipps Oil in 1976, having previously been associated with the company and the consultancy interests of Colin Phipps. The company attracted a large group of investors to back it, though Singer and Friedlander retained an important stake and Colin Phipps had one of the largest personal holdings.

Supply and Service

The Scottish financial sector became highly involved in the supply and service sector as well as in exploration, though Scottish industrials were also active in supply and service. The main arm of the financial sector in this area has been North Sea Assets. This company was set up by Ivory and Sime in 1972 under the joint management of Edward Bates and Noble Grossart and aimed to establish joint ventures with existing companies. The company intended to acquire substantial minority holdings in companies operating both onshore and offshore. The original board of the company was recruited from its managers and institutional backers: Lord Clydesmuir from the Bank of Scotland, James Gammell from Ivory and Sime, Dennis Barkway of Edward Bates, Angus Grossart of Noble Grossart, Gavin Boyd of Stenhouse, and L.M.H. Gow of Christian Salvesen, together with Robin Fox the

managing director of Oil Exploration. Initially the company bought
into established companies such as Bett Brothers (2.5 per cent) and
Hewden-Stuart (1.7 per cent), though it also backed companies such as
Iain Noble's Seaforth Maritime. Between 1973 and 1975 the company
decided to sell off its quoted investments and concentrate on holdings
in unquoted companies, one of its most important acquisitions being a
39 per cent stake in BLOC. With the failure of Bates, Noble Grossart
became sole managers of the company, though the only board change
was that Peter de Vink became a director. By 1978 its stake in BLOC
had fallen to 28 per cent but the company had acquired important
holdings in Salvesen Offshore Holdings (20 per cent) and Viking Jersey
Equipment (20 per cent). The latter had, in fact, been an early investment of North Sea Assets and was a company formed to own the
Viking pipe-laying barge. North Sea Assets followed the pattern of the
oil exploration companies in enabling investment trusts to participate
at one remove from the actual operating companies and the Ivory and
Sime group took this principle one step further when they set up
Viking Resources Trust in 1972 as an investment trust specialising in
the shares of companies involved in oil developments. Viking Resources
held 10.3 per cent of Oil Exploration (Holdings) and had smaller stakes
in Bett Brothers, Brown and Tawse, Hewden-Stuart, and Weir. In the
same year, Ivory and Sime set up the foreign-registered Viking
Resources International as a similar medium for foreign investors.

A number of shipping companies moved into oil industry supply
activities. In addition to BLOC and Salvesen Offshore there was also
Lyle Offshore formed by Lyle Shipping. Lyle Shipping and H. Hogarth
were jointly involved with Sidlaw Industries in the formation of Seaforth
Maritime with the backing and advice of Noble Grossart. Lyle and
Hogarth both had minority stakes in Pict Petroleum and in 1972 they
got Noble Grossart to set up Seaforth Maritime with the two companies
taking 30 per cent each, Sidlaw and Noble Grossart taking the balance.
The company was originally formed to build and operate supply vessels
but soon diversified into engineering, land transport and plant hire.
Lyle Offshore Group was set up in 1975 to carry out onshore and
offshore maintenance, its main backers being Lyle Shipping with 40
per cent and the balance being taken by Scottish trusts, particularly the
Martin Currie Group, Scottish United Investors and Scottish National
Trust. As part of its expansion plans James Finlay not only bought
into LSMO and SCOT but also into Servoil, a supply and service
company. Initially Finlay took 60 per cent and Culter Guard Bridge
took the remaining 40 per cent, but the whole share capital of the

company was eventually acquired by Finlay.

Conclusion

We have given only the briefest outline of the involvement of Scottish capital in North Sea oil developments, but we hope to have produced enough evidence to show the crucial importance of the investment trust sector and of a relatively small number of industrial companies. Industrials such as Lyle have done well out of the oil boom, others such as Burmah have had to cope with serious problems. Yet other companies have been totally unaffected by the oil industry. By and large, the whole of the Scottish financial sector has had to come to terms with oil, whilst the impact of oil on industrial companies depended very much on their particular industrial background.

Oil has had a variable impact on Scottish companies, just as it has had a differential impact on Scottish employment. By 1974 about 19,000 new jobs had been created in Scotland as a result of the oil developments: 6,000 in exploration and located mainly in the North East, 8,700 in manufacturing located mainly in the Highlands, 3,500 in construction and pipelaying located mainly in the North East and Edinburgh, and 800 in production which were evenly spread across the country. The impact on Glasgow and the West of Scotland where the traditional heavy industry is concentrated has been minimal and so there has been little effect on the general pattern of Scottish employment. The lasting effects of the oil boom may prove to have been the restructuring of the financial sector which was already more consistently successful than the Scottish industrial companies.

CONCLUSION: THE TRANSFORMATION OF SCOTTISH CAPITAL

Scottish industrialisation as the junior partner in British imperial expansion established a basic pattern of export-oriented manufacturing companies and overseas-oriented investment companies. Scottish capital has been concentrated in the heavy industries (coal, iron, steel and ship-building), textiles (linen, wool, jute and linoleum), and in investment trusts and mortgage companies, with lesser involvement in drink production, chemicals and overseas merchanting. The wheels of Scottish capital were kept moving by an efficient banking and insurance sector which was allied very closely to the other sectors of Scottish capital. The development of this capital system can be described in terms of three overarching processes. First, the periodic reconstruction of Scottish capital which led to a long-term restructuring of the system: a story of concentration and monopolisation and of the changing balance of power between various interests within Scottish capital. Second, the progressive 'Anglicisation' and 'Americanisation' of Scottish industry which led to an increase in external ownership and orientation, and to the increased interdependence of the Scottish and English economies. Third, the managerial reorganisation of the propertied class consequent upon changes in the pattern of capital ownership.

The Restructuring of Scottish Capital

The primary means of transforming the entrepreneurial firm into the modern corporation in Scotland has been the holding company. Towards the end of the nineteenth century there were a great many company amalgamations, often based around cartels and 'trusts' and associated with horizontal and vertical linkages. Similarly, the 1920s were a period in which a large number of mergers and acquisitions occurred following the immediate post-war boom. In virtually all cases the holding company form was the means through which the entrepreneurial firms were combined. The Scottish amalgamations do not seem to have been quite so unwieldy as some of the larger English combines, but the companies seem to have continued with the decentralised holding company structure until after the Second World War. Only gradually during the post-war period did companies begin

258

to adopt a more centralised structure and subsequently the multi-divisional form. Nevertheless, many of the companies, including some of the amalgamations, remained quite small in British terms and remained concerned with one group of products. In the smaller companies there was little need for a fundamental managerial restructuring.

Managerial restructuring was associated with a transformation in the pattern of ownership. Family shareholders were gradually reduced as a larger proportion of shares were sold through the stock exchange or sold to other interests. Many of these shares eventually found their way into the hands of the insurance companies, investment trusts, unit trusts and pension funds which became the major source of capital from the 1920s onwards. These financial 'institutions' mobilised the resources of large numbers of beneficiaries and invested the funds in company stock and became the most significant feature of the post-war capital market. In the case of the larger companies, family shareholdings were reduced to a minimal level and effective ownership passed into the hands of the constellation of financial institutions which owned a controlling block of the companies' shares. Nevertheless, family control or influence persisted in even the largest companies, and traditional controlling groups were able to retain their dominant positions so long as the institutions did not intervene. This continuity of control was most marked in the investment trust sector where the nature of recruitment to legal and accountancy partnerships ensured long lineages for many families. The lawyers and accountants were able to retain control over the trusts which they managed or for which they provided secretarial services, and the investment trust directorate as a whole was a major element in the 'pool' of people from which directors of banks, insurance companies and industrial companies were recruited.

The structure of interlocking directorships over time shows that the density of the network fell as a result of the business boom of 1919-20 and then rose continuously until the late 1950s. The rapid fall in density through the 1960s and 1970s corresponded to the growth of English and American ownership. The connectivity of the network followed the same trend but the fall during the 1960s and 1970s was not quite so marked, showing that the network included a smaller number of separate companies than in former years. The number of companies in the largest component increased steadily from the 1920s. The proportion of plural lines in the network fell from its peak in 1937-8, though the absolute number of plural lines did not peak until 1955-6. This suggests that the clustering of the network increased

during the inter-war period but that the pattern of interlocking subsequently became more diffuse, with the various spheres of influence
being less tightly integrated and more likely to overlap.

Over the period studied the whole structure of the network of
interlocking directorships was transformed. There was a move away
from groups of functionally interrelated companies and the 'empires'
of wealthy men to a structure of overlapping spheres of influence. By
the end of the period, industrial companies were most likely to be
linked into the network through financial companies rather than
through interlocks with other industrials. The banks had always
occupied key positions in the network but by the 1970s their centrality
was unchallenged. The banks had links to important industrial, insurance
and investment companies and a number of the largest insurance
companies fuctioned as 'bridges' between the various banking centres.
Within the structure, the overlapping spheres of influence showed a
considerable continuity with the tighter groupings of earlier years.
Instead of functionally interlocked industrial groups the Scottish
economy of the 1970s was dominated by large vertically and horizon-
tally integrated corporations with predominantly financial interlocks.
The industrial interlocks had, as it were, been internalised into the large
modern business corporation.

The Branch-Plant Economy

The Scottish economy has moved away from being a more or less
separate economy in the nineteenth century — at least as autonomous
as any politically independent nation might have been — and has
become merely a relatively autonomous sub-system of the British
economy. Political union between England and Scotland happened in
1707, but economic union is only now being completed. While new
industries have come under English or American dominance, many of
the basic industries have been nationalised. This effect of the political
union has reinforced the tendency towards a progressive integration of
the Scottish and English economies and has further narrowed the sphere
of Scottish capital.

Increased interdependence with the English economy has occurred
at two levels: technical and financial. The processes of production
carried out in Scottish companies have become progressively more
dependent upon English production as the whole technical division of
labour has become more complex. It is no longer the case that the
output of one Scottish industrial is the input to another. It is far more
likely to be the input to an English industrial; and its own inputs are

likely to come from English suppliers. Thus, the matrix of inter-industry exchanges becomes more and more sparse as companies and sectors become more externally oriented. The Scottish economy shows signs of 'disarticulation': it no longer operates as an autonomous unit. At the same time, financial links with England have grown as Scottish companies are taken-over or find themselves net debtors to English financials.

This is not to postulate some decline from a 'golden' past; industrial Scotland has always had strong technical and financial relations with England. The point is that there has occurred a fundamental change in the *degree* of interdependence. The Scottish registered companies form less and less a distinct and autonomous entity. They comprise the rump of old Scottish capital, increasingly subject to English ownership, together with a smattering of more recent Scottish companies, and a number of English and American subsidiaries which have Scottish registration as a matter of simple convenience or because they are based on old Scottish companies. It may well be that a devolved Scottish Assembly, if one is set up in the near future, may make Scottish registration a more meaningful economic fact, though this is only likely if the Assembly has economic powers over and above those minimal powers presently possessed by the Scottish Development Agency. An independent Scottish state would certainly make Scottish registration a positive act and might lead companies such as Sidlaw Industries and Grampian Holdings to take up Scottish registration, whilst companies such as Burmah Oil would have to decide whether to transfer their registration to London. But an important point must be made. While political union can be subject to a devolution of power, economic union cannot so easily be disentangled. Britain is part of an increasingly internationalised world economic system, and it is difficult to envisage an unravelling of the chains of interdependence while the prevailing international relations of production remain unchanged.

Nationalisation and the take-over of Scottish companies by outside interests have, however, also opened-up possibilities for Scottish capital by making available large sums of money to the former owners of the companies involved. By and large it would seem that this wealth has not found its way into the industrial sector; instead it has gone into the financial sector. Indeed, the investment trusts had their origins in the 1870s as a way of channelling the surplus funds of the jute industry into more profitable channels, and this process seems to have continued. And perhaps the one area where Scottish registration and Scottish identity have consistently been important, and particularly in the most recent period, has been the financial sector. Scottish capital in finance has been more dynamic than industrial capital and has not suffered as greatly from nationalisation, Anglicisation, or Americanisation, though the relationship between the English and Scottish banks has become very close. Scottish capital has, it might be argued, a relatively over-developed financial sector. While this may have been a sign of weakness in the past — with capital flowing abroad through the investment trusts rather than being invested in local industry — it has proved something of a strength in relation to the recent challenge posed by North Sea oil. The ability of Scottish capital to move into oil and compete with foreign capital derived from the expertise which the financial sector had developed over the course of the present century. Scottish fund managers have played a leading part in oil development, which has consequently been seen from a 'financial' point of view rather than being seen as an 'industrial' problem. It is noticeable that the non-financial companies which have moved into oil-related work come predominantly from shipping and commerce (e.g., Lyle Shipping and James Finlay) rather than from heavy industry, though it should be remembered that much of the old Scottish heavy industry has been nationalised and that British Steel and the National Coal Board have both been active in oil development. Equally, engineering firms such as Weir and Hewden-Stuart have been involved in oil-related activities. Nevertheless, the balance of Scottish involvement in North Sea oil has been on the financial side.

The North Sea sums up the basic principle of the Scottish economy: a dynamic financial sector in alliance with foreign capital in the development of a high technology growth industry. The Scottish economy has no doubt benefited from the fact of Scottish participation, though the benefits may have been greater if the industrial response had been greater. The significance of this is that the Scottish financials have mainly serviced Scottish industrials which have moved into oil and, particularly, have financed various specialised oil investment companies. Many of the industrial 'branch plants' have secured finance from the associates of their parent companies. The relative lack of Scottish industrial involvement in North Sea oil reduces the potential market for the services of the Scottish financial companies. The long-term viability of Scottish finance is very dependent upon that of its industrial base.

Oil has offered an important challenge to Scottish capital; it has given the opportunity for the funds of the investment trusts to be invested in North Sea developments rather than in Australia, America, or the Far East. We have shown in Chapter 5 that there has been some response to this challenge and that this reponse has invigorated the whole Scottish financial system. We have tried to point out here that the 'branch plant' character of the Scottish economy is manifest in the response to oil: and therein lies both the promise and the threat of North Sea oil.

The Managerial Reorganisation of the Propertied Class

We have already pointed to the continuity of family control and influence in Scottish companies, and it is worth considering some of the implications of this for the notion of a 'managerial revolution'. The main cases of companies in which executive managers dominate the board are those companies which are subsidiaries of English and American companies and are therefore special cases, since they are merely semi-autonomous profit centres within a large organisation. In the majority of companies studied there was little evidence of a managerial take-over. Those managers who did rise to board positions — and there were many of them — have often established their own family dynasties or have remained loyal to the controlling interests.

The major characteristic of the period studied has not been a managerial revolution but a managerial reorganisation of the propertied class. In the very largest companies it is no longer the case that a particular company is owned by a particular family. Rather, the propertied families own shares, often in relatively small blocks, in a large number of companies. At the same time, these propertied families constitute the pool from which the company boards are recruited. The multiple directors can be seen as the leading and active element in a propertied class. Their relatively high level of education shows that they have increasingly acquired the managerial skills necessary in a modern economy, and they have adopted a more 'professional' attitude to their work. The proportion of directors with two or more directorships remained constant from 1904 to 1938, apart from its low point after the 1919-20 boom, but has fallen steadily in the post-war period. This period of decline has, of course, corresponded to the growth of English and American influence when a number of Scottish companies became directly linked to outside interests. Within Scotland there has emerged a relatively small corps of multiple directors who manage the affairs of the business system as a whole and who tend to be active in the various business and economic policy groups which relate to the overall structure of Scottish capital. These men show considerable continuity with the old controlling families, though the basis of their power differs.

Future Research

In this book we have concentrated on presenting the data which will
permit more detailed investigations of more specific issues to be
studied. In the final part of this Conclusion we should like to outline
some of these possible areas of future research.

A major task is to begin to give more specific explanations of the
trends which we have observed in the characteristics of the business
system. In particular, it is to be hoped that studies will be carried out
for years other than those which we have studied in order that more
detailed trends can be observed and turning-points in the various
variables can be identified. It is important to investigate further into
the role of the banks: how active have they been in restructuring
industry, have they moved willingly into new areas or have they had
to be pushed, and so on. Important contributions can be made through
case studies of actual decision-making processes in particular companies.
What kinds of decisions are taken by company boards and what are left
to management? How active are the institutional shareholders and the
bank trust companies, both overtly and behind-the-scenes? What are the
forces which lead to the financial collapse of a company, and what
determines whether or not it will go into liquidation or be restructured?
All these crucial questions concerning business decision-making remain
to be answered.

In the area of the external relations of the Scottish economy there
are also a number of important areas of future research. There is
considerable scope for an investigation into the ownership of the
investment trusts, their original backers, and their general sources of
capital. In particular it is necessary to examine whether they have
consistently channelled industrial surpluses abroad. The whole question
of the involvement of English and foreign capital in Scotland is an
under-investigated area. It is necessary to investigate the links which
have been established between Scotland and other economies, both
in terms of capital and personnel, and to study the gradual incorporation
of the Scottish business system into an overarching British system.
Whilst studies of the branch-plant economy of the 1960s and 1970s
have been carried out, the early development of Anglo-Scottish
relations has not been studied fully.

There are, finally a number of important research problems in
relation to class and political power. When did the decline in family
ownership begin, and when did 'institutional' share ownership begin?
At what pace did these developments occur? Was the withdrawal of
families from positions of active control associated with the rise to

power of career managers, and did the managers constitute a distinct
social class? Our study of kinship links has merely scratched the surface
of this phenomenon and future investigations must carry out detailed
and systematic analyses which look at the origins of the families involved
in the different types of company, their connections with the land-
owning families, the role of the aristocracy, and so on. This whole area
raises crucial problems for the analysis of class structure and social
mobility in Scotland. It is necessary to study the linkages between the
dominant people of business and the political power of the state in
relation to areas such as nationalisation, regional policy and North Sea
oil. What have been the main lobbying forces involved in political
decisions and to what extent do the lobby groups reflect the interests
of Scottish capital? What has been the extent of the involvement of
Scottish businessmen in policy-making, advisory and regulatory bodies?

The oil industry offers an extremely useful laboratory in which to
study many of these topics. But there is also a need for a substantial
amount of historical research, since present structures can only
adequately be understood as developments from earlier structures.
This book is intended as a contribution to that task, and has concentrated
on setting-out the base line data from which other topics can be
investigated.

APPENDIX: METHODS AND DEFINITIONS

Our aim in selecting companies for analysis was to select by issued share capital so as to obtain at least 100 companies for each year studied. The years included are those given in Table A.1, but owing to different reporting dates each 'year' will not be exactly 12 months. In each case the *Stock Exchange Official Year Book* (formerly *Stock Exchange Official Intelligence*) covering the appropriate year was used as the basis for selection. Thus, for example, the data for 1904-5 came from the *Intelligence* for 1906. Unless otherwise indicated all the tables included are drawn from our own data. The information for the most recent period relates to 1973-4 and ownership information has generally been updated to 1974-5. In the case of exceptionally important events we have updated the information to the beginning of 1979. In addition to the above sources we have consulted company annual reports, the official share registers and company files lodged with the Registrar of Companies in Edinburgh, the financial pages of newspapers and magazines, and innumerable company histories.

Table A.1: Distribution of Top Companies (1904-74)

Sector	Number of Companies Selected				
	1904-5	1920-21	1937-8	1955-6	1973-4
Non-financial	64	76	59	55	62
Banking	8	8	8	6	4
Insurance	14	13	14	14	9
Investment and Property	22	17	30	34	45
TOTALS	108	114	111	109	120

For 1904-5 the cut-off point for issued share capital was £300,000, and in cases where no capital had yet been issued authorised capital was used. The list includes all industrial and investment companies with share capital in excess of £300,000. As in other years, banks were selected by deposits and insurance companies by life and general funds. The 1920-21 list includes all companies with share capital of £500,000 or more. In the list for 1937-8, the cut-off point for industrials was

£700,000 or more and the cut-off for investment companies was raised to £800,000. The higher cut-off for investment companies resulted in the exclusion of 14 companies with capital of £750,000 each. Most of the 14 excluded investment companies were 'Second' and 'Third' trusts of companies already on the list. The cut-off point for industrials in 1955-6 was £1,000,000, with investment companies having capital in excess of £1,100,000, being selected. This again resulted in the exclusion of an additional 14 companies, mainly 'Second' and 'Third' trusts. For 1973-4 a cut-off point of £1,200,000, was used for both industrial and investment companies. Tables 1.A, 2.A, 2.B, 3.A, and 4.A give the company listings for each of the years together with capital, industry and multiple directors. In Table 4.A the fifth column of Section A gives the rank of each company in the *Times 1000*, where British non-financial companies are ranked by turnover. The figure in brackets gives the company's turnover rank amongst the Scottish companies included in the *Times 1000*. Similarly, the fourth column of Section D gives the rank of the investment trusts in the *Times 1000*, where the British trusts are ranked by assets. The figure in brackets gives the asset rank for the Scottish companies alone. Table 4.B lists the multiple directors with their directorships in the top companies and gives a separate column for primary business interests. Much of the information on directors was obtained from the *Directory of Directors* and from the year books of the Institute of Chartered Accountants in Scotland. The company listings do not normally include 'Company', 'Limited', etc., in a business title unless it is an integral part of the name. Apart from abbreviations of company names (in the multiple director lists) and conventional abbreviations, the following abbreviations are used:

G	Governor
DG	Deputy Governor
P	President
VP	Vice President
HP	Honorary President
C	Chairman
VC	Vice Chairman
DC	Deputy Chairman
M	Manager
MD	Managing Director
GM	General Manager
JMD	Joint Managing Director
AMD	Assistant Managing Director

S   Secretary
T   Treasurer

Owing to the complexities of the laws relating to peerages and successions, the numbering of titles has often changed. For example, a man referred to as the 6th Earl of X may suddenly become the 12th Earl of X. In general, we have tried to follow the numbering given in the most recent volume of *Burke's Peerage*. We have not normally distinguished Scots and UK peerages, nor have we distinguished courtesy titles. Our tabulations of titles do not include 'Hon.' since this was not always given in the original sources. Men having the same name and sitting on different companies are assumed to be the same man only if there is no doubt. In cases of doubt, they are counted as two separate individuals. Hyphenated names and family names used as forenames are not always distinguished, particularly if the original source is not clear. We use whichever form of name occurs most commonly, though we recognise that this may not be the way the person himself would write his name. The reader wishing to trace a particular individual should, therefore, check the index and alphabetical lists for both parts of a surname – e.g. check for John Smith Brown under both 'Smith' and 'Brown'.

The diagrams of family trees have often been truncated, giving only those names and links most relevant to this study. Equally, we have not followed strict genealogical conventions in drawing the diagrams. The diagrams of company connections generally use a circular arrangement as a matter of convention and this arrangement is not intended to have any mathematical precision.

A company as opposed to a partnership is defined in the Introduction. A private company (not legally recognised until the early 1900s) has a limited number of shareholders, restrictions on the sale of its shares, and is exempt from certain disclosure requirements. A public company has no such restrictions or exemptions. A quoted company is simply a public company having a Stock Exchange quotation for one or other of its classes of shares or for its loan stock. Many of the insurance companies are organised not as proprietary companies but as mutual companies. A mutual company (like a Friendly Society) has no share capital but is jointly owned by its policyholders. Companies may register with the Registrar in Edinburgh or in London and our definition of a Scottish company for this analysis has been a quoted company registered in Scotland.

In the text we frequently use 'industrial' to refer to 'non-financial' companies rather than in the more restricted sense of manufacturing industry. Similarly, the text uses 'firm' as a synonym for 'company' and 'corporation' as well as to refer to the more restricted sense of business partnership. Finally 'finance' is used in its general sense as well as referring specifically to banking, insurance and investment companies. The context should always make the meanings of these terms clear.

In Chapter 4 we refer to various modes of control. Majority control is the situation where more than 50 per cent of a company's shares are held by a particular group. Minority control refers to control based on between 10 per cent and 50 per cent. Each of these is qualified as 'exclusive' or 'shared' depending on whether one or more interests are involved. Limited minority control is the situation where a particular interest has slightly less than 10 per cent of the shares but has strong board representation. Control through a constellation of interests occurs when the largest 10 or 20 shareholders collectively have minority control. A nominee company is a company set up purely to act as the registered owner of company shares and does not always have beneficial ownership. Nominee companies are frequently subsidiaries of banks and hold shares on behalf of banking clients.

A number of terms which have been used to describe the networks of interlocking directorships must be defined here. There is a 'line' between two companies when they have one or more directors in common. The 'value' of a line refers simply to the actual number of common directors. The network of plural lines consists of all those lines with a value of two or more. The 'centrality' of a company is measured by the number of companies with which it is directly connected. Thus, the sum of the centrality scores for all companies is equal to twice the number of lines in the network. The 'density' of a network is simply the ratio of the actual number of lines to the total possible number of lines as a percentage. Similarly, the 'connectivity' of a network is the probability that any two companies will be connected through a continuous series of lines. A 'component' in a network is a set of companies all of which are connected through a series of lines, and the connectivity of a network will normally be lower when there is a large number of components. A 'clique' is a set of companies with particularly close links. As used here, a clique is a group of three or more companies in the network of plural lines, where the group does not have more than a one-third overlap of membership with any other group. A clique is therefore a group of companies which have closer links to one another than they have to other companies. We should perhaps mention here that we frequently say that a person 'sat on Company X' rather than saying he 'sat on the board of Company X'. Although some readers may find the phrasing objectionable we have used it as a necessary form of shorthand.

BIBLIOGRAPHY

In order not to make the text too complex we have not given footnote references to our sources. Apart from standard reference books and newspapers the main sources which we have used are given below. The bibliography is not intended to be comprehensive: a full, but somewhat dated, bibliography is given by Marwick in the Payne volume cited below. A discussion of some of the general features of the development of modern capitalism can be found in John Scott's *Corporations, Classes, and Capitalism* (Hutchinson, London, 1979).

Arnaud, A.A. *Investment Trusts Explained* (Woodhead-Faulkner, Cambridge, 1977)

Arnold, G. *Britain's Oil* (Hamish Hamilton, London, 1978)

Bain, A.D. *et al. The Financing of North Sea Oil*, Research Report no. 2, Committee to Review the Functioning of Financial Institutions (HMSO, London, 1978)

Barclay, J.F. *The Story of Arthur & Co.*(Arthur & Co., Glasgow, 1978)

Blair, Sir A.C. *Edinburgh American Assets Trust Ltd.* (Edinburgh, 1978)

Bremner, D. *The Industries of Scotland* (Adam & Charles Black, Edinburgh, 1869)

Brown, Gordon (ed.) *The Red Paper on Scotland* (Edinburgh University Student Publications Board, Edinburgh, 1975)

Bullock, H. *The Story of Investment Trust Companies* (Columbia University Press, New York, 1959)

Burrow, E.J. *The Book of the Anchor Line* (E.J. Burrow, London, 1932)

Burton, H. & Corner D.C. *Investment and Unit Trusts in Britain and America* (Elek, London, 1968)

Cairncross, A.K. (ed.) *The Scottish Economy* (Cambridge University Press, Cambridge, 1954)

Callow, Clive *Power from the Sea* (Gollancz, London, 1973)

Campbell, R.H. *Carron Company* (Oliver & Boyd, Edinburgh, 1961)

Carvel, J.L. *The Coltness Iron Co* (T. & A. Carvel, Edinburgh, 1948)

Carvel, J.L. *Stephen of Linthouse* (Alex. Stephen & Sons, Glasgow, 1950)

Cazenove & Co. *The North Sea: The Search for Oil and Gas and the Implications for Investment* (Cazenove, London, 1972)

Cazenove & Co. *North Sea Oil: Investment Recommendations* (Cazenove, London, 1972)

Checkland, S.G. *The Mines of Tharsis* (Allen & Unwin, London, 1967)

Checkland, S.G. *Scottish Banking: A History* (Collins, Glasgow, 1975)

Clayton G. *British Insurance* (Elek, London, 1971)

Cooper, B. & Gaskell, T.F. *The Adventure of North Sea Oil* (Heinemann, London, 1976)

Crowdy, M. *History of Lyle Shipping* (World Shipping Society, Kendal, 1966)

Dunnett, A.M. *The Donaldson Line* (Jackson & Co., Glasgow, 1960)

Fairfield 1860-1960 (Barbour & Maclaren, Glasgow, 1960)

Firn, John 'External Control and Regional Policy', in Brown (ed.), *The Red Paper on Scotland*

Forsyth, D.J.C. *US Investment in Scotland* (Praeger, New York, 1972)

Gaskin, M. *The Scottish Banks* (Allen & Unwin, London, 1965)

Gilbert J.C. *A History of Investment Trusts in Dundee* (P.S. King, London, 1939)

Glasgow, George *The English Investment Trust Companies* (Eyre & Spottiswoode, London, 1930)

Glasgow, George *The Scottish Investment Trust Companies* (Eyre & Spottiswoode, London, 1932)

Gray, W.F. *A Brief Chronicle of the Scottish Union and National Insurance Co* (Scottish Union, Edinburgh, 1924)

Haldane, R.A. *Investment Trusts and Unit Trusts* (William Blackwood, Edinburgh, 1972)

Hood, N. & Young, S. 'US Investment in Scotland — Aspects of the Branch Factory Syndrome', *Scottish Journal of Political Economy*, 23, 3, 76

Jackson, W. Turrentine *The Enterprising Scot* (University Press, Edinburgh, 1968)

James Finlay & Company (Jackson Son & Co., Glasgow, 1951)

Johnston, T.L. *et al. Structure and Growth of the Scottish Economy* (Collins, Glasgow, 1971)

Johnston, Tom *Our Noble Families* (Forward Publishing, Glasgow, 1919)

Keir, David *The Younger Centuries* (W. Younger, Edinburgh, 1951)

Keith, A. *The North of Scotland Bank* (Aberdeen Journals, Aberdeen, 1936)

Kerr, A.W. *A History of Banking in Scotland* (A. & C. Black, London, 1926), 4th edition

Lea, K.J. *A Geography of Scotland* (David & Charles, Newton Abbott, 1977)

Lenman, Bruce *An Economic History of Scotland* (Batsford, London, 1977)

Lenman, Bruce & Donaldson, Kathleen 'Partner's Incomes, Investment and Diversification in the Scottish Linen Area, 1850-1921', *Business History*, 13, 1971

Lewis, T.M. & McNicoll I.H. *North Sea Oil and Scotland's Economic Prospects* (Croom Helm, London, 1978)

Lythe, S.G.E. & Butt, J. *An Economic History of Scotland* (Blackie, Glasgow, 1975)

McEwen, John *Who Owns Scotland?* (Edinburgh University Student Publications Board, Edinburgh, 1978)

McLaren, M. *The History of the United Wire Works* (H. and J. Pillons and Wilson, Edinburgh, 1947)

McLean, Angus (ed.) *Local Industries of Glasgow and the West of Scotland* (British Association for the Advancement of Science, Glasgow, 1901)

MacKay, D.I. and Mackay, G.A. *The Political Economy of North Sea Oil* (Martin Robertson, London, 1975)

Macmillan, D.S. *Scotland and Australia* (Clarendon Press, Oxford, 1967)

Malcolm, C.A. *The Bank of Scotland* (R. & R. Clarke, Edinburgh, 1945)

Malcolm, C.A. *The History of the British Linen Bank* (T. & A. Constable, Edinburgh, 1950)

Marwick, W.H. *Scotland in Modern Times* (Cass, London, 1964) Unwin, London, 1936)

Merwick, W.H. *Scotland in Modern Times* (Cass, London, 1964)

Mathias, P. & Pearsall, W.H. (eds.) *Shipping: A Survey of Historical Records* (David & Charles, Newton Abbott, 1971)

Maxwell, Sir Herbert *Annals of the Scottish Widows Fund & Life Assurance Society* (Scottish Widows, Edinburgh, 1914)

Muir, Augustus *The Fife Coal Company* (Fife Coal, Leven, no date)

Muir, Augustus *The Story of Shotts* (Shotts Iron, Edinburgh, 1952)

Munro, N. *The History of the Royal Bank of Scotland* (R. & R. Clark, Edinburgh, 1928)

Murphy, W.S. *Captains of Industry* (Wm S. Murphy, Glasgow, 1901)

Murray, Robin *UCS: The Anatomy of A Bankruptcy* (Spokesman Books, Nottingham, 1972)

North British & Mercantile Insurance Co. A Centenary (North British & Mercantile, Edinburgh, 1909)

Oakley, C.A. (ed.) *Scottish Industry* (Scottish Council, Edinburgh,

1953)

Oil Over Troubled Waters (Aberdeen People's Press, Aberdeen, 1976)

Orbell, J. *et al. From Cape to Cape: The History of Lyle Shipping* (Paul Harris, Edinburgh, 1978)

Payne, Peter L. (ed.) *Studies in Scottish Business History* (Frank Cass, London, 1967)

Pottinger, G. *The Winning Counter: Hugh Fraser and Harrods* (Hutchinson, London, 1971)

Rait, R.S. *The History of the Union Bank of Scotland* (John Smith, Glasgow, 1930)

Reader, W.J. *Imperial Chemical Industries* (Oxford University Press, Oxford, 1970)

Robertson, P.L. 'Shipping and Shipbuilding: The Case of Wm. Denny'. *Business History*, 16, 1974

Rosie, G. *Cromarty* (Canongate, Edinburgh, 1974)

Scotland's Top 500 Companies (Jordan Dataquest, London, annually)

Scott, John & Hughes, Michael 'Ownership and Control in a Satellite Economy', *Sociology,* 10, 1, 1976

Scott, John & Hughes, Michael 'Finance Capital and the Upper Class', in Brown (ed.), *The Red Paper on Scotland*

Scott, John & Hughes, Michael 'Capital and Communication in Scottish Business', *Sociology*, 13, 1, 1980

Scott, John *et al.* 'Patterns of Ownership in Top Scottish Companies', *Scottish Journal of Sociology*, 1, 1, 1976

Scottish Clearing Banks *Evidence on the Financing of Industry and Trade* vol.6, Committee to Review the Functioning of Financial Institutions (HMSO, London, 1978)

Shields, John *Clyde Built* (William MacLellan, Glasgow, 1949)

Slaven, Anthony *The Development of the West of Scotland* (Routledge & Kegan Paul, London, 1975)

The Carpet Makers, (A.F. Stoddard & Co., Johnstone, 1962)

The Third Statistical Account of Scotland, particularly volumes on Glasgow (1958) and on Edinburgh (1966) (Collins, Glasgow)

Two Hundred and Fifty Years of Shipbuilding (Scotts of Greenock, Glasgow, 1961)

Turnock, D. *The New Scotland* (David & Charles, Newton Abbot, 1979)

Underwood, Robert (ed.) *The Future of Scotland* (Croom Helm, London, 1977)

Vaizey, John *The History of British Steel* (Weidenfeld & Nicolson, London, 1974)

Vamplew, Wray *Salvesen of Leith* (Scottish Academic Press, Edinburgh, 1975)

Wilson, R. *Scotch: The Formative Years* (Constable, London, 1970)

Wood Mackenzie & Co. *Investment Trust Annual Review* (Wood Mackenzie, Edinburgh, 1974)

INDEX

Multiple directors in Tables 1A, 2A, 2B, 3A have not been indexed for reasons of space. A full list of these directors together with their directorships (*Multiple Directors in Top Scottish Companies 1904-1956*) has been lodged with the British Library, British Lending Library, and Leicester University Library. Similarly, the multiple directors in Table 4B have not been separately indexed since they are listed alphabetically in the Table. Primary business interests in Table 4-B are indexed only if they also appear elsewhere in the text. 'Second' and 'Third' trusts are not indexed separately unless they have a distinct history from the main trust.

276